PRAISE

Redefining RHEMA

I am excited to endorse *Redefining Rhema* by David Lake and Ed Delph. This is an important teaching on the concept of RHEMA and how it is to be used in the life of a believer. I have been teaching on the relationship between RHEMA and faith for some time and appreciate the insights of this book. It goes beyond how to receive RHEMA to the why of RHEMA. It then goes on to address practical applications and the significance of these applications for the time in which we live. This book is needed to bring a better balance to the teaching about RHEMA, and RHEMA's relationship to LOGOS. Thank you, David and Ed, for this most needed contribution.

RANDY CLARK, DMin, ThD Overseer of the Apostolic
Network of Global Awakening, founder of Global Awakening
Mechanicsburg, Pennsylvania

Every day we are bombarded with thousands of marketing messages in the form of billboards, television, magazines, newspapers, and the Internet. As the intensity of these words grows louder, we need to stop, listen, and hear the RHEMA voice of God. If we do not clearly recognize God's voice, then we are vulnerable and can easily be persuaded by each commentator who adds his or her voice. In this book, Ed Delph and David Lake help us rediscover and trust God's RHEMA before we say what we think. God still speaks to His children, and this is the time to *know* and not to merely *think* so that God's voice can pierce the darkness.

GRAHAM POWER
Founder of Global Day of Prayer and Unashamedly Ethical
Cape Town, South Africa

Listening well and walking in balance are two primary marks of emotional and spiritual maturity—something each one of us needs to know more about. I don't think this book could come into our lives at a more critical time. It's the right season for us to hear, redefine, and move forward. Thanks, Ed and David, for helping the church to come to full stature.

Dr. David Cannistraci
Lead Pastor, GateWay City Church
San Jose, California

Dr. Ed Delph is an amazing urban practitioner who understands the kingdom of God. In *Redefining Rhema*, Ed Delph and coauthor David Lake unveil the secret of their effectiveness, which is hearing the voice of God. In this day, when so many Christian leaders depend more on business strategy than acting on a divine RHEMA, this book is both timely and prophetic!

Dr. Joseph Mattera
Mattera Ministries International
Brooklyn, New York

God is smarter than we are, and the amazing thing is that He wants to share His thoughts with us! This is the basic premise of this incredible book that will help leaders tune in to the frequency of God's voice as the fundamental building block to every great endeavor to which they may give their lives. Ed and David are two seasoned leaders in the kingdom who have masterfully brought an apostolic and prophetic vantage point on this ageless truth, presenting it in a fresh and relevant way to inspire the global church. Read it and live it!

Alan Platt
Doxa Deo Global Visionary Leader
Pretoria, South Africa

God is using my anointed apostolic friend Ed Delph and coauthor David Lake to impact the nations of the world with the gospel of the kingdom of God. In their new book, *Redefining Rhema*, they have written a masterfully clear, insightful, and practical handbook on the vitally important spiritual principle of a RHEMA word from God. With each chapter, Ed and David lead us on a journey of understanding and illumination that empowers us to grasp the meaning of what a RHEMA is and then apply it in our walk with Christ. They give us great insight by connecting RHEMA to the wisdom of Solomon, to see, say, and share. What makes this book so powerful is knowing Ed has practiced what he preaches and lived out for many years by example what he teaches us about in these pages! Dig in, for you're going to love *Redefining Rhema*!

Dr. Michael Maiden
Lead Pastor of Church for the Nations
Phoenix, Arizona

Hearing the voice of God is essential to discovering and walking in God's purposes. Ed Delph and David Lake define how to listen, hear, and practically apply what God says in the everyday decisions of life.

Mel C. Mullen
Founder of Home Church
Red Deer, Alberta, Canada

We were talking over a light lunch at the Johannesburg International Airport when Ed shared with me the essence of *Redefining Rhema*. It surely warmed my heart. Ed's ministry and writings have been a blessing to many people across the globe. I believe your experience when reading Ed Delph and David Lake's book will echo that of the two people from Emmaus: "Were not our hearts burning within us while He was speaking to us on the road, while He was explaining the Scriptures to us?" (Luke 24:32).

Dr. Isak Burger
Author and former president of the Apostolic
Faith Mission of South Africa
Pretoria, South Africa

We live in an attention-deficit, overstimulated world that is quickly moving in a direction that lacks clarity. If ever we needed to truly hear from God, it's now! *Redefining Rhema* is a timely read. My friend Ed Delph and coauthor David Lake do a masterful job reclaiming and explaining the life-changing experience of RHEMA to a new generation.

Dan Steffen
Senior Pastor, Pure Heart Church
Glendale, Arizona

The book in your hands deals with one of the most wonderful aspects of the Christian walk: the ability and right of every believer to hear God's voice on a regular basis. Hearing and obeying is an essential key to successfully living the Christian life and fulfilling God's call. Clear biblical teaching on RHEMA is desperately needed in today's world of many conflicting voices.

With new insights and a fresh perspective, I am sure this book will be a valuable resource to you that will result in a more successful, intimate, and powerful walk with God.

Tak Bharna
Senior Pastor, Church Unlimited
Auckland, New Zealand

Having used NationStrategy as a tool to pry open community awareness in pastors attending my TLC (Training Leaders for Christ) Center, I am not surprised that Heaven has once again chosen Dr. Ed Delph and coauthor David Lake to receive a revelation that fits perfectly with the past, present, and future of the community and the church. By learning the real and often misunderstood meaning of one word, you will have the key to perfectly fulfill God's purpose for you and the world around you. You will never regret reading this book.

Dr. Iverna Tompkins
Training Leaders for Christ
Scottsdale, Arizona

I have had the pleasure of knowing my good friends Ed Delph and David Lake to be men of practical wisdom and deep spiritual insight. Their new book, *Redefining Rhema*, brings to clarity that God's Word is full of life and power. It sharpens your spiritual eyes the moment you start reading the book. You will encounter that everything about God and you is personal!

Peter M. Kairuz
President and CEO, CBN ASIA, INC.
and host of *The 700 Club* Asia

Redefining Rhema is a book that is so apt for this time and season of our lives. It teaches us how to accurately see and hear what God wants to say and show us. God wants us to accurately download what is in His heart so that we know what to do in this season of our lives. Jesus says in Matthew 13:16, "But blessed are your eyes, because they see; and your ears, because they hear." It is a blessing from God to be able to accurately see and hear, not only that we walk in the perfect will of God, but so that, like the sons of Issachar, we can tell the people what to do. This book is a gem and a guide toward this end. Read it and be thoroughly blessed!

Dr. Chew Weng Chee
Pastor, SIBKL Church (Sidang Injil Borneo Church Kuala Lumpur)
Kuala Lumpur, Malaysia

I wholeheartedly endorse Ed Delph and David Lake as men who are living out their message. Recently, David spoke to our church about "hear first, speak second," and it was outstanding. I have heard and spoken on faith, but the clarity of revelation David brought was on another level altogether. I believe this work is just in time for those who have ears to hear so that the body of Christ can advance the kingdom of God in the earth.

Dave Dishroon
Lead Pastor, Change Point Church
Tauranga, New Zealand

In *Redefining Rhema*, the collaborative genius of Dr. Ed Delph's apostolic gifting has joined with David Lake's prophetic gifting to create a brilliant revelatory work that will illuminate God's direction for your life and endow you with power to effect change by hearing first and speaking second. This book is a must read for everyone seeking to move with the truth of God's Word.

Karen Drake, DMin
President/Overseer, Phoenix University of Theology
Phoenix, Arizona

DESTINY IMAGE BOOKS BY ED DELPH

The Five-Minute Miracle

Learning How to Trust

Redefining RHEMA

RESPONDING TO GOD'S VOICE
RELEASING HIS PURPOSES ON EARTH

ED DELPH
& DAVID LAKE

DESTINY IMAGE® PUBLISHERS, INC.
P.O. Box 310, Shippensburg, PA 17257-0310
"Promoting Inspired Lives."

This book and all other Destiny Image and Destiny Image Fiction books are available at Christian bookstores and distributors worldwide.

Cover design by Eileen Rockwell
Interior design by Terry Clifton

For more information on foreign distributors, call 717-532-3040.
Reach us on the Internet: www.destinyimage.com.

ISBN 13 TP: 978-0-7684-1478-3
ISBN 13 eBook: 978-0-7684-1479-0
ISBN 13 HC: 978-0-7684-1644-2
ISBN 13 LP: 978-0-7684-1645-9

For Worldwide Distribution, Printed in the U.S.A.
1 2 3 4 5 6 7 8 / 21 20 19 18 17

This book is dedicated to those who, since humankind began, have endeavored to know God by listening to or hearing from Him. Many who have come and gone prior to the writing of this book have aided the church in learning how to hear from the Lord. We celebrate their contribution. We have been inspired and influenced by their mentoring and writings about hearing God.

We stand among many others, adding to their contributions on this subject. If we see more than they did, it is only because of the perspective we received from sitting on their shoulders. We sincerely hope to build on their teachings, mixing our contribution with their contributions, equipping those who come after us to have a clearer understanding of hearing God.

Many coming after us will add to the contributions of this book. Our only desire is to bring those who want to know God by hearing Him into a fuller understanding of how to use both LOGOS *(the written Word) and* RHEMA *(an utterance from God presently speaking) for the advancement of fulfilling the purposes of God for their generation.*

If we were to dedicate this book to any one individual, it would be to Pastor Joshua Churchyard of Benoni, South Africa. For many years without fail, the first thing he says to us when we see him is, "What is the Lord saying to you?"

—DAVID LAKE and ED DELPH

CONTENTS

FOREWORD

by Lance Wallnau

Dr. Ed Delph and David Lake have come up with something that is both timely and profound. Jesus said: "It is written, 'Man shall not live by bread alone, but by every word that proceeds from the mouth of God'" (Matthew 4:4 NKJV). Notice that Jesus did not say, "Christians shall not live by bread alone"; He said "man." The Word of God applies to all people and all areas of life. It is the hour when believers need to hear and speak the counsel of God into every sphere. There is a fresh Word proceeding out of God's mouth to your ear—can you hear it? Everything changes the moment you do.

I first learned about hearing God and distinguishing His inward voice, RHEMA, and His Word in Scripture, LOGOS, from Kenneth Hagin and Derek Prince. That was over twenty years ago. It makes sense that a fresh perspective would emerge in this strategic hour when so many conflicting ideas and opinions are being broadcast 24/7. Anyone with discernment can see that the collision of spiritual realms has heated up in a cosmic war of words. That is the reason I am excited about this book—*Redefining Rhema.*

The spirit of antichrist is described by Daniel as a "little horn" with a large and *dangerous mouth*: "This horn had eyes like the eyes of a human being and a mouth that spoke boastfully" (Daniel 7:8 NIV). The last days will be characterized by the clashing of swords in the mouths of messengers. In each sphere or realm in conflict—political, cultural, or religious—the battle in the heavens will be fought through competing narratives and voices.

Nothing could be more important than the practice of hearing and speaking what the Lord is actually saying. In this unique book, Dr. Ed and David have combined forces and thus synergized their research and anointing to produce something fresh. Ed is undeniably a spokesman for releasing kingdom transformation in culture, while David brings a fresh prophetic edge to the message.

Redefining Rhema is a vital message because societal reformation can only be released to the degree that the church exits its own mountain and engages every other mountain of society. For kingdom transformation to take place on a cultural level, the church mountain needs to stop trying to replicate preachers to expand the church mountain and, instead, start sending men and women with the mind of Christ into the mountains of culture that are presently under the influence of false messages and demonized messengers. We need a few more anointed educators, school administrators, journalists, filmmakers, mayors, lawyers, and entrepreneurs and fewer Sunday sermon critics.

Words *are* being released into the earth; there's no doubt an army of unsuspecting Millennials are drinking it all in. What's going to cut through the strategies of darkness? Laborers who wield the sword of the Lord in their respective mountains of influence. This sword is God's RHEMA. I believe a defining hallmark of these laborers will be this: they will know how to *hear* and *speak* the utterance proceeding out of the mouth of God. Their words will stick fast in the minds and hearts of those who hear them. They will be Heaven's apologists, and when the enemy tries to hem them in Jesus will show up through them: "For I will give you words and wisdom that none of your adversaries will be able to resist or contradict" (Luke 21:15 NIV).

So, I invite you to consider where *you* are right now. Consider *your* sphere of influence. Consider *your* present assignment. Celebrate it, because this is where God wants to designate you as a mouthpiece, a catalyst of transformation. Preachers have their place, but their calling is not superior to yours. In the same manner the preacher releases words that are *Spirit and life* (see John 6:63) from a pulpit, you will find your words just as powerful in the marketplace sanctuary where God has placed you. Ed Delph and David Lake have delivered a work that will position you to hear words from Heaven and release the transformation strategies of the kingdom into whatever sphere you are called to in this season.

LANCE WALLNAU
Author of *God's Chaos Candidate*
Founder and President of Lance Learning

POWER THOUGHTS ON THE *Introduction*

On the voyage to Rome, Paul did not hide in his cabin when the storm arose; he went to the deck and took command of the situation. Too many Christians huddle in staterooms these days, discussing Euroclydon (a stormy wind from the north or northeast which caused the ship on which Paul was travelling to be wrecked) instead of rising to the occasion in the name of the Lord. It is much easier to stay hidden and deplore the tempest. We need to be on deck with a word from God for the passengers.

—Vance Havner[1]

Desire RHEMA and acquire RHEMA, because we all require RHEMA.

—Ed Delph

As a Christian, our most important sense of the five senses is hearing. Faith comes by hearing a word from God. We are not the 'sight and sound' generation. We are the 'sound then sight' generation.

—Ed Delph

"But Mary treasured up all these [RHEMAS], pondering them in her heart" (Luke 2:19). The birth of Christ was a [RHEMA] revival orchestrated by the Holy Spirit illuminating the Word just born. The word [RHEMA] appears seven times in the first three chapters of Luke. What did Mary do? She treasured the [RHEMA]. She thought about what this meant. We hope that you, our readers, now armed with the why, what and how of [RHEMA], will be like Mary and treasure [RHEMA] for [RHEMA] is treasure.

—Ed Delph and Dave Lake

INTRODUCTION

> Trust comes from knowing God; faith comes from hearing God.
>
> —DAVID LAKE

Here's a question for you: Of the five senses—seeing, hearing, touching, smelling, or tasting—which sense is the most imperative for you? If you say that your answer depends on the situation, then you're correct. But from a spiritual perspective, hearing would be the most important sense. Why? It is because we were designed by God to listen to Him.

In Genesis 1, the first thing we learn about the person of God is that He *speaks*. The Bible is called the *Word of God*. Creation was brought into being through the vehicle of *speech*. This idea is important because navigating today's complex, tumultuous, chaotic, and unpredictable world without God's direction makes us candidates for a shipwreck.

Look around you. There is a whole lot of shaking going on. Read Second Timothy 3:1-7. In times like these, you need to hear from God first. God is the ultimate hearing aid. He is not just a resource; He is the source. God is broadcasting all the time. If people aren't hearing from Him, the problem is not the broadcaster but the receiver. We need to tune in to God's channel for decision making, direction, and discernment. This book is about getting a revelation on the often-addressed subject of hearing God. But this book is not going where you think it's going. It's different. We (Ed Delph and David Lake) call the concept "hear first, speak second."

Did you know you can know something but not really know it? Did you know you can see something but not see it? Did you know you can hear something but not hear it? Jesus said to His disciples, "Having eyes, do you not see? And having ears, do you not hear? And do you not remember?" (Mark 8:18). In other words, you can have cognition of a Bible truth but not re-cognition of that truth. Cognition is knowledge, but re-cognition is understanding. This is why people can know something profound and powerful without it affecting their attitude, faith, or behavior. A shift in behavior happens after re-cognition, not cognition. It takes an aha moment; it takes light and truth. It takes an epiphany.

Do you remember the story in Mark 8:22-26 about the blind man Jesus had to pray for twice for him to see? The first time Jesus prayed for him, He asked, "Do you see anything?" The man replied, "I see men like trees walking about." That was the wrong answer. People don't have branches and leaves growing out of their heads, and neither do they have bark for skin. The blind man saw people, but he didn't see them clearly. He had cognition of others, but not re-cognition. Jesus touched him again...a second time. The result was that "he looked intently, and was restored, and began to see everything clearly." He got an aha. Shift happened in him after the second touch. God speaking through Jesus opened the eyes of the blind man's mind in the first encounter, but God speaking through Jesus opened the eyes of the blind man's heart in the second encounter. The result was that the blind man transitioned from information, to revelation, to transformation.

We have written this book because of our deep concern we see in the church today. Too many Christ-followers resemble this blind man after Jesus's first touch—they see the truth of their need to hear from God before speaking or acting, but they see like trees. They see it, but not clearly. They hear it, but not clearly. They know it, but they don't know it clearly. They don't know the *implications*, so they are weak in the *applications*. How do we know this? By their words, by their actions, and by the outcome in their lives.

This book is about the second touch, the aha moment, when you begin to see everything clearly. In today's world, clarity is a rarity. There's a difference between believing *in* Jesus and *believing Jesus.* Clarity helps you make that shift.

This book's mission is nearly impossible. First, we must address the biblical reality of hearing first and speaking second. Then we must move our readers from *knowing about* this principle to *knowing it by revelation and thus acting upon it.* We desire, with the Holy Spirit's help, to create a *shift* in behavior much like Jesus did with the blind man. How? *By the second touch*! Our desire is for you to grasp at first touch, clearly, one of the most powerful and fruitful truths in the Bible: hear first, speak second. In fact, it's a pattern throughout the whole Bible, as we will see.

Psalm 43:3 gives insight into this concept: "O send out Thy light and Thy truth, let them lead me; let them bring me unto Thy holy hill" (KJV). In other words, it takes both light and truth to lead you to that elevated place where you can look out on the spiritual landscape. The light is the Holy Spirit and the truth is God's Word. To clean yourself thoroughly, you need *both* soap and water. Soap without water won't clean you, but neither will water without soap. The same holds true with truth and light. Both working together is what gets you clean. So let there be light empowered with truth!

This book is about transformation; it's not just a transaction. It is not about information; it's about revelation. It's about the Greek word RHEMA. RHEMA is *a faith-infused, biblically correct, and spiritually accurate utterance from God to a person or persons for a specific occasion, reason, or revelation*. You don't find RHEMA; rather, RHEMA finds you.

We will seek to redefine and refine RHEMA. We will uncover RHEMA and discover RHEMA so you can recover RHEMA. This is an upgrade from what you may have heard before. We believe the first time RHEMA became a popular subject, people saw it like a tree. But this book is about the second touch. It's about listening. It's about clearly and accurately hearing utterances spoken to a present situation, and, most importantly, applying it God's way. It's a key to the kingdom, but the key still needs to be turned the right way to open the gates of Heaven. It's relevant for times like these. It's current. It's clarion. It's better than a smartphone app for how to live in shifting and ambiguous times.

As we said, this book is not going where you may think. It's written from two different yet valid perspectives. David Lake, more prophetic by nature and calling, addresses RHEMA from a prophetic perspective, while Dr. Ed Delph, who is more apostolic by nature and calling, focuses on the absolute necessity and implications of hearing first and speaking second. With equal status and different roles, we provide both spiritual and practical perspectives. We start from Heaven and then bring truth to the Earth. Grafting our gifts, we bring a fuller perspective applicable to all, arriving at balance through fullness, presenting the whole picture of hearing first, speaking second. This blending of perspectives will enhance what you have learned about RHEMA.

It is our hope that this book will surprise you. It is not about a formula for success. It's not about finding a path to prosperity. It's not about receiving an early inheritance. There's no formula to hear from God or to talk God into something you want or to get your breakthrough. We won't tell you how to talk God into your timing or how to seek first His kingdom for your own benefit. This book is not about finding a new source or significance by saying, "The Lord just told me to tell you..." It's not about showing off how much faith you have. And it is not about trying to please God. Rather, it is about knowing God by hearing God.

Redefining Rhema is about accessing God and what He is doing in the earth today. It's about moving from a slave to a friend by knowing what God wants. This book is about being proactive rather than reactive. It's not about adjusting to change; it's about anticipating change in each season, and what to do in each season as you hear first and speak second. This concept works well in both perilous times and good times. It keeps you alive in the wilderness and it will keep you alive in the land of milk and honey.

It is our hope that *Redefining Rhema* will shift your spiritual reality. This book is about you—from a pure heart and mind—releasing spiritual shockwaves from Heaven into Earth after you hear God tell you to do it. This book is about, "Thy kingdom come, Thy will be done on earth, as it is in heaven" (Matthew 6:10 KJV). It is about hearing, speaking, and walking in the magnificent fear of the Lord. In fact, after you read and understand this book, the fear of the Lord should take on a whole new meaning for you.

Redefining Rhema is about you giving God a supernaturally natural and incredibly credible voice and face on earth. It's about knowing whose voice you are hearing and engaging culture with a word of wisdom and clarity for such a time as this. This book is for everyone who desires to hear first and speak second. It is strategic for everyone working and ministering in the seven mountains (spheres of influence) of society—family, education, media, arts and entertainment, business, religion, and government. This book is about allowing the Word to speak His word before you speak a word.

Our twofold desire is that you will live your life in all areas by the "hear first, speak second" paradigm. Second, we desire for you to receive a RHEMA on RHEMA. It's your birthright. As a result, God has a voice—your voice—on Earth as it is in Heaven. Here is a world-changing, society-transforming, giant-slaying, runaway culture-shifting statement for you: If you truly hear from God, then God speaks through your words a relevant, personal truth that is biblically correct and spiritually accurate for the hearer's situation. That's high octane. Use, but use it wisely.

A Special Note from David Lake

I was asked by my good friend Ed Delph to cowrite this book. At a home fellowship group in the early '90s, we had talked about the importance of hearing God first and speaking second. I was young in the Lord then. Until Ed recently brought up that conversation at breakfast, some twenty-five years later, I had forgotten about it. Ed pulled out a notebook and showed me notes and the date when that conversation occurred. Though we did not know it twenty-five years ago, that is when the idea for this book was conceived.

Through many lunches and breakfasts over the years, Ed and I have met and talked about God. Many of our discussions have been centered on hearing God. Lots of good books have been written about hearing God, so we knew this was not a new subject. Our desire was to bring a perspective that reveals the character of God. We want you to know Him. John 17:3 (AMP) says, "And this is life eternal: [it means] to know (to perceive, recognize, become acquainted with, and understand) You, the only true and real God, and [likewise] to know Him, Jesus (as the) Christ (the Anointed One, the Messiah), Whom You have sent." Hearing God is imperative to knowing God. In fact, the most important reason to hear God is to know Him.

This world continues to manifest a wickedness and sinfulness that was hard to imagine just a few years ago. Trials and tribulations continue to increase at an alarming rate. Never has there been a more important time to know God and to hear His voice. Never has there been a time when faith has had to manifest itself so strongly as a light in a world that continues to grow increasingly dark. Romans 10:17 says, "So faith comes from hearing, and hearing by the word of Christ." We need to hear Him if we are to get faith.

I never seriously considered writing a book because it sounded so complicated, and I had no idea where to start. Besides that, who would read a book I wrote? I've been in the construction business my entire life. My life experiences didn't seem much different from anyone else's;

I don't have a big crowd that gathers to hear me speak weekly. But God put in me a deep desire to hear His voice and to know Him.

When I talk to people about hearing God, they usually admit the value of hearing but don't connect that hearing directly to faith. I had never heard anyone speak on the dynamic that faith comes from God. I had a lot of good reasons not to write a book! The task was too big, too complicated, and impossible to imagine. But the process required me to listen to God as I never had before. It sounded to me like God was talking.

Note

1. Vance Havner, *Pepper 'n' Salt* (Grand Rapids, MI: Fleming H. Revell Company, 1966).

Section I

THE BIBLICAL PATTERN OF HEAR FIRST, SPEAK SECOND

by Ed Delph

> O send out Thy light and Thy truth; let them lead me; let them bring me to Thy holy hill, and to Thy dwelling places.
>
> —PSALM 43:3 KJV

Redefining Rhema is about how truth needs revelation to work for a clear understanding. God didn't create truth to be alone; truth needs light for illumination, direction, clarity, wisdom, and intimacy with God on His holy mountain, the place where He dwells. Sight and insight require light. We will use several words throughout this book that refer to the concepts of light and truth. Here are their definitions:

- Illumination: an interpretation that removes obstacles to understanding; clarification that follows from the removal of ambiguity.

- Revelation: an usually secret or surprising fact that is made known; an act of making something known; an act of revealing something, usually in a surprising way.
- Epiphany: A manifestation occurring as an experience of sudden and striking realization. It can apply in any situation in which an enlightening realization allows a problem or situation to be understood from a new and deeper perspective. Epiphanies generally come from the inside, whereas discoveries are made from the outside.
- Recognition: The perception of something as existing or true; a realization. To acknowledge or know again; understanding by a knowing again. A deeper understanding.
- Understanding: the mental process of a person who comprehends; comprehension; personal interpretation: superior power of discernment; enlightened intelligence.
- Awareness: feeling, experiencing, or noticing something.
- Quickening: To make more rapid; to cause (a body or soul, for example) to become alive; vitalize. To excite and stimulate; stir.
- Awakening: to cause to wake up; to cause (someone) to become aware; alert or enlighten.
- An aha moment: a moment of sudden realization, inspiration, insight, recognition, or comprehension.
- Word of wisdom: The application of knowledge that is given by God. This type of wisdom is a gift that cannot be gained through study or experience; but the recipient should by no means try to replace study

or experience with a word of wisdom. The word of wisdom is seeing life from God's perspective.

- Word of knowledge: A definite conviction, impression, or knowing that comes to a person in a similitude (a mental picture), a dream, through a vision, or by a scripture that is quickened to the recipient. It is supernatural insight or understanding of circumstances, situations, problems, or a body of facts by revelation; it comes without assistance by any human resource, but solely by divine aid.
- Discerning of spirits: Recognizing what is of God versus what comes from the world, the flesh, and the devil. Discerning of spirits must be done by the power of the Holy Spirit; He alone bears witness with our spirit when something is from God. The gift of discerning of spirits is the supernatural power to detect the realm of spirits and their activities. It implies the power of spiritual insight—the supernatural revelation of plans and purposes of the enemy and his forces.[1]

Note

1. The last three definitions are adapted from http://www.christcenteredmall.com.

Chapter 1

Shift Your Spiritual Reality to Shift Their Spiritual Reality

If you truly hear from God, then God speaks through you as you speak. That is quite a statement, isn't it? This type of thinking can be dangerous or used wrongly by power-hungry leaders. But I'm not referring here to adding or subtracting from the Bible or the LOGOS of God. Rather, I'm talking about a specific, timely, wise, faith-infused utterance from God for a specific occasion.

Some people go too far in claiming to speak for God. They think everything they hear is from Him. I have a friend who, as a teenager, thought he was Jesus Himself. Doctors had to sedate him to bring him back to reality. Fortunately, this teenage "Jesus" has developed into a faithful pastor in the Phoenix area. It's one thing to hear from God, but it's another thing to think you are God or Jesus. So the statement, "If you truly hear from God, then God speaks through you as you speak," is worth exploring. A heap of people in our world need Christians to give God a voice within the community in which they live.

Communication without Illumination

This book is about you and me hearing from God first and then speaking what God has said after He's said it to you. Did you get that?

Hear first, speak second. Enthusiastic people often speak before hearing from God. They think they speak in the name of the Lord, but they just speak in the name of themselves. Usually, everyone knows it except for those doing doing it. Talk about awkward.

Jesus emphatically said in Matthew 6:32-33, "For the Gentiles eagerly seek all these things [money, clothes, material possessions, prestige, long life, position, and power]; for your heavenly Father knows that you need these things. But seek first His kingdom and His righteousness, and all these things shall be added to you." Jesus's point is that we first seek the kingdom of God for God's sake, not for our own sakes. God's kingdom is not self-serving. It is not about finding a means to our own end. God's kingdom is about His will being done on earth as it is done in heaven: "Thy kingdom come, Thy will be done..." (Matthew 6:10 KJV). This means God's will for our lives is attached to us advancing His kingdom. Our purpose and reason for existence is a kingdom purpose. If we aim at earth, then we get nothing; if we aim at Heaven, then we get earth thrown in too.

As a result of other people using God's kingdom principles for their own purposes, many believers have shrunk into silence. They don't want to speak for God at all, not even to quote the Bible. They don't want to be tagged as spiritual kooks who make a mockery of God. These believers think they are wise, but unbelief is not wisdom. Wisdom knows whose voice you are hearing, when to speak, and when to listen. If you haven't heard anything from God, it's better to not speak at all. But if you have heard something from God and you don't speak, that is unbelief—probably even disobedience. Because of hesitation, we have lost a voice, a necessary voice, in engaging our modern culture. Part of our purpose here on earth is to give God a face and a voice in every place we go and with everyone we meet.

Do you see the problem here? One side is too enthusiastic, narcissistic, and ridiculous, while the other side justifies silence in the name of wisdom. The voice God gave to us to reveal His voice—His wisdom, power, and values—is either silent or discarded. If no "God voice" exists within the community, then another voice will take its place, and thus we will have many voices competing for the culture's ear. The culture will only get worse, lost in the rhetoric of agenda-driven media. This is because people were created to listen. They will listen to something. They will turn on the "Tell-A-Vision" and let it tell them a vision; they will go to universities and listen to the professors Tell-A-Vision. They will go to politicians and let them Tell-A-Vision; and they will go to their teenage friends and let them Tell-A-Vision.

The apostle Paul said it best: "And how will they hear without a preacher? And how will they preach unless they are sent?" (Romans 10:14-15). With what have they been sent? They have been sent with a word from God about the gospel and Heaven, wisdom for a better life, common sense, and the power to back it up. How do churched people respond to this? Extreme actions create extreme reactions. If they feel they can't or decide they won't speak for God, then why should they listen to Him in the first place? This produces Christians who don't listen to God and won't speak for Him.

Look at our culture. The results speak for themselves. Many competing voices have marginalized God's voice, at least God's voice spoken via Christian voices. Those voices don't know what to say because they have nothing worthwhile to say. Christians aren't hearing from God, so they can't speak for God; rather, they speak only for themselves. But that voice is flesh-based and erased because it's not graced with God's voice.

Illumination *then* Communication

The truth is that both of these positions are untenable. Both are equally impotent. One moves from faith to presumption, while the other moves from faith to unbelief. The result is that the church and the community both underachieve. The blind lead the blind, and the deaf lead the deaf. But where do we go from here? Is there a better way than presumption or unbelief? Of course, there is. That's why we wrote this book. We want to be part of the church's repentance and returning and restoration as described in Acts 3:19-21:

> *Therefore repent and return, so that your sins may be wiped away, in order that times of refreshing may come from the presence of the Lord; and that He may send Jesus, the Christ appointed for you, whom heaven must receive until the period of restoration of all things about which God spoke by the mouth of His holy prophets from ancient time.*

Could it be that hearing first and speaking second is one of the priorities needing to be restored in Christians today in order for Jesus to return? We believe it is. We believe a time of refreshing is coming to not just freshen us but to refresh us to accurately, powerfully, and profoundly hear from God and speak for God. As God speaks to Jesus (see John 8:26), Jesus speaks to the Holy Spirit (see John 16:13-14; Romans 10:17), and the Holy Spirit in turn speaks to us (see 1 Corinthians 2:10-12).

By talking about hearing the voice of God, we do not mean adding to existing Bible scripture or the LOGOS of God. Rather, we mean using the Word of God in the power of the Holy Spirit to give the "now" word for the occasion. The "now" word is both biblically correct and spiritually accurate. It brings a connection that gives direction for the best outcome for all parties involved. God's "now" word is what is best for both the individual and the community. It's not about having our way, but about having God's way, which is the best way for all parties involved. It's a word of wisdom that is clear to all. Some people may not receive it as valid, but it is undeniably from God. And all concerned parties have a far better voice to listen to than someone else's voice. That voice is God's RHEMA—fully from God and wholly personal and appropriate for a specific person or persons in a precise situation.

Getting a Rhema on Rhema

God's voice speaks in a RHEMA that will increase in clarity and spiritual volume. A future amplification of this voice is coming, much like at times in the past, as in Acts and Exodus. We have needed that voice for a long time. God's voice is given for a reason and a season. It is like a hammer that shatters the rock of barriers to God's will. There will be no doubt when that voice comes. People will know it. It will have a clarity people are not used to. And many more people, with wisdom and faith, will hear from God so that when they speak, others will hear God speaking specifically to them or to their situation. That does not make these RHEMA speakers God; rather, it makes them the carriers and couriers that we, as Christians, were created to be. It's not our word; it's God's specific word for the occasion. God illuminates, and we communicate.

Will these RHEMA words change the Bible? Of course not. Will they add to Scripture? Not one iota. Both David and I are writing this for people who worry about adding to the LOGOS. Listen carefully: We are not professing that RHEMA words spoken by God through any person hold greater authority than the Bible. We affirm the powerful tool of speaking what God is presently speaking to people, issues, and entities. It's biblical. It's essential. It's powerful. It's current and relevant. It's God-breathed and inspired. It's Daniel speaking to the king, Joseph speaking to Pharaoh, or Peter addressing the Jewish leaders of his time. It's not Scripture, but it is from God. And it has the power to create shift.

We shift our spiritual reality by tuning in to God's channel. We are created to hear so that we can fill the earth with the knowledge of the glory of the Lord just like the waters cover the sea as we hear first, speak second. If we shift *our* spiritual reality, then we can shift the spiritual reality of others.

The Three-Legged Stool of Life

As you begin reading this book, David and I want to explore the process of learning with you. Teaching involves mental assent. Learning is when you integrate into your life what you have been taught through revelation or illumination—you own the truth internally and externally.

Two forces compete for the minds of people: the kingdom of God and the kingdom of man. The kingdom of God governs by wisdom—"Let there be light!"—while the kingdom of man governs by knowledge—"Hath God said?" Satan promised Adam and Eve wisdom but gave them knowledge. The result in their lives was the same as in satan's life: Adam and Eve and the rest of humanity made in their image became puffed up and arrogant. Knowledge, if not turned into wisdom, only produces pride.

The kingdom of man builds its own house—nation, culture, and legal system—by knowledge and legislation. How does God build His house? God builds His house by wisdom and transformation: "By wisdom a house is built, and by understanding it is established; and by knowledge the rooms are filled with all precious and pleasant riches" (Proverbs 24:3-4). Wisdom, understanding, and knowledge comprise the three-legged stool of life. We need all three legs for the stool to balance and hold its occupant. Knowledge is where everything starts: "My people are destroyed for lack of knowledge" (Hosea 4:6). Understanding is comprehending what the knowledge implies or means: "... which things we also speak, not in words taught by human wisdom, but in those taught by the Spirit, combining spiritual thoughts with spiritual words" (1 Corinthians 2:13). Wisdom is the proper application of knowledge through understanding: "But by His doing you are in Christ Jesus, who became to us wisdom from God..." (1 Corinthians 1:30).

If you picture wisdom as a house, then understanding is its rooms and knowledge its furnishings. Most people in the world, and some in the church, have built their houses with knowledge rather than wisdom. Wisdom has an illumination aspect to it in order to know how to apply it correctly, which is called understanding. Understanding is knowing the "why" of the "what."

Knowledge is the "what," understanding is the "why," and wisdom is the "how." Knowledge has to do with the head (God opens the eyes of our minds), understanding has to do with the heart (God opens the eyes of our hearts), while wisdom has to do with the feet. It's not only where we apply what we know and understand, but it is also where we have an *internal desire* to know and apply what we have learned. *We own it.* Application comes from the inside out, not the outside in. Knowledge is knowing, understanding is being, and wisdom is doing. The world has knowledge and some understanding, but it has little godly wisdom. Paul called the world's wisdom the wisdom of man.

The church holds the keys of wisdom. Wisdom is a pearl of great price. It is proactive and planned, not reactive or fearful. It's building-orientated and sees the big picture. In fact, God designed the church so that the "manifold wisdom of God might now be made known through the church to the rulers and authorities in the heavenly places" (Ephesians 3:10). God's wisdom is what makes queens "come from afar," like the Queen of Sheba did, "to hear the wisdom of Solomon" (Luke 11:31; see also 1 Kings 10:1). And Paul first prayed for wisdom and understanding so the Ephesian church could use knowledge correctly: "That God of our Lord Jesus Christ, the Father of glory, may give to you a spirit of wisdom and of revelation [understanding] in the knowledge of Him" (Ephesians 1:17).

Let's summarize the progression from knowledge to wisdom, from the external to the internal. Knowledge was never created to be the end; it is a means to an end called wisdom. Knowledge is the alpha, but wisdom is the omega. The key to moving from the alpha to the omega is illumination—God shedding light on everything He created. We need light and we need truth. Knowledge is not what builds the house of God; wisdom is needed for that.

KNOWLEDGE	UNDERSTANDING	WISDOM
What	Why	How
Knowing	Being	Doing
Head	Heart	Feet
Information	Illumination	Transformation
Furniture	Rooms	House

The key to this three-legged learning process is the middle column, where truth and light intersect. That is where one moves from being taught to learning. Don't discount the aha factor in moving truth from the head to the heart to the feet. The key to hearing God's voice is to learn to shift your spiritual reality so that you can shift the spiritual reality of others.

POWER THOUGHTS FOR *Chapter 2*

In the beginning, the Spirit or ruach of God was vibrating, quivering, and wanting to hear something. God spoke, the Holy Spirit listened, and there was illumination and creation. There's the pattern. All the Holy Spirit wants to do in us is listen for what God says and then do it.

—Ed Delph

The word *listen* contains the same letters as the word *silent*.

—Attributed to Alfred Brendel

A good time to keep your mouth shut is when you are in the middle of deep water.

—Unknown

The devil has nothing in Jesus, because Jesus doesn't listen to or give any credence to the devil's words (see John 12:30).

—Ed Delph

The number one issue in today's world is, whose voice are we listening to?

—Alan Platt

Hear first, then speak or act second. The Lord's Prayer is a holy God who is in Heaven speaking to us, His people, what to pray so that His kingdom comes and His will is done on earth as it is in Heaven.

—Ed Delph

Chapter 2

An Encounter with the Ultimate Hearing Aid

*They brought to Him one who was deaf
and spoke with difficulty.*
—Mark 7:32

In January 1997, David and I had a life-changing encounter with God at a cell group meeting in my home, which we have been digesting ever since. We were co-teaching on Mark 7:31-37 when the encounter occurred. We hope that the context of this story helps explain why Jesus did what He did in this passage.

The preceding chapter of Mark describes Jesus feeding five thousand people, a "fish and chips" service for Israel. After that event, Jesus sends His emerging apostles for a stormy boat ride to a Gentile area. In Mark 8, Jesus feeds another four thousand people in a Gentile area called Decapolis, a Gentile "fish and chips" service. Jesus is showing the people in both areas, both Jew and Gentile, as well as His emerging apostles, that everyone is included in God's kingdom—no one is excluded.

After both of these miraculous feedings, the Pharisees approach Jesus and argue with Him. They want to see a sign from Heaven in order to test Him. Jesus doesn't want to play the arguing game because He is aware of a reality of which they aren't aware: even if they saw a miracle, they wouldn't believe it. Rather, they would dissect it, debate it, analyze it, and eventually reject it. They *couldn't* see it because they *wouldn't* see it.

Right after the encounter with the Pharisees, the apostles notice they had just one loaf of bread left, and, like the Pharisees, they began to heatedly discuss their lack of sustenance. Look at Jesus's response in Mark 8:17-21:

> *And Jesus, aware of this, said to them, "Why do you discuss the fact that you have no bread? Do you not yet see or understand? Do you have a hardened heart? Having eyes, do you not see? And having ears, do you not hear? And do you not remember, when I broke the five loaves for the five thousand, how many baskets full of broken pieces you picked up?" They said to Him, "Twelve." "When I broke the seven for the four thousand, how many large baskets full of broken pieces did you pick up?" And they said to Him, "Seven." And He was saying to them, "Do you not yet understand?"*

Whether you are Jew or a Gentile, a Pharisee or an apostle, it is possible to *hear* something yet *not hear* it. You can *see* something, yet *not see* it. You can *know* something, yet *not understand* it. And that's a problem if you were designed to hear, see, and understand. Jesus provides an aha regarding the cause of their lack of understanding spiritual realities: "Why do you not understand what I am saying? It is because you cannot hear My word" (John 8:43). This is a problem for people who are designed by God to hear, see, understand, speak for, and represent Him in the earth today.

Born to Win, Conditioned to Lose

Now let's pick up the narrative beginning with Mark 7:31-37:

> *Again He went out from the region of Tyre, and came through Sidon to the Sea of Galilee, within the region of Decapolis. They brought to Him one who was deaf and spoke with difficulty, and they implored Him to lay His hand on him. Jesus took him aside from the crowd, by himself, and put His fingers into his ears, and after spitting, He touched his tongue with the saliva; and looking up to heaven with a deep sigh, He said to him, "Ephphatha!" that is, "Be opened!" And his ears were opened, and the impediment of his tongue was removed, and he began speaking plainly. And He gave them orders not to tell anyone; but the more He ordered them, the more widely they continued to proclaim it. They were utterly astonished, saying, "He has done all things well; He makes even the deaf to hear and the mute to speak."*

Here is a disabled Gentile man, who is made in the image of God, who speaks with difficulty and a lack of clarity. Perhaps at one time he could clearly hear and speak, but he lost his hearing through an event. And now he was losing his ability to speak because he couldn't properly hear. So his friends brought him to Jesus. They thought, "Jesus, bless him. We like him but we can't understand him. Maybe You can do something with him. He is awkward. No one knows what he is saying." This man was marginalized because he had lost his ability to hear. He was on the outside looking in.

Because he could not hear, the man spoke with difficulty. There was no clarity, no power, no authority, and no life when he spoke. He'd lost the power of his tongue, the power of speech. But the loss of speech was only a symptom of a greater problem that was going on: *He couldn't hear.* One's ability to speak is directly tied to one's ability to hear. A baby hears before speaking clearly; in fact, a baby can't speak what he or she hasn't heard. One must hear first and speak second. We were designed by God, in both the natural and the spiritual realms, to hear first and speak second.

So it is with many people and leaders in the church and marketplace today. In a spiritual sense, they used to clearly hear the voice of God; there was two-way communication with Him. When they heard from God, they powerfully, clearly, and authoritatively spoke. They inspired others. They created shift. They produced fruit that remained. They were transformational. That kind of clear, powerful speaking from Heaven to earth attracted others. These people heard from God and demonstrated love in word and deed. People were blessed and happy to be with them. But they lost their way. Somewhere along the way, they lost their ability to hear, and now they "speak with difficulty." Unintelligible rhetoric and shallow explanations, political maneuvering and cronyism, denominational doctrinarism and career building have taken the place of clear speech.

People don't do this intentionally. But somewhere, somehow, some way, something gets in the way and they lose their ability to clearly speak. They trade God's voice for that of another. Naturally, they justify and explain away this idea. But is it the "now" word of the Lord that creates shift and forward momentum when they speak? Where is the power? Where is the hammer that shatters the rock? My observation is that when a Christian loses the ability and desire to hear from God, the result is that he or she speaks with difficulty.

The truth is that people tolerate leaders like this. Like the men in the gospel story, they say, "Just bless him, Jesus. We like him, but we don't know what he is saying. We can't understand him anymore. Touch him, Jesus, because he needs help." And that is unfortunate. Any church or marketplace leader in that sort of condition needs a hearing aid. It's not about being wrong; it's about being life giving. After all, in the spiritual realm, *if God doesn't say it, then we probably don't have much to say.*

God-Style Prophetic Activation

Jesus had more in mind than just blessing the deaf man and sending him on his way. Jesus wanted to prophetically activate him. He didn't want the man marginalized; He wanted him to hear so he could speak. Jesus wanted the man back in the game of quality life. Observe what Jesus did to put this man back in circulation through prophetic activation: Jesus restored his *hearing first*, then his *speaking second.* Hear God first, then speak to others. We probably don't have much to say if we don't hear anything, but God has a lot to say. If He can heal this man's hearing, then He can do it for us too!

How did Jesus activate the man, bringing him back into his purpose, calling, vision, and destiny? First, Jesus took the man away from the multitude. He understood that the village had a voice. Jesus wanted the man to hear His voice, not all the other voices from the multitude. Think of it: many of those around him were just as spiritually deaf as the man was physically deaf. Jesus took the man out of his comfort zone; He "turned off the television" of others telling him their vision. Jesus got him alone so that God could speak to him though Jesus. The man got alone with God so that he could speak to others the words God spoke to him.

Second, Jesus put His fingers in the man's ears before doing anything else. Why did Jesus do this? It is because people can't speak clearly until they hear clearly. On this occasion, Jesus put His fingers into the man's ears, and after spitting on whatever came out of his ears, He touched the man's tongue with His saliva. Why do you think Jesus put His fingers into the man's ears first? Why do you think Jesus spit on whatever came out of the man's ears? Why did Jesus then touch the man's tongue with His saliva? It was because God told Him to do it in that order. Jesus only did what the Father spoke. God spoke, Jesus responded, and the man was healed.

Can you imagine what Jesus thought about this? Perhaps He was thinking, "This doesn't make sense. This is disgusting! Father, You have told Me to heal other people, and I have never had to do it this way before! What will the people who are watching Me think? Father, are You sure about this? Do You realize that there will be really enthusiastic Christians in the future who will read this and try to do this to other people when You never told them to do it?" (Just kidding!) Perhaps that is why Jesus sighed. Whatever Jesus was thinking in the moment, there is a lesson that God gave during that encounter. To speak properly, we first need to hear properly. Hear first, speak second. That's how God's kingdom comes and His will is done on Earth as it is in Heaven.

Third, Jesus, after hearing what the Father told Him to say, said to the deaf man, "Ephphatha! Be opened!" Isn't it interesting that after the man's ears were opened, "the impediment of his tongue was removed," and then "he began speaking plainly"? The crowd was "utterly astonished." They saw the miracle. But even more importantly, they heard the kingdom lesson from Heaven. Notice what they observed and the order in which they said it: "He makes even the deaf to hear and the dumb to speak." Hear first, speak second. This changes everything.

Whose Voice Are We Hearing?

Let's focus on what Jesus spoke to the deaf man as well as to the people in the surrounding multitude from the village. Remember that everything Jesus did was for the benefit of those who were watching. While the "Be opened" statement was specifically for the deaf man's ears, there was an additional story behind the story—Jesus was telling all of us to be open to God's voice. The multitude heard the village's voice, peoples' voices, Gentile voices, and their culture's voice. But Jesus was introducing all of them to *the* voice, the voice of God.

The multitude were listening to, obeying, and serving the voices of entities that were as spiritually deaf as the man was physically deaf. The village's voice had nothing to say because its message didn't come from God. The village spoke with difficulty because its populace couldn't clearly hear. Jesus was telling them in this encounter, "You are just as deaf as the deaf man you brought to Me. And because you are spiritually deaf, you speak with difficulty, telling lies from the father of lies and calling it truth. You assess the times with humanity's fallen wisdom. Because you are *hearing* the wrong voice, you are *speaking* the wrong message. In the same way, My Father physically healed this man, and I want to spiritually heal you. But you will have to 'be open!' Listen! Do you hear who and what I hear? If so, then you will speak what I speak. Allow the Word to speak a word before you speak a word."

Be Open

Like He did with the deaf man in Mark 7, Jesus is taking us away from the multitude of voices, distractions, and obstacles that keep us from hearing the Father's voice. As He did with the deaf man, Jesus wants to open our ears. After the deaf man's ears were opened, his mouth suddenly opened too. He no longer spoke with difficulty. Because he could now hear clearly, he could also speak clearly. In today's world, clarity is a rarity.

Be open and be wise. Jesus didn't say to throw away discernment. However, He didn't say to throw away faith either! Let me spring into prophetic mode: Be open! Open your ears before you open your mouth. If you can't hear God, then you can't speak what God is speaking. If you can't hear the whole truth, then you won't speak the whole truth. If you can't hear faith, you won't speak faith. If you can't hear cultural transformation, you won't speak cultural transformation. If you can't hear engaging and influencing the seven mountains of culture, then you won't speak to and engage and influence the seven mountains of culture. If you can't hear what the Spirit is saying, then you will never say what the Spirit is saying. If you can't hear apostolic ministry, then you won't speak apostolic ministry.

John, the beloved apostle of God, demonstrates this reality: "I was in the Spirit on the Lord's day, and I heard behind me a loud voice like the sound of a trumpet" (Revelation 1:10). Notice that John didn't speak until God first spoke. If we can't hear wisdom, then we won't speak wisdom. If we can't hear love, then we won't speak love. If we can't hear victory, then we won't speak victory. If we can't hear forgiveness, then we won't speak forgiveness. If we can't hear the value of prayer, then we won't speak the value of prayer. If we can't hear marketplace ministry, then we won't speak marketplace ministry. If we can't hear character, then we won't speak character. If we can't hear hope, then we won't speak hope. If we can't hear the fruit of the Spirit, then we will never speak the fruit of the Spirit. If we can't hear the gifts of the Spirit, then we will never speak the gifts of the Spirit. If we can't hear valuing others, then we will never speak value to others. If we can't hear unity, then we won't speak unity. The source of what we hear is vitally important, for it determines what we speak.

Whose voice are you listening to? If you are truly hearing God's voice, then be open! This truth applies to you, your marriage, your family, your business, your finances, your spiritual life, and your education. It applies to your spending habits; where, when, and how to invest; and how to build your business. The culture has a voice but it is not God's voice.

Being open requires having both an open mind and open ears. Many Christians have it backward: they are close-minded to what God is saying and open-minded to what the multitude is saying. Clean out your ears that are plugged with the earwax of the village so your ears can clearly hear God when He speaks. Then the impediment of your tongue will be removed as well. Then you'll be positioned for an abundant life in lean times. Jesus did this when He was tempted by satan in the wilderness, showing us how to live in tumultuous times: "Man shall not live on bread alone, but on every word [RHEMA—an utterance from God for a specific occasion] that proceeds out of the mouth of God" (Matthew 4:4).

What You Hate May Be That Which Activates You

Do you know the definition of *poor*? POOR means Passing Over Opportunities Repeatedly. This book, if applied correctly, will have the outcome of RICH: Radiant, Inspired, Competent, and Healthy. Don't be closed. Quit focusing on the way circumstances appear; quit focusing on the confusion and tumult that surrounds you. God is not surprised by any of these situations. God wants to move you from the outhouse to the penthouse. In fact, you are already there; you are already seated with Christ in heavenly places. God has everything under control. The big picture is secure. Don't be intimidated. The village wants you to focus on the smaller picture—don't fall for it.

Christians in today's world often start wondering whether God really exists. I've noticed many Christians who are like the man in Mark 7: they used to hear clearly and they could speak clearly, but now they are speaking a kind of semi-God, semi-village-type of rhetoric that sounds "difficult." The deaf man didn't know that he was speaking with difficulty because his hearing was blocked. Likewise, many of us don't know we are speaking with difficulty because, either intentionally or unintentionally, our hearing is impaired, which causes our speaking to be impaired. We think we are wiser than others, we justify our actions, we are "contemporary," and we compromise in crucial areas. As a result, there is no power in our lives anymore—and we don't even know it! But believe me, everyone else notices.

As you continue reading this book, David and I suggest that you allow the Holy Spirit to speak to you. Maybe Jesus will stick His fingers in your ears. Maybe Jesus will do something that offends you. Maybe He will spit on whatever He takes out of your ears and then touch your tongue. Don't get mad at Jesus. He only does what the Father tells Him to do. You can be sure that if it comes from God, then it is good for you because God is good. What you think you hate may be that which activates you! Mike Murdock says it even better: "Sometimes you've got to do something you hate to get to something you love."[1]

Listening

As I was writing this book, I was amazed to discover a significant addition in two familiar biblical accounts I have been aware of for years. The first time this account is mentioned is at Jesus's baptism and the second time is atop a mountain that was transfigured because the person at the top was being transfigured. Notice the small but life-changing difference:

> *And after being baptized, Jesus went up immediately from the water; and behold, the heavens were opened, and he saw the Spirit of God descending as a dove and lighting upon Him, and behold, a voice out of the heavens said, "This is My beloved Son, in whom I am well-pleased'"* (Matthew 3:16-17).

> *While* [Peter] *was still speaking, behold, a bright cloud overshadowed them; and behold, a voice out of the cloud said, "This is My beloved Son, with whom I am well-pleased; listen to Him!"* (Matthew 17:5)

The voice has the same source, the Son is the same, the two "beholds" in each account are the same, and the bright clouds in each account are the same. Everything is the same until we get to the last two words in the second account. The second account adds, "Listen to Him!" Some other versions say, "Hear Him!" Why should we hear Jesus? It is because He hears the Father. Why should we listen to Jesus? It is because He listens to the Father. God interrupted Peter's speech and accolades—Peter didn't have much to say, but God did. God gives us crucial insight here: God speaks *to* us so that God can speak *through* us. The first time this happens in Mathew, God makes a declaration; the second time this happens in Matthew, God gives a command. When you want to transfigure cultural mountains, you must first be transfigured yourself by hearing Jesus.

Since becoming a Christian, I have often struggled in my practice of prayer. I have been through the "Could you not pray with Me for one hour?" prayer programs. I have been through the "binding and loosing" prayer movements, and I have been through the "soaking prayer" movements. I thought I was not a prayer person until I saw those last two words of Matthew 17:5: "Hear Him." It was like God was speaking to me: "Listen to Me. Get understanding. Learn the story behind the story."

As I was reflecting on this, I heard God say: "Ed, you don't realize it, but you are a competent prayer person. While the 'Peter types' talk, you listen. You are tuned into Me and what I am saying. You think about Me all the time. You have stumbled into something many aren't yet aware of. You listen. You hear Me. You don't ask for much. You don't request much. You just listen. You have an ear for revelation. You find gold. You have something to say because you listen to Me. If you open your mouth wide, I will fill it."

Me? A prayer person? I admit that I do think about God as often as I can. I tune into the God channel regularly. I don't have to try to think about God; it's just who I am. It's my nature. There are other types of prayer people, too, and I am honored to know them. There are intercessors who stand in the gap, spiritual prayer warriors, meditators and chanters, and prayer-of-faith people. Maybe the prayer army that needs to be raised up in today's world is an army of listeners, who become learners, and learners who become doers. Maybe God is raising up people who have real wisdom because they hear Him. History has shown many of the strongest prayer people are people who hear first then speak or act second on what they heard. After all, as Alfred Brendel says, the words *listen* and *silent* have the same exact letters in them.[2]

Notes

1. Mike Murdock, *Wisdom for Crisis Times: Master Keys for Success in Times of Change* (Ft. Worth, TX: The Wisdom Center, 1992).
2. This portion of this chapter was taken from an article that appeared in Ed Delph's newspaper column "The Church-Community Connection" in September 2016. Ed has written this column since November 2004 for the Glendale Star and Peoria Times in the Phoenix-Metro area, as well as for outlets in other cities outside of the United States

POWER THOUGHTS FOR *Chapter 3*

God's Words Create God's Worlds, "By faith we understand that the worlds were prepared by the word (RHEMA) of God, so that what is seen was not made of things which are visible." Hebrews 11:3

The first thing we learn about God is He speaks! The second thing we learn about God is whenever God wants to make the invisible visible, He illuminates. Logos was concealed until God spoke "Let there be light." The Holy Spirit created what God spoke. God's truth is revealed by God's light.

—Ed Delph

Let me share with you what my wife and I experienced during a cave tour in Indiana. We were several hundred feet below the ground in a big cave. The leader of the tour said, "Now we would like you to experience what real darkness is. We are going to turn off the lights in this cave for a short period of time. What you formerly thought of as darkness is not darkness at all. There was always a bit of light for your pupils to adjust to. In this cave, the pupils in your eyes are ineffective. This is real darkness."

She was right. I could not see anything. The Bible calls it "gross darkness." I noticed something though: even though I couldn't see, I could hear.

All seven mountains of society think they have a corner on the truth, but it takes real insight to know what truth is and what truth is not. Insight comes from hearing God. If we don't have God's insight, or truth with light, then we will be groping in that dark cave with no lights on.

Catch God's frequency. Frequent seeing comes by frequently hearing God. Let the Word speak to you a word before you speak a word. In a spiritual sense, whenever you have illumination, light, or insight, someone heard something.

—Ed and Becky Delph

The best vision is insight.

—Malcolm Forbes

Prayer is not a monologue, but dialogue.

—Andrew Murray[1]

Walking and talking with God in the cool of the evening is what life was like before the fall.

—Ed Delph

God whispers because He's close.

—Steven Furtick[2]

Jesus could go through Calvary because He had prayed in Gethsemane.

—Harvey Lifsey[3]

Illumination comes before communication. We must first hear spiritual thoughts from God before speaking what God had said to the person God wanted us to talk to. We're the conduit, not the spring.

—Ed Delph

Chapter 3

UNLEASHING SPIRITUAL SHOCKWAVES FROM HEAVEN

Let's explore a kingdom reality in a practical way starting with the question we posed in the Introduction: which is more important, the sense of hearing or the sense of seeing? Before answering this question, consider what God reveals to us in the first words of the Bible:

> *In the beginning God created the heavens and the earth. And the earth was formless and void, and darkness was over the surface of the deep; and the Spirit of God* [ruach] *was moving over the surface* [a waste or emptiness] *of the waters. Then God said, "Let there be light," and there was light* (Genesis 1:1-3).

The first thing we learn about God from the Bible is that He speaks. The Father spoke, and the Holy Spirit heard and responded to the Father's voice. Speech activated the Holy Spirit to create something called light. The Hebrew language explains what God said better than the English translation: "Light, be!" The spoken word of God created the world of God. After God spoke, it was "on earth is it is in heaven." No hesitation, no time taken, just, "Light be!" and it was. God spoke, the Holy Spirit listened, and *boom*, there was light. Once again, we see the principle of hear first and speak second. God speaks what is on

His mind, then the Holy Spirit responds. The result was that God saw what was created by hearing His voice was good.

The answer to the question I asked above is that hearing is more important than seeing, especially when it comes to the spiritual realm. God designed us to be responsive to His will being done on earth as it is done in Heaven. We were designed, as children of God, to listen and respond to what God says in the same way that the Holy Spirit responded to what God said at creation.

What we see often gets in the way of what God is saying. Our eyes speak one thing and God speaks another thing altogether. Our eyes have a voice like that village—unspiritual sight influences our minds more than our spiritual hearing does. We all have experienced that at some time in our lives. Generally, the result of us choosing the way of natural sight over spiritual hearing is like Adam without a wife—it is simply "not good."

Hear First, Speak Second: The Ministry of Jesus

As David and I began to explore the idea of hear first, speak second, we noticed a powerful prophetic pattern throughout the Bible that impacted us in an unprecedented way. We had an aha moment. We noticed that usually in the Bible, hearing appeared before seeing. How are we, as believers, to interpret what we see until we have heard about and understand what we are seeing? Here are some examples from the life of Jesus:

> *Jesus therefore answered them, and said, "My doctrine is not Mine, but His who sent Me"* (John 7:16 NKJV).
>
> *... but He who sent me is true; and the things which I hear from Him, these I speak to the world* (John 8:26).
>
> *... and I do nothing on My own initiative, but I speak these things as the Father taught Me* (John 8:28).

> *He who is of God hears the words of God; for this reason you do not hear them, because you are not of God* (John 8:47).
>
> *For I did not speak on My own initiative, but the Father Himself who sent Me has given Me commandment as to what to say and what to speak* (John 12:49).
>
> *I know that His commandment is eternal life; therefore the things I speak, I speak just as the Father has told Me* (John 12:50).
>
> *Do you not believe that I am in the Father, and the Father is in Me? The words that I say to you I do not speak on My own initiative, but the Father abiding in Me does His works* (John 14:10).
>
> *No longer do I call you slaves, for the slave does not know what his master is doing; but I have called you friends, for all things that I have heard from My Father I have made known to you* (John 15:15).
>
> *For I have given unto them the words which Thou gavest Me; and they have received them, and have known surely that I came out from Thee, and they have believed that Thou didst send Me* (John 17:8 KJV).

Jesus heard first from the Father and then spoke and ministered out of what He heard. The Word doesn't speak a word unless the God of the Word speaks a word first.

Hear First, Speak Second: The Ministry of the Holy Spirit

The Holy Spirit does His ministry in much the same way. The Father speaks a word to the Holy Spirit before the Holy Spirit says a word to us. Consider some of these passages of scripture:

> *I have many more things to say to you, but you cannot bear them now. But when He, the Spirit of truth, comes, He will guide you into all the truth; for He will not speak on His own initiative, but whatever He hears, He will speak; and He will disclose to you what is to come* (John 16:12-13).
>
> *For to us God revealed them through the Spirit; for the Spirit searches all things, even the depths of God. For who among men knows the thoughts of a man except the spirit of the man which is in him? Even so the thoughts of God no one knows except the Spirit of God. Now we have received, not the spirit of the world, but the Spirit who is from God, so that we may know the things freely given to us by God, which things we also speak, not in words taught by human wisdom, but in those taught by the Spirit, combining spiritual thoughts with spiritual words.*
>
> *But a natural man does not accept the things of the Spirit of God, for they are foolishness to him; and he cannot understand them, because they are spiritually appraised. But he who is spiritual appraises all things, yet he himself is appraised by no one. For who has known the mind of the Lord, that he will instruct Him? But we have the mind of Christ* (1 Corinthians 2:10-16).

Christians, in a corporate sense, have the mind of Christ because we have the Holy Spirit dwelling within us. As Jesus hears the Father speak, and as the Holy Spirit hears Jesus speak, so we hear the Holy Spirit speak so that when we speak, we know that God is speaking to the world in Jesus's name. Hear first and speak second. God has a voice—your voice—speaking to today's confused world. That's the way God designed us to live. In fact, that's our sweet spot. That's where we become X factors and difference makers. God has a voice, our voice, if we can truly hear first and speak second.

Hear First, Speak Second: The Ministry of the Kingdom of God and Heaven

From the beginning of Jesus's ministry, His central theme was the kingdom of God. God's invisible person, kingdom, jurisdiction, power, and glory in Heaven were to be made visible on the earth. How was God going to do that? This coming of God's kingdom is going to happen by speaking the word of God to reveal the will of the God of the Word. God spoke from Heaven to those on earth who were to first hear then speak God's word and His will to the world.

The kingdom of God. That's quite a concept, isn't it? How does it work? How does God's kingdom come and His will get done on Earth as it is in Heaven? How does God reveal Himself? How does an invisible God make Himself visible? How will we, as people, ever know that His "is the kingdom and the glory and the power forever" (see Matthew 6:13)? To know how the kingdom of God operates, we must understand the mother of all parables. If we don't understand this parable, then we will never understand all the other parables. In fact, the interpretive key to all other parables, as well as to understanding the kingdom of God, is in the parable of the sower and the seed.

In each of the accounts of the sower and the seed, Jesus spoke what the Father said: "He spoke many things to them in parables" (Matthew 13:3), and "He spoke by way of a parable" (Luke 8:4). Perhaps the best account of this is what Mark wrote: "Listen to this! Behold, the sower went out to sow" (Mark 4:3). See the pattern here? Listen, then behold; hear, and then see. Jesus wanted His disciples to open their ears to God so they could understand what they were about to see; Jesus wanted them to know what to say to those who were waiting for answers.

"And He said to them, 'Do you not understand this parable? And how will you understand all the parables?'" (Mark 4:13). The interpretive key to understanding all the parables is this: "Now the parable is this: the seed is the word of God" (Luke 8:11). God fills the earth with the knowledge of the Lord by sowing His Word into people. Let's connect these thoughts: "The kingdom of heaven is like a man who sowed good seed," and "the seed is the Word of God" (Matthew 13:24 NKJV; Luke 8:11). From this we can see that the Word of God comes from the God of the Word first. What the God of the Word spoke is the Word of God—that Word we sow into the earth and into the lives of others. This is how His kingdom comes and His will is done on Earth as it is in Heaven.

As Jesus goes on to tell the parable, we are presented with a problem. The problem in this parable is not the seed; the problem is not that the seed wasn't sown. Rather, the problem occurs where the seed *was* sown. Three times the seed was sown into the ears of people who couldn't or wouldn't hear. But the fourth time the seed was sown into the ears of people who could hear. Jesus used four types of soil as examples of the types of hearts the seed was sown into, thereby revealing the condition of the hearers' ears and hearts. The Greek word for *seed* used here is *sporos*, meaning "a scattering of seed" or "scattered seed." The word used here and throughout this parable for God's Word is LOGOS. LOGOS is the entire Bible, the totality of God's Word. Let's look at the four different types of soil:

1. Shallow soil: "Those beside the road are those who have heard; then the devil comes and takes away the word from their heart, so that they will not believe and be saved" (Luke 8:12). Matthew recorded this idea in a kingdom context: "When anyone hears the word of the kingdom and does not understand it, the evil one comes and snatches away what has been sown in his heart. This is the one on whom seed was sown beside the road" (Matthew 13:19).

2. Rocky soil. "Those on the rocky soil are those who, when they hear, receive the word with joy; and these

have no firm root; they believe for a while, and in time of temptation fall away" (Luke 8:13).

3. Thorny soil. "The seed which fell among the thorns, these are the ones who have heard, and as they go on their way they are choked with worries and riches and pleasures of this life, and bring no fruit to maturity" (Luke 8:14).

4. Good soil. "But the seed in the good soil, these are the ones who have heard the word in an honest and good heart, and hold it fast, and bear fruit with perseverance" (Luke 8:15).

What is good soil? It's people who have heard and understood the Word of God that was sown into them, and thus it takes root and produces fruit. They are fruitful and they multiply the fruit that they bear. These people are called Christians or "little Christs." They can only be sustained by living one way: hearing first and speaking second. As Acts 17:28 says, "for in Him we live and move and have our being" (NKJV).

You may recall that after Jesus told the parable of the kingdom, He ended with this admonition to all people: "And as He said these things, He would call out, 'He who has ears to hear, let him hear'" (Luke 8:8). Then He spoke to His listening disciples before He explained the parable: "To you it is granted to know the mysteries of the kingdom of God, but to the rest it is in parables, so that seeing they may not see, and hearing they may not understand" (Luke 8:10). Why couldn't they see? It was because if they can't hear God's voice, then they will never be able to understand what they are seeing. Jesus then concluded this parable by speaking to them a Word from God: "So take care how you listen; for whoever has [the ability to hear God clearly], to him shall more [ability to hear God clearly] be given; and whoever does not have [the ability of hear God clearly], even what he thinks he has [the ability to hear God clearly], shall be taken away from him" (Luke 8:18).

If you are worried about being able to understand spiritual realities, parables, the Bible, and hearing the voice of God, don't worry. The disciples were in the same shape as you (and me too). Look at how Jesus handled this issue with His disciples: "And with many such parables He was speaking the word to them as they were able to hear it" (Mark 4:33). Relax, because God wants you to truly hear Him more than you want to hear from God.

Hear First, Speak Second in the Names of God

As I was writing this book, a voice spoke within me (the Lord spoke to me in my mind like in First Corinthians 2:10-14). The voice said, "Check out all the names of God in the Old and New Testaments. I want to show you something." Allow me to uncover it for you and hopefully recover it for the church. Here is what I discovered:

1. In every place where a different name of God is mentioned, the Lord spoke before, during, or immediately after the His name was mentioned.

2. God is revealing to us not only His names but His nature. His names are like a prism. As light hits a prism, it bursts into different colors and hues that show what light is made of. In the same way, God wants to reveal Himself as well as His will. These bursts expose some amazing aspects and revelations about God.

3. Each time God revealed an aspect of His nature, He spoke. The reason He spoke was for our benefit and our ever-increasing revelation of God. We get to know God better through understanding His names. God spoke another aspect of His glory so that we could ascend with Him, going from glory to ever-increasing enlightening, and illuminating glory. When He speaks, our response is to listen. Hear first, speak second. God initiates by speaking, and we respond by

doing. It's our responsibility to respond to His ability as He speaks first.

Here is a list of most of the Hebrew names of God representing His multifaceted character. Notice that God speaks in each example:

- *Who God is: Elohim* means Creator, mighty and strong. Since it is a plural word, it contains the Trinity. It represents the one, true God and His mighty and sovereign work (see Genesis 1:1). *What God spoke*: In the beginning, *Elohim* created the heavens and the earth (see Genesis 1:1), and then *Elohim* said, "Let there be light," and there was light (see Genesis 1:3).
- *Who God is: El Shaddai* means "God Almighty." This speaks to God's ultimate power over all things; it represents that God is omnipotent and omnipresent. *What God spoke*: "Now when Abram was ninety-nine years old, the Lord appeared to Abram and said to him, 'I am God Almighty [*El Shaddai*]; walk before Me, and be blameless. I will establish My covenant between Me and you, and I will multiply you exceedingly.' Abram fell on his face, and God talked with him..." (Genesis 17:1-3).
- *Who God is*: Yahweh/Jehovah. Strictly speaking, this is the only proper name for God, translated in English Bibles as "LORD" to distinguish it from Adonai, which is translated as "Lord." This name specifies an immediacy, a presence. Yahweh is present, accessible, and near to those who call on Him for deliverance (see Psalm 107:13), forgiveness (see Psalm 25:11), and guidance (see Psalm 31:3). *What God spoke*: "And God said to Moses, 'I AM WHO I AM' [Yahweh]; and He said, 'Thus you shall say to the sons of Israel, "I Am [Yahweh] has sent me to you"'" (Exodus 3:14).

- *Who God is*: Adonai, which is translated as "Lord" throughout our English translations. It was used in place of Yahweh, which was thought by the Jews to be too sacred to be uttered by sinful men. In the Old Testament, Yahweh is more often used in God's dealings with His people, while Adonai is used more when He deals with the Gentiles. This signifies that God is Lord over all of us collectively and as individuals. *What God spoke*: "After these things the word of the Lord came to Abram in a vision, saying, 'Do not fear, Abram, I am a shield to you; your reward shall be very great.' Abram said, 'O Lord God [Adonai], what will You give me, since I am childless...?'" (Genesis 15:1-2).
- *Who God Is: Jehovah-Jireh* means the Lord Will Provide. This name of God was memorialized by Abraham when God provided the ram to be sacrificed in place of Abraham's son Isaac. *What God spoke*: "Abraham called the name of that place The Lord Will Provide [*Jehovah-Jireh*], as it is said to this day, 'In the mount of it will be provided.' Then the angel of the Lord called to Abraham a second time from heaven, and said, 'By Myself I have sworn, declares the Lord, because you have done this thing and have not withheld your son, your only son, indeed I will greatly bless you, and I will greatly multiply your seed as the stars of the heavens and as the sand which is on the seashore; and your seed shall possess the gate of their enemies. In your seed all the nations of the earth shall be blessed, because you have obeyed My voice'" (Genesis 22:14-18).
- *Who God is: Jehovah-Rapha* means the Lord Who Heals. God heals both in body and in soul. In body,

God heals by preserving from and curing diseases, and He heals in soul by pardoning iniquities. *What God spoke*: "And He said, 'If you will give earnest heed to the voice of the Lord your God, and do what is right in His sight, and give ear to His commandments, and keep all His statutes, I will put none of the diseases on you which I have put on the Egyptians; for I, the Lord, am your healer [*Jehovah-Rapha*]'" (Exodus 15:26).

- *Who God is: Jehovah-Nissi* means the Lord Our Banner. Banner is to be understood as a rallying place of the Lord. This name commemorates the desert victory over the Amalekites in Exodus 17. *What God spoke*: "Then the Lord said to Moses, 'Write this in a book as a memorial and recite it to Joshua, that I will utterly blot out the memory of Amalek from under heaven.' Moses built an altar and named it The Lord is My Banner [*Jehovah-Nissi*]; and he said, 'The Lord has sworn; the Lord will have war against Amalek from generation to generation'" (Exodus 17:14-16 NKJV).
- *Who God Is: Jehovah-Shalom* means the Lord Our Peace. This is the name Gideon gave to the altar he built after the angel of the Lord assured him he would not die as he thought he would after seeing Him. *What God spoke*: "When Gideon saw that he was the angel of the Lord, he said, 'Alas, O Lord God! For now I have seen the angel of the Lord face to face.' The Lord said to him, 'Peace to you, do not fear; you shall not die.' Then Gideon built an altar there to the Lord and named it The Lord is Peace [*Jehovah-Shalom*]..." (Judges 6:22-24).

- *Who God is: Jehovah-Shammah* means the Lord Is with Us. This name is revealed in the last verse in the book of Ezekiel. It was spoken by God in the design of the new city and the inheritances to the tribes of Israel. *What God Spoke*: "The city shall be 18,000 cubits round about; and the name of the city from that day shall be, 'The Lord is There'" (Ezekiel 48:35).[4]

Do you see the pattern here? It is always hearing first and then speaking second. I could have gone on and described many more names of God, but I think with the above examples, my point has been made. Every place we see another one of God's names, God always spoke surrounding that event. The only exception to this might be *Jehovah-Rohi* (The Lord Is My Shepherd) in Psalm 23. However, we can assume that David, the shepherd boy who slew the giant Goliath, wrote this after getting a revelation of God in a way he could understand. No doubt the Lord had been speaking to him.

Hear First, Speak Second: Other Occurrences in the Bible

Isn't it interesting that the story of Jesus healing the deaf and mute man appears in Mark 7 and then the story of Jesus healing the blind man appears in Mark 8? Hearing is the most important sense that we can have when it comes to the spiritual realm. Here are a few other verses that contain the hear first, speak second principle:

> *But* [Jesus] *answered and said, "It is written, 'Man shall not live on bread alone, but on every word that proceeds out of the mouth of God'"* (Matthew 4:4).

> *He who has an ear, let him hear what the Spirit says to the churches* (Revelation 2:7).

For the testimony of Jesus is the spirit of prophecy (Revelation 19:10).

Everyone must be quick to hear, slow to speak and slow to anger (James 1:19).

I, the Lord, am your God, who brought you up from the land of Egypt; open your mouth wide, and I will fill it (Psalm 81:10).

And they were utterly astonished, saying, "He has done all things well; He makes even the deaf to hear, and the mute to speak" (Mark 7:37).

... and the ears of the deaf will be unstopped. Then the lame will leap like a deer, and the tongue of the mute will shout for joy (Isaiah 35:5-6).

A lion has roared! Who will not fear? The Lord God has spoken! Who can but prophesy? (Amos 3:8)

And I will keep watch to see what He will speak to me, and how I may reply when I am reproved. Then the Lord answered me and said, "Record the vision and inscribe it on tablets that the one who reads it may run" (Habakkuk 2:1-2).

He said to me, "Prophesy over these bones and say to them, 'O dry bones, hear the word of the Lord.'"...so I prophesied as I was commanded" (Ezekiel 37:4,7).

Then I heard the voice of the Lord, saying, "Whom shall I send, and who will go for Us?" Then I said, "Here am I. Send me!" He said, "Go, and tell this people: 'Keep on listening, but do not perceive; keep on looking, but do not understand'" (Isaiah 6:8-9).

So faith comes from hearing, and hearing by the word [concerning] *Christ* (Romans 10:17).

A more accurate translation for Romans 10:17 would be, "So the faith to be saved by believing and confessing Christ came by hearing a specific, personal, clear word from God concerning Christ that 'Jesus is Lord.'"

> *But before all these things, they will lay their hands on you and will persecute you, delivering you to the synagogues and prisons, bringing you before kings and governors for My name's sake. It will lead to an opportunity for your testimony. So make up your minds not to prepare beforehand to defend yourselves; for I will give you utterance* [a mouth] *and wisdom which none of your opponents will be able to resist or refute* (Luke 21:12-15).

Other Mothers and Other Brothers

Right after this encounter with the mother of all parables, God gives us the bottom line with another unusual encounter:

> *And* [Jesus's] *mother and brothers came to Him, and they were unable to get to Him because of the crowd. And it was reported to Him, "Your mother and Your brothers are standing outside, wishing to see You." But He answered and said to them, "My mother and My brothers are these who hear the word* [LOGOS] *of God and do it"* (Luke 8:19-21).

I like that. Being a brother of Jesus would look good on our résumé, wouldn't it? How does "mothership" and "brothership" happen anyhow? Hear first, speak second. That's what we were designed by God to do; it is only then that we are in our sweet spot. We are fulfilling the purposes of God for our generation as we hear what God says and then faithfully say what He has given to us. We aren't listening to other competing voices in society and we aren't listening to our own voice; rather, we are listening to God's channel: "Your kingdom come, Your will be done." We are the good soil that produces fruit, some thirtyfold, some sixtyfold, and some a hundredfold.

The Chicken with Its Head Cut Off

Jane Cherney, one of NationStrategy's intercessors, recently shared with me some Bible verses that stunned her regarding the principle of hear first, speak second:

> *Therefore no one is to act as your judge in regard to food or drink or in respect to a festival or a new moon or a Sabbath day—things which are a mere shadow of what is to come; but the substance belongs to Christ* (Colossians 2:16-17).

The literal translation of the last part is "but the body of Christ belongs to Christ." Let's look at the next two verses.

> *Let no one keep defrauding you of your prize by delighting is self-abasement and the worship of the angels, taking his stand on visions he has seen, inflated without cause by his fleshly mind, and* ***not holding fast to the head, from whom the entire body, being supplied and held together*** *by the joints and ligaments, grows with a growth which is from God* (Colossians 2:18-19).

We can see that the body of Christ belongs to Christ, who is the Head of the body. But these misguided leaders have lost their head. They are running around with their heads cut off. When Jane saw these verses, she asked the Lord what they meant. And the Lord told her, "That's my church."

My grandfather owned several cattle ranches. I will never forget the "harvest time" of preparing for a night's dinner. It wasn't a pretty sight, to say the least. The decapitated chicken's body would run all over the place with blood spurting everywhere in big pulses. When a chicken loses its head, there's heaps of activity for a few brief moments with no direction, but then the end comes quickly. Never confuse motion with direction.

Don't worry. Neither Jane nor I want to bash the church. But we thought this revelation and its interpretation were interesting considering writing this book. Certainly, at times, Christ-followers and churches have acted like headless chickens—lots of motion with no direction. Without our Head (Jesus), we've stopped listening because we have no head. We can't hear what the Head is saying and therefore we lack any productive or significant direction. We have stopped hearing first and speaking or doing second. We don't know it, but Christ's life is draining from us, leaving us headless and soon-to-be lifeless.

Think of it. Why did David slay Goliath? He listened for God's direction and heard what God wanted him to do. Faith came to David by God's direction. David spoke God's direction, and then he did God's direction. As a result of hearing first and speaking second, David experienced a great victory for himself, his people, and his God. He had his head. His body and head were connected. He even got his name in the Bible.

But why did David get in trouble with Bathsheba? It was because he lost his head. The sight of that beautiful woman spoke louder to him than what he had heard. And just like that, there he was—the great warrior king, a man after God's own heart, a prophet—running around with his head cut off, doing exactly what the body always does without its Head, which is lose direction. The results would haunt him for the rest of his life. And this all happened because in the moment his head was severed from his body in a figurative sense. He quit hearing first and speaking second.

The Bible is loaded with headless people running around in chaos. Thank God that many of them eventually rediscovered their lost head. For example, let's take Peter, a man who was full of faith and a glorious future, denying Christ three times. Jesus even warned Peter about this before it occurred. Perhaps it is no coincidence it was a chicken crowing three times that jolted Peter back into reality. Peter didn't listen first and speak second; he went headless for a short season. Then later he got his head back.

This happens to church people, churches, pastors, communities, cities, and even countries. When the body of Christ is severed from the Head (who is Christ), the body or flesh will do what it always does, which is sin, miss the mark, underachieve, and do meaningless activity that has little outcome. Some nimrod from the body will always come along with something that sounds good but is not from God. Remember, the wages of sin is death. Where does sin ultimately come from? Sin comes from not listening to God, not hearing God, and not acting on what God speaks. This is why the principle of hear first, speak second is so important. Otherwise, we end up making quite a spectacle of ourselves—just like that chicken.

Here's a takeaway for kingdom ministry: Hear from God first and then speak, see, act, and do second. Illumination comes before communication. Revelation takes place, then impartation. That's the kingdom. That's how the spiritual realm works. That's how we were designed to work. It's also how businesses work, churches work, nations work, cities work, governments work, media works, athletics works, and science works. Everyone was created by the God of the Word to hear the word of God. Anything less than that will eventually underachieve.

We unleash spiritual shockwaves into Heaven as we report for duty and do what God says to do. Ministry is doing what God told us to do in prayer. We hear first, then speak second, making our part on Earth as it is in Heaven. We make the invisible become visible by making the inaudible become audible. Intimacy with God is our source.

What is Rhema?

You might be saying to yourself, "Okay, let's get on to the subject of RHEMA." In order to understand what RHEMA is and how it works, we wanted to give you the "why" of RHEMA first. RHEMA needs a context if it is to be effective. The biblical pattern of hear first, speak second is what RHEMA was designed for. What do you hear first and speak second? What God tells you.

If we just gave you a Bible study on RHEMA, you would know the "what" of RHEMA but not the "why." You would have knowledge but little understanding. Knowledge without understanding is like seeing men walking as trees—we wouldn't be able to see clearly—which would lead to the abuse and misuse of RHEMA, as occasionally has happened in the past. RHEMA is a means to an end, not the end itself. RHEMA is what we "hear" in the hear first, speak second biblical pattern. It is the vehicle. Hear first, speak second is the driver; it is the second touch. We want you to see clearly.

Notes

1. Andrew Murray, *With Christ in the School of Prayer* (New Kensignton, PA: Whitaker House, 1981).
2. Steven Furtick, *Crash the Chatterbox: Hearing God's Voice Above All Others (Multnomah Books,* Colorado Springs, CO, 2014).
3. I heard Harvey Lifsey say this in a message years ago while we were in India.
4. This list of the names of God are largely adapted from the website gotquestions.org.

Section
II

Redefining Rhema: Faith Comes from Hearing God

by David Lake

POWER THOUGHTS FOR *Chapter 4*

What's the real story on the parables of the minas (see Luke 19:11-27) and the talents (see Matthew 25:14-30)? Two of the people listened and heard a RHEMA from God; one didn't. They did what the nobleman said. Hearing first, obeying second changes everything. Two lost their lives, which ultimately saved their lives; one saved his life and that lost his life. Two listened, while one didn't, resulting in two completely different outcomes.

—ED DELPH

Listen when Jesus speaks. Jesus had to specifically say "Lazarus, come forth" (John 11:43), or the whole graveyard would have come alive.

—ED DELPH

We spend much time and money learning how to speak when we need to learn how to listen. "... And while hearing they do not hear, nor do they understand" (Matthew 13:13). "If anyone hears my sayings" (John 12:47). "... He who has ears to hear, let him hear" (Mark 4:9). After all, we have two ears to hear with and only one mouth to speak with—thank the Lord!

—VANCE HAVNER[1]

Today's foolproof formula for hearing the voice of God: shut up!

—DAVID LAKE

Chapter 4

Redefining and Refining Faith

What is faith? Let's begin with Hebrews 11:1. The writer of Hebrews says that "faith is the assurance of things hoped for, the conviction of things not seen" (ESV). Most Christians who have studied the Bible for any length of time will say that Hebrews 11:1 is the verse that defines faith. But that verse explains what faith does; it doesn't define what faith means.

The King James version says that "faith is the substance of those things hoped for; the evidence of things not seen." This word translated *assurance* or *substance* comes from the Greek word *hupostasis*, which basically means "support." Faith is the actual support for what a person hopes for. Or we could say that faith supports hope. The Christian's hope is to spend eternity with God, and so faith manifests by action that supports hope. Our actions show that we believe that God is who He says He is and that He does what He says He'll do.

The Greek word we translate as *faith* is *pistis*, meaning moral conviction. More specifically, *pistis* refers to a moral conviction of religious truth or truthfulness, especially a reliance upon Christ for salvation. To put it simply, faith it is what you believe. A moral conviction or belief causes an action. James 2:18-20 says:

> *But someone may well say, "You have faith and I have works; show me your faith without the works, and I will show you my faith by my works." You believe that God is one. You do well; the demons also believe, and shudder. But are you willing to recognize, you foolish fellow, that faith without works is useless?*

Basically, James is saying that faith should look like something. Faith has a work that follows it. It has fruit. James continues in 2:21-26:

> *Was not Abraham our father justified by works when he offered up Isaac his son on the altar? You see that faith was working with his works, and as a result of the works, faith was perfected; and the Scripture was fulfilled which says, "And Abraham believed God, and it was reckoned to him as righteousness,' and he was called the friend of God. You see that a man is justified by works and not by faith alone. In the same way, was not Rahab the harlot also justified by works when she received the messengers and sent them out by another way? For just as the body without the spirit is dead, so also faith without works is dead.*

You can talk about having faith, but if your life shows no action that testifies of your faith, then you're lying. Faith always produces something.

Here's where we make faith confusing. We all want to say we're people of faith, so what do we want to do? We want to "take steps of faith," or make faith happen. And here we encounter the buzz words we've grown so accustomed to in the church: "When are you going to step out in faith?" Those words imply that faith is something you do or an action you perform.

Don't get me wrong: faith produces action. But that is not to be confused with an action-producing faith. I believe; therefore, I do. I have a moral conviction that the light switch will turn on the light; therefore, I flip on the switch. I have a moral conviction that if I get into the car and turn the key, the car will start; therefore, I get into the car and turn the key. I have a moral conviction that Jesus will speak to me; therefore, I ask and listen to Him. In each situation, faith produces an action.

Actions testify of what we really believe. In the course of daily life, everything we do is caused by what we believe. Does anyone analyze how to turn on a light switch? No. It's a habit. It's second nature. Why? Because the light switch has predictably performed what it was designed to do for decades. Faith in the light switch causes us to flip the switch with no doubt that the light will turn on or off. When will Christians start instinctively trusting in God like that? "God, You said You would do what You said You would do. God, You said that all things work for the good of those who love You and are called according to Your purpose. God, You said You would provide for my need according to Your riches in glory." Then if we really believe that God is that way and that He spoke these things to our hearts, if we have revelation of who He is, then our actions should testify to that belief.

God is the CEO of the business I am involved with. My first question every day is, "God, what do You want to do in the business today?" There are times and seasons when God will give me directives that are counterintuitive to how business is normally run. But I do them anyway. This is because that instruction comes from God, and the beautiful thing about God is that when He speaks, "His word will not return void, but will accomplish what He pleases and prospers on the thing where He sent it" (see Isaiah 55:11).

God's specific word to me necessarily becomes an important part of how the business is run. I love Psalm 46:10, which says, "Be still and know that I am God" (NKJV). Why? Because, according to James 1:4, when you let patience have its perfect work within you, you become complete and desire nothing. This is because God fulfills the things He said He was going to do. I see people spending a lot of emotional energy chasing their tails for no reason whatsoever. I ask them, "Did that help? Are you worried? Did that change the circumstances? Didn't

God say He would take care of it?" If God is who He really says He is, then He necessarily will do what He promised.

When I first got saved, I did not attend church for a couple of years. I wanted to know if God was real. I did not want to be influenced by what others thought about God. And so I said, "God, You're either true or You're a liar." As I reflect on that now, I can see that was a result of God speaking and imparting faith. I opened the Bible, read and prayed. That's how I spent my first three years getting to know God—listening to Him and reading His Word. As I read His Word, the Holy Spirit began to reveal who He is and how He acts. The Bible says in First John 2:27 that we have an anointing and that anointing teaches us about all things.

A day would be different if I ever woke up and didn't have a cup of coffee with God. I read His Word and talk to Him about how He thinks the day should go. You see, when you know God is who He says He is and does what He says He'll do, then your prayers become a reminder that He is in control. I have no doubt where I'm thinking I must change His mind; there's no manipulating or having to draw something from Him.

Relax and Let God Be God

The Bible says in Hebrews 4:11 to "labor to enter into His rest." When we know God for who God is, then guess where we go in times of stress and worry? We go to God. We rest because we can't help it. It's time to enjoy the journey. Faith should not be confused with presumption. Presumption is an idea taken to be true and then used as a basis for other ideas, even though the original idea is not a certainty. The problem with presumption is that it supposes on itself but doesn't come true every time.

Presumption often works like this: God speaks that He's going to do something regarding a specific time or situation, then we want to paint the whole world with that paintbrush. We think that God should act the same way in similar situations. But Jesus knew better than to try to make God play with that sort of rulebook. Jesus said, "I only do what I see the Father do; I only speak what I hear the Father speak" (see John 5:19).

The Son's example for us was to do everything that He heard from the Father. He had no concern about being the Son of God. He had no concern that all creation was subject to Him. What did He do? He said He only wanted to do what He saw the Father do; He only wanted to speak what He heard from the Father. That's how I challenge Christians all the time: "Don't tell me what He showed you about Himself a year ago or what you think He wants to do; tell me what He told you about who He was last week and what He plans today." If you ask me for advice, the first thing I want to ask you is, "What did God tell you?" And when you tell me you don't know what He said, then it's time for us to sit down and listen.

You see, God is real. He's alive and He affects my life; He's a part of every aspect of my life. That's how real He is to me. When is the church going to start walking like that's a reality of who they are? I don't need to manipulate God. I know what's coming. I know what He is. I know that He makes promises. I know that He talks to me. I can't wait to see the next adventure. I can't wait till He tells me the next thing about Him that I didn't know. God is so big that we will spend eternity discovering who He is. So why don't we start living it now? Don't wait till you die. God's alive and well.

People often say, "I think God is going to do something," and just I laugh. Has anybody ever had a prayer not answered? Let's just examine this issue for a moment. It's easy to criticize and say we didn't have enough faith to see our prayer answered, but the fact is that God did not speak specifically about that situation. Rather, we presumed that God would act on our behalf.

When I first got saved, God was teaching me He was the healer. I could pray for anybody and they'd get healed. Then suddenly, I would pray for people and no one was healed. It seemed that the faucet dried up. Did the character of God change? No, but God said, "I want you to understand something, David. You see, that's a part of who I am. I heal in My time, and you will always know that. Let's go and discover who else I am." Does that mean I don't pray for someone's healing, believing and trusting and asking God for mercy? Do I think He can't heal them? Not at all! I know that He will do what He needs to do because His vision is much bigger than any human's, including mine. God delivers, God heals, God provides, and He is our protector; He's the one who watches over us; He's the one we trust; He's the Rock on which we stand. That reality is who He is.

I don't want to be the spoiled little child who says, "My daddy is the King." You know what I want? I want to be the child who says, "Daddy, what would You like me to do now? What do You want me to do with what I've got? How do You want me to deal with this situation?" I want to be the obedient son who says, "God, love that person through me. God, You've got to forgive through me. I know I can't do it. God, love my wife through me because I fail so often in loving my wife. God, love my children through me. Let Your will be done, God. What do you want me to do?"

Presumption will always expose itself by not coming true. Understand this: We must be comfortable enough in our relationship with God to say, "God, I missed it." Once I was sitting in a business meeting, and the guy was telling me what his big, audacious God-given goals were. He wrote them in 2013 and this meeting took place in 2015. He said, "This is what God promised to give."

I said, "Whoa, whoa, whoa, whoa! You said this was going to happen in 2013. Has it happened yet?"

"No," he said.

"Does that mean it was from God or not?" I asked him. He just looked at me. I said, "It could be from God, but I don't think He gave you the calendar on it."

We always want to put things into in our time frame, don't we? The fact of the matter is that this guy shouldn't have put a time frame on what God said He would do, even if God promised to double the size of his business. When he put that time frame on it, it only reflected when he wanted it done. It had nothing do with God. When I questioned him about it, he said, "You know what? I shouldn't have put that there. That wasn't God."

But we do stuff like that all the time. We can hope and we can beg for His mercy, but when God gives us a revelation of who He is, there's nothing that will stop Him. Nothing. That's the difference between faith and presumption—hearing the voice of God.

In Hebrews 11:3, faith means "moral conviction" or belief, so every time we read that word, let's soak in that meaning. The verse says, "By faith we understand that the worlds were prepared by the word of God, so that what is seen is not made out of things which are visible." The Greek term used here for *word* is RHEMA. This is important because biblical Greek uses two different terms, LOGOS and RHEMA, both translated as "word" in our English Bibles.

As I study the Bible, I use reference books called *Strong's Exhaustive Concordance of the Bible* and *Vine's Expository Dictionary of New Testament Words*. These books catalog their entries using a numerical system. I've studied this subject so much that my Bible is marked up with these numbers, and I recognize them when I come across them. As I'm reading, I know which word is being translated as *word* in any verse.

You will be amazed at what you start to understand when you recognize the difference between these two words. Remember, RHEMA means "an utterance from God"; it implies something current regarding a particular situation. It is something that He gives to you individually. On the other hand, LOGOS implies something written that was spoken in the past. For instance, Jesus is called the LOGOS, that is, the historical, written Word, in John 1:14.

Hebrews 11:3 tells us that we understand by faith that the worlds "were prepared by the word of God," or an utterance from God. Think of RHEMA as present tense. I think if you're like most readers of this book, you believe that God speaks. You probably praise God and ask Him for things depending on the severity of your situation: "God, I need something." Hopefully, this is your daily practice—"God, I just want to hang out and talk." It is by faith that we understand that the word of God prepared the world. We could retranslate this verse to say, "By faith (or moral conviction and belief), we understand that the worlds were prepared by a word (or an utterance from God) so that what we see was not made from things that are visible."

Romans 10:17 says that faith comes by hearing a RHEMA from Christ. To have faith, one must hear God's voice. When a person hears God's voice, he or she may not necessarily recognize it at first. Here's a case in point: Hebrews 11:4 says, "By faith Abel offered to God a better sacrifice than Cain, through which he obtained the testimony that he was righteous, God testifying about his gifts, and through faith, though he is dead, he still speaks." Abel's sacrifice was better than Cain's because Abel's sacrifice was by faith. What had to happen for him to sacrifice by faith? He had to hear from God. Faith comes by hearing. By faith Abel offered a better sacrifice to the King. The fact is that God told Abel what to sacrifice. That was a RHEMA.

A lot of people say when they first got saved, "Man, I just knew then that I needed God." This implies you did something. Truth be told the reason you realized you needed God is because the Father spoke to you regarding your need. He uttered something to you though you didn't recognize His voice at the time. When He spoke to you, RHEMA, He imparted faith which caused you to ask Him to be a part of your journey. The impartation of faith by hearing an utterance from God is a process that begins at salvation and continues our entire lives. God designed faith to operate like that. He created you to have fellowship with Him and the fruit of that fellowship is an impartation of faith from Him. When we're witnessing, we often tell people, "God wants to hang out with you. He wants to talk to you. Ask Him. Let's see what He wants to do." That is why the Bible says that faith comes by hearing the RHEMA of God.

We can go on to a theological debate and ask if God spoke to Cain too. I would contend that yes, God did speak to Cain, but Cain was a type and shadow of the flesh. And does the flesh ever chase God? No, it doesn't. We know that God can speak and people don't get it. We speak to people about God just like God spoke to Cain, and they just don't get it. Like Cain, they hear with their ears but never get RHEMA. They never decide for Christ. In my flesh dwells no good thing; apart from God, I can do nothing. The New Testament tells us this all the time.

Let's tie these two concepts together: Faith and an utterance from God are inseparable. It is by faith that we understand that RHEMA prepared the worlds. We understand that these godly men had a moral conviction because they heard a word from God. In fact, Abel had faith (or moral conviction) because he heard God and thus he offered God a better sacrifice than Cain because God gave him a RHEMA, A FAITH INFUSED WORD FROM GOD, of what would be pleasing to Him.

If you're saved, then you have heard from God, which is why you responded to Him in the first place. So now when you read Hebrews 11 and all the stories of the people of faith, you can go back and think of faith as being imparted and manifests as a moral conviction that comes from RHEMA, an utterance from God. Abel had to have a divine interaction with God to execute what he knew was pleasing to Him.

The clearest illustration of an utterance from God imparting faith to do the impossible happened in my marriage. My wife and I have been married for thirty-two years. About sixteen years ago, I had an affair. I was involved in the church, pastoring, involved in missions, and home fellowship groups. I was also working and coaching sports. I fell into an affair and was stuck for three years. I did every lick of spiritual warfare I could possibly do; I went to counselors and talked to friends. I repented of absolutely everything I was aware of, but I remained stuck where I was. I continued to make bad decisions that hurt my wife and my family. I could not get free.

My wife and I went back and forth several times, trying to make our marriage work. I would move back in and then would have to leave again due to me picking up the affair again. For years, we struggled to get things resolved. We were two wounded people trying to make something broken better. Anyone who does any counseling knows that those situations usually don't work out very well. Finally, My wife got to the point where she said to me, "I need a divorce."

I got it; I kept making wrong choices. My wife is a woman who loves God and believes in the power of prayer. She prayed and asked God what any woman of faith would pray: "God, please heal this marriage! God, set him free." At least seven times I broke it off with the other woman, but then I would fall back into sin once again. And every time my wife asked, "Are you seeing this lady?" I'd tell her no because at that minute I wasn't seeing her. Then I'd find myself back in the same mess within days.

My wife is a woman of faith! She's an angel or at least should be nominated for sainthood in my eyes. One day, long after she had filed for divorce, my wife was in church listening to the message. We were about a week and a half from arbitration—this is the time when it all comes to an end. The pastor's message was about God's ability to do anything. God spoke to her heart, deeper than words heard by her ears, and said, "Nothing is impossible with Christ." My wife knew this truth from reading her Bible—she trusted God—but all of a sudden, this word took on a life of its own. God gave her a RHEMA.

This experience occurred three days after she told me she needed the divorce. There she was, weeping in church. She went home, sought God, and spent time journaling again, and she wrote down what God spoke. "Now is the time!" She began to weep again as the thoughts and fears of trying again consumed her. The next day my wife called me, and I was at my sister's house—with my girlfriend. My wife said to me, "We need to try this again."

At that point, I felt like I couldn't go on. I had no power to reconcile my life with my beliefs. All I could do was try to make peace with God and say, "God, I have screwed up my life. I have screwed up ministry. There is nothing I can do to make it better." I had failed so many times, and I had no hope of making it better. And now my wife was telling me we needed to try again. I told my wife, "You do what you think God wants you to do." Then I hung up the phone.

Three days later, I got a phone call from my lawyer. He said, "David, your divorce is over."

"What?" I asked.

"It is off," he said. I was stunned. I knew that the ball was back in my court. For the first time in three years, I had an enabling grace to look at that other woman and tell her, "I am going back to my family," and not have one emotional tie to her. What happened? God gave my wife a RHEMA. He spoke to her and imparted faith to do what she could not do before—try again. And God gave me a RHEMA too. He spoke to me that the time was now for healing and imparted faith to walk away from the affair. When God gives you RHEMA, there is no possibility of it not happening.

My wife and I had a personal experience of God speaking to us about our marriage, which gave us the faith to accomplish what we could not accomplish before—to walk through healing and the restoration of our marriage. Our lives changed 180 degrees. By the end of that week, I was shopping with my children for my wife's Mother's Day present. I hadn't done that in three years. By the end of that month, I had moved back home with no more problems to deal with regarding the other woman.

Over the next three months, God gave my wife and me the ability to purchase our first house. By the end of the year, He sent us on the honeymoon we never had when we first married. Why? Because God spoke and imparted faith to us. As I continue to grow in my understanding of what happens when God speaks, I look forward to those moments when He gives me a RHEMA. When He speaks a word, there is no possibility of it not happening.

There was another time when God was teaching me about healing. I was working construction and sitting in a fast-food restaurant with two other guys. An older woman, who was helped by her husband, came into the restaurant. I looked at this woman, and suddenly the Holy Spirit said to me, "I want you to go pray for her." I was in a public place, filthy and sweaty from working, and I thought there was no way that was from God. The Holy Spirit came on me so strongly that I began to shake. I sat at the table trying to ignore the feeling coming over me and the loss of bodily control I was experiencing. My buddy sitting across from me was a Christian too—he looked at me and said, "David, either God is talking to you or you got a devil."

I told him, "Hey, God wants us to go pray for this lady." I said that "God wants *us* to" because it is a lot easier dragging somebody else down with you when you're going to sink. Trying to eat my salad, I sat there and ignored all those feelings, shaking like a leaf. Then I got up with all the boldness of nothing and walked past her into the bathroom and washed my hands five times. When I came back, I finally prayed, "God, You are going to have to give me the strength to do this."

We got up and walked over to the woman. I looked at the husband and said, "Sir, I think God wants to heal your wife. Can we pray for her?"

"Yeah," he said.

She looked at me, and then I said to her, "Ma'am, may I pray for you?"

"If you think it is going to work," she said.

I was still shaking; I couldn't control myself. I had my bottle of anointing oil on me, so I anointed her with oil and prayed one of those deep spiritual prayers. It went something like this: "Oh God, heal her in the name of Jesus." The prayer lasted a good five seconds and then we headed for the door! We were gone without looking back. We were embarrassed and scared. When I got into the truck, I was trembling. My two friends sat there silent. As I began to back the truck out, I started to prophesy: "You did not stay around to see that I healed her, but I healed her." The peace of God hit me and I stopped shaking on the spot.

I tell this story because it was a RHEMA, an utterance from God, where He spoke to me and imparted faith to do what I had no power on my own to do. It was a specific word for a specific circumstance at a specific time. The fact is that I've prayed for a lot of people all over the world. I've been involved with missionary work since 1993; I've counseled and done all kinds of ministry. But do you know what? When God speaks a RHEMA, it is beyond the knowledge obtained by reading the Bible; it's an impartation of faith to change what He wants to change in that moment.

That doesn't mean I don't tell people to make right choices, and it doesn't mean I don't tell people to trust God. But here is what I know: If God doesn't speak, there is no faith for your life to change. There is a difference between RHEMA and LOGOS. In Isaiah 55:8-11, God says:

> *"For My thoughts are not your thoughts, nor are your ways My ways," declares the Lord. "For as the heavens are higher than the earth, so are My ways higher than your ways and My thoughts than your thoughts. For as the rain and snow come down from the heaven, and do not return there without watering the earth and making it bear and sprout, and furnishing seed to the sower and bread to the eater, so will My word be which goes forth from My mouth: it will not return to Me empty, without accomplishing what I desire, and without succeeding in the matter for which I sent it."*

That is the beauty of God's Word going forth from His mouth. When God gives you a RHEMA about a situation, then you know it will not return void and do what it was supposed to do. In fact, that is God's character. That is the importance of hearing His voice.

This is why you can't just be a "study" person and not be a "hearing" person. The Pharisees and Sadducees were study people; they probably had more biblical knowledge than the disciples, but the difference was that they didn't have RHEMA. The disciples asked Jesus "Why do You speak to them in parables?" And He told His disciples, "For it has been given unto you to know the mysteries of the kingdom of God, but to them it has not been given" (see Mark 4:10-11).

The fact is that knowing God's mysteries has everything to do with receiving a RHEMA that comes by hearing the voice of God. Maybe you know what I am talking about: you have read a certain scripture many times, and then suddenly that scripture takes on new life. You never looked at it that way before. It's an aha moment; it's the RHEMA. And suddenly, you can do something or believe like you never could before.

In my wife's situation, for example, our marriage was over, but God said, "I can do anything!" He imparted into her a supernatural faith to try to reconcile one more time regardless of her fears and the desire to move on with her life. God also imparted something to me and set me free to do what I was unable to do for three years before that—turn from my sin to be a godly husband and dad. That is faith imparted by a RHEMA from God.

Note

1. Vance Havner, *Pepper 'n' Salt* (Grand Rapids, MI: Fleming H. Revell Company, 1966).

POWER THOUGHTS FOR *Chapter 5*

Presumption will always expose itself by not coming true.

—David Lake

To have faith, you necessarily have to hear God's voice.

—David Lake

At some point, Christians must stop trying to be Christians or stop trying to act like Christians and start simply being Christians. How? They begin by looking at everything through the Father's eyes. They hear what the Father says.

—David Lake

I want you to understand something: It was a small miracle that Paul could shake off the viper and not die. The most important part of this story is that all creation was subject to what God had already spoken. In Acts 27, God told Paul that he was going to testify in Rome. So it did not matter what demons in hell tried to do—the challenge of a snake in a fire, the powerful winds of a storm, being shipwrecked, or the threat of guards—nothing was going to stop what God had already spoken to him. Paul knew God. He shook off the snake not because he had authority but because God had already told him what he was going to do. And what God utters, there is no possibility of that not happening!

—David Lake

Chapter 5

RHEMA FIRST, FAITH SECOND

If we are to have the faith God longs for us to have, then we need to understand where it comes from. Paul writes in Romans 10:17 that "faith cometh by hearing, and hearing by the word of God" (KJV). Paul uses RHEMA here when talking about the *word of God.* So when Paul uses *word* in Romans 10:17, he is telling us where faith comes from.

When we begin to study the idea that faith comes from hearing, and hearing comes from a RHEMA, we can see in the LOGOS when God imparted faith to people and how it changed their lives. Faith becomes the evidence of God speaking. Once that happens, we'll begin to ask questions like, "When Jesus could not heal many because there was little faith, what was really happening? If faith comes by hearing, then what really happened in that region?" There was little faith in that region because God spoke little RHEMA in that area, which is why just a few were healed. When we begin looking at what was really happening, we see how faith and RHEMA are directly tied together.

Let us not throw out everything we have learned in the past about faith. God has graced us as He matured us in Him. Rather, what we are doing here is adding to what we have already learned. RHEMA is about recognizing what has been happening all along—we heard God and that is why we had faith to believe.

I have learned a lot from my teachers in the past. But part of the beauty of God is that He takes us on a journey to know Him even more. He teaches us something one day so He can teach us something new in the future. Yesterday's revelations pale in comparison to the revelation He wants to give us tomorrow. God is so big that we will spend eternity getting to know Him. We want to camp out at yesterday, and so we make yesterday's revelation the end. The fact is that it is not the end; it is only the beginning of what God wants to show us about who He is.

The more I see that faith and RHEMA walk hand in hand, the more I desire to hear God's voice. Without faith, it is impossible to please Him. Without Him speaking first to our hearts, it is impossible to please Him, which means it is impossible to have faith without Him first speaking to our hearts. To be a person of faith requires that He speaks. I am reminded of the weakness of my flesh and my absolute need of Him!

In Matthew 4:4, Jesus was tempted by satan in the wilderness. "But He answered and said, 'It is written, "Man should not live by bread alone, but on every [RHEMA] that proceeds out of the mouth of God."'" Jesus was not talking about LOGOS in that context; rather, He was talking about RHEMA, hearing a present word from God. Satan was using LOGOS to tempt Jesus. Jesus was emphasizing the need of RHEMA to correctly use LOGOS.

The Bible says that before Jesus comes back, this world is going to get worse. That means it's even more important to hear a RHEMA from God giving us the strategies to navigate the way He wants us to in these times. Our reaction to any given situation should not be a proclamation to God of our desired result; rather, it should be going to the throne of grace and asking how He desires us to deal with the issues. When we know God, we can't help but cast our cares upon Him. We need to be like a professional athlete who goes out on game day, not thinking about what we are going to do, but reacting to the changing environment. The athlete's training has become part of who he is, so his reactions to game situations are automatic.

When will Christians start reacting to specific situations because it is part of who they are? Think about a doctor who has earned college and medical school degrees, and completed internships and residencies. Along the way, he's had to think about how to the make the right choices for each case. But there comes a day (many years down the road) when he no longer thinks about being a doctor because he *is* a doctor. He starts acting like a doctor and looking at everything through a doctor's eyes. At some point, Christians must stop trying to act like Christians and start simply being Christians. We must start looking at everything through the Father's eyes, hearing what He says, knowing that when He speaks He gives us faith to overcome. The most important question any of us can ask is, "God, how do You want to deal with this situation? What do You want to do with it?" God will do it because that is who God is.

There is a story in Luke that demonstrates God moving a person from doubt to faith by a RHEMA from Him:

> *Now the sixth month, the angel Gabriel was sent from God to the city in Galilee called Nazareth, to a virgin engaged to a man whose name was Joseph, of the descendants of David; and the virgin's name was Mary. In coming in, he said to her, "Greetings, favored one! The Lord is with you." But she was very perplexed at this statement, and kept pondering what kind of salutation this was* (Luke 1:26-29).

Would you be distressed by this event? I know I would be. Let's continue:

> *The angel said to her, "Do not be afraid, Mary; for you have found favor with God. And behold, you will conceive in your womb and bear a son, and you shall name Him Jesus. He will be great and will be called the Son of the*

> *Most High; and the Lord God will give Him the throne of His father David; and He will reign over the house of Jacob forever, and His kingdom will have no end." Mary said to the angel, "How can this be, since I am a virgin?"* (Luke 1:30-34)

Did that sound like a statement of faith to you? Women don't have babies if they are virgins. Mary had never heard of this happening before; this word she was given was way bigger than she was.

Has God given you a word that is too big for you to believe? Has He given you a word that, unless He moves on your behalf, there is no possibility of it happening? That may be an indication that the word is from God. If it is from God, then He will give you the faith to see it happen regardless of how impossible it may seem in the natural realm. You see, when God gives you a word, it should be bigger than what you have the capacity to believe for. That is what a big, audacious, God-given goal is—it is given by God and will only happen if He moves. That is a RHEMA! A God-given goal isn't something that we do; it is God telling you what He is going to do.

Let's look at Mary's interaction with Gabriel. Notice that Mary does not have a testimony of faith at this point. Mary said to the angel, "How can this be, since I am a virgin?"

> *The angel answered and said to her, "The Holy Spirit will come upon you, and the power of the Most High will overshadow you; and for that reason the holy Child shall be called the Son of God. And behold, even your relative Elizabeth has also conceived a son in her old age; and she who was called barren is now in her sixth month* (Luke 1:35-36).

Then here comes the important verse: "For nothing will be impossible with God" (Luke 1:37). The word translated as *nothing* comes from three Greek words. One of these words is *ou*, one of them is *pas*, and the last one is RHEMA. Here is what Gabriel told her: "Mary, what

God has uttered, there is no possibility of that not happening." That is what a RHEMA is. *If God utters something to you, then there is no possibility that it won't happen.* Mary responded and said, "Behold, the bondslave of the Lord. May it be done to me according to your word" (Luke 1:38). Mary moved from doubt to faith because of a RHEMA from God.

Acts 27 is a clear illustration of a RHEMA coming from God. Paul is on a boat, sailing to Rome so he can testify to what has happened to him:

> *When considerable time had passed and the voyage was now dangerous, since even the fast was already over, Paul began to admonish them, and said to them, "Men, I perceive that the voyage will certainly be with damage and great loss, not only of the cargo and the ship, but also of our lives." But the centurion was more persuaded by the pilot and the captain of the ship than by what was being said by Paul. Because the harbor was not suitable for wintering, the majority reached a decision to put out to sea from there, if somehow they could reach Phoenix, a harbor of Crete, facing southwest and northwest, and spend the winter there.*
>
> *When a moderate south wind came up, supposing that they had attained their purpose, they weighed anchor and began sailing along Crete, close inshore.*
>
> *But before very long there rushed down from the land a violent wind, called Euraquilo; and when the ship was caught in it and could not face the wind, we gave way to it and let ourselves be driven along. Running under the shelter of a small island called Clauda, we were scarcely able to get the ship's boat under control. After they had hoisted it up, they used supporting cables in undergirding the ship; and fearing that they might run aground on*

> *the shallows of Syrtis, they let down the sea anchor and in this way let themselves be driven along. The next day as we were being violently storm-tossed, they began to jettison the cargo; and on the third day they threw the ship's tackle overboard with their own hands. Since neither sun nor stars appeared for many days, and no small storm was assailing us, from then on all hope of our being saved was gradually abandoned.*
>
> *When they had gone a long time without food, then Paul stood up in their midst and said, "Men, you ought to have followed my advice and not to have set sail from Crete and incurred this damage and loss. Yet now I urge you to keep up your courage, for there will be no loss of life among you, but only of the ship. For this very night an angel of the God to whom I belong and whom I serve stood before me, saying, 'Do not be afraid, Paul; you must stand before Caesar; and behold, God has granted you all those who are sailing with you.' Therefore, keep up your courage, men, for I believe God that it will turn out exactly as I have been told. But we must run aground on a certain island"* (Acts 27:9-26).

In the beginning of the chapter, Paul gave a warning about the loss of the ship, the loss of cargo, and a loss of life. After he received a RHEMA, however, he knew he was going to stand before Caesar and that God was going to save all their lives. They end up running aground and find out they're on an island called Malta. A native takes pity on them in that awful weather and cold and helped them find shelter and light a fire.

Paul gathers a bunch of sticks to add to the fire, but the heat drives out a poisonous viper, and the snake bites him, fastening its fangs on his hand. The natives think this was God's justice. Paul must be a murderer; even though he had been saved from drowning in the sea, he was now going to die from a snakebite. But Paul simply shook the viper off his hand, and he was fine.

It was a small miracle that Paul could shake off the viper and not die from its bite. The most important part of this story is that all of creation is subject to what God has already spoken. God had already told Paul that he was going to testify in Rome, so it did not matter what demons in hell tried to do—the challenge of a snakebite, the powerful winds of a storm, being shipwrecked, or the threat of guards killing the prisoners—nothing was going to stop what God had already spoken to him. Paul intimately knew God. He shook off the snake not because he had authority but because God had already told him what he was going to do. And whatever God utters, there is no possibility of that not happening!

POWER THOUGHTS FOR *Chapter 6*

A lesson of listening to God in tough or troubling times: "Listen. I love you more than you currently understand, I'm not paying you back. I'm bringing you back."

—Craig D. Lounsbrough

Maybe I've got to be sufficiently broken by life's many broken promises to be sufficiently compelled to seek out God's unbreakable promises.

—Craig D. Lounsbrough[1]

A season of silence is the best preparation for speech with God.

—Samuel Chadwick[2]

Read the Bible through the lens of knowing God rather than pleasing God.

—David Lake

Mary listened; Martha worked. There is nothing wrong with work. There are times to work and times to listen. Martha was doing work at a listening time. The right thing to do requires the right time to do it in. Martha had the first part right but missed the timing.

—Ed Delph

Discipleship: a journey on how to listen to God and then know that it is God.

—Ed Delph

Chapter 6

TRUST COMES FROM KNOWING GOD, BUT FAITH COMES FROM HEARING GOD

Faith comes from God. It's not what we do that produces faith, and it is not an assumption of what God wants to do in and through us. Faith is not moving in presumption. For example, when you're experiencing a challenge in life, the best thing anyone could ask you would be, "What did God tell you to do?" If you don't have that answer, then wait on God and see what He wants to say to you. And if waiting on God takes four hours, then wait on God four hours. The important part is to hear from God and get the RHEMA God wants to give you.

It seems that people get confused about the difference between faith and trust. Biblical Greek translates several different words as trust in our English Bibles. According to *Strong's Concordance*, the King James Version of the New Testament uses the word *trust* twenty-seven times. The Greek term *elpizo* means "to expect or confide," *peitho* means "to convince," while *pisto* (which is related to *pistis*) means "to have faith." *Webster's Dictionary* defines trust like this: "assured reliance on the character, ability, strength or truth of someone or something in which confidence is placed." I have my own definition of trust that I would like to offer here: *Trust in God is a reliance on Him to be who He says He will be and that He will do what He says He will do.* Trust only comes from knowing God.

Faith, on the other hand, is imparted when God speaks. That kind of faith is different than trust. The point is this: just because Christians have confused the meanings of faith and trust, and have often combined them, we have eliminated the divine connection of faith. Faith can be a *now word for a specific situation.*

The Difference between Faith and Trust

We are going to walk through some scriptures that I've labeled either as trust or faith. In the process of looking at these verses, I realized that *faith is an impartation from God regarding a current circumstance, while trust is continuing with God regardless of the current circumstance.* It's a subtle difference in the wording, but in the reality of life's situations, the two are miles apart. Let's not confuse them.

God gives us RHEMA, which is a faith-infused word from God for particular situations at particular times. And it has everything to do with God initiating it. This is different from LOGOS, which is God's written Word about Himself. LOGOS reveals the character of God. For example, there is a scripture in Isaiah that says "by His stripes we've been healed" (Isaiah 53:5 NKJV). That is a LOGOS word that reveals that God has healed us through the cross of Christ. But it may not reveal *when* God will heal us. As Christians, we ask God for healing, and we *know* He can heal. We trust Him with our health but we have no authority to tell Him when He should heal us. We are supposed to go to God for healing, but there are times when God says, "I need you to pray for this person right now; speak healing over him in My name." That is a faith-infused word from God. It's an utterance from God for a specific situation, a "now" word for that time. That is what a RHEMA is all about.

When I began to look at trust, I realized that trust had something to do with *standing over time*. Trust has to do with the realization that God is who He says He is and that He does what He says He's going to do. Trust is what you do when things don't go your way or your expectations are not met. You trust that God knows what He is doing. We take Isaiah 53:5 and we keep trying to force everybody to be healed or to become healers. Really? Is that what God wants to do? If He really wanted to do that, would He not manifest Himself in such a way? We trust He is our healer.

I'm by no means saying that we shouldn't pray for people to be healed. On the contrary, we should pray for everyone God leads us to pray for; that is the character of God. James 5:14 says, "Is anyone among you sick? Then he must call for the elders of the church and they are to pray over him, anointing him with oil in the name of the Lord." Don't put God in a box regarding when He should do something He has promised in His Word to do. And don't put burdens on the sick as though they can make the healing happen.

In the end, people may get healed in the life that is now or in the life that is to come. We have a timing mechanism by which we'd like to see that happen. The fact of the matter is that is it up to God when a person will be healed. We simply trust He will do what needs to be done when it needs to be done. Trust has to do with who God is, His sovereignty over all, and how the depth of that sovereignty impacts your life. And I'm okay with that—I'm really excited about it!

The King James Version of Matthew 12:21 says, "And in His name shall the Gentiles trust." We know this scripture is about Jesus, and the fact is that the Gentiles are the non-Jews who are going to be people who trust God. The Greek word used for trust here means "to expect and confide." Those are two of the things we do with Jesus: we expect that we're going to have eternal life with Him, and we confide in Him in everything that has to do with our lives. That kind of trust happens in day-to-day life. But that trust is different from the faith we've mentioned in the context of receiving revelation.

Let's look now at Matthew 8:5-10. In this story, a centurion came to Jesus at Capernaum, begging Him to heal his servant. When Jesus said that He would come to the centurion's house to heal the servant, the centurion replied that he was unworthy for Jesus to come, but if

Jesus would just say the word (the LOGOS) from where they were, he knew his servant would be healed. The centurion continued:

> *"For I also am a man under authority, having soldiers under me. And I say to this one, 'Go,' and he goes; and to another, 'Come,' and he comes; and to my servant, 'Do this,' and he does it." When Jesus heard it, He marveled, and said to them that followed, "Assuredly, I say to you, I have not found such great faith, not even in Israel"* (Matthew 8:9-10 NKJV).

Consider again the meaning of faith—it is a persuasion, a moral conviction. And where does faith come from? Faith comes from a word, a RHEMA, from God. What's so incredible about this story is what Jesus says about this Roman soldier. It wasn't the Jews who were getting the RHEMA in this context; it was a Gentile. The only thing that this centurion understood was the concept of authority. This was his world, being a soldier. But God had spoken to him about the reality of the authority Jesus had. How do I know this? Because Jesus said, "Assuredly, I say to you, I have not found such great faith, not even in Israel."

The Spirit of God had to speak (RHEMA) and impart the faith that allowed the centurion to believe and communicate in the context in which he lived. The Roman soldier said something like this: "Listen, Jesus. I know something about You. You have authority over sickness. I understand how authority works. I tell people to do this and that and it happens. You speak the word (LOGOS) and my servant is healed." The centurion had a revelation of the authority of Christ. He didn't get that from being a soldier; rather, he got that from the Father speaking directly to his heart.

Jesus marveled that He hadn't seen anyone in all of Israel with that kind of faith. And He went on to say that Gentile people from all over the world would find their way into God's kingdom, but "the children of the kingdom shall be cast out into the outer darkness: there shall be weeping and gnashing of teeth. And Jesus said to the centurion,

Go thy way; and as thou hast believed, so be it done unto thee. And his servant was healed in the selfsame hour" (Matthew 10:12-13 KJV). The centurion should not get the glory for believing; his faith was the result of God speaking.

Faith comes by hearing, and hearing comes by the RHEMA of God (see Romans 10:17). The centurion heard the voice of God and faith was produced in his heart. How does what happened to him when he heard the voice of God affect us? What should happen to us for us to go to Jesus? John 6:45 has the answer: "Everyone who has heard and learned from the Father comes to Me." The Father spoke to the centurion, and the centurion said to Jesus, "Please heal my servant," because he had a revelation. The centurion had a RHEMA from God. That's faith in that context, faith that God imparted.

Sometimes at church, I want to ask people, "How are you feeling today?" I can tell by how they look that they're sick, that they're ready to drop off their feet. But we have Christianized faith so much that many are afraid to say they don't feel well. They're going to make a "confession of faith" as though that will manipulate their circumstances. But the answer is this: "You know, I don't feel too good, but I'm trusting God to get me through this." That's the reality of what they're dealing with. They are trusting that He is going to heal them, but He hasn't given them a specific revelation that He was going to do something in this instance. He is our Great Physician, so we can rest in Him. We can trust Him, which is a bit different than trying to overspiritualize faith in God for our health. Let's not try to make faith something that we're going to make happen.

Years ago, the wife of a friend of mine was diagnosed with leukemia. However, one day at their church he received a RHEMA, and his wife was healed for many years. Then she had a debilitating stroke. Praying for her was awkward. All people could do was trust that God knew what He was doing in her life. As much as they wanted to see her healed, nobody got a specific word of faith to pray for her healing. Nobody could get up because God didn't get up. But her husband had to trust. He had to place her in God's hands. Their church begged God and praised Him, but the truth was that nobody received a RHEMA from God. People questioned, "Why didn't God heal her? He was *supposed* to heal."

In these types of situations, people try to perform and get God to move on their behalf. We try to conform God to our image. Our churches put a burden on the people for whom they are praying. We're all guilty of it. We put a burden on a person that we can't even carry ourselves. That's what our religious spirit does, which is just what the scribes and Pharisees did. They put burdens on people they couldn't bear themselves. And what did Jesus call them? Whitewashed tombs.

This husband's attitude was, "Okay, we have faith in You. Heal my wife again." The fact is that God revealed to them that He was the healer; He then revealed that He was sovereign. We can't lean on our own understanding regarding how and why He does things the way in which He does them. We can trust that in whatever He does, all things work together for the good of those who love Him, to them who are called according to His purpose (see Romans 8:28).

God's grace empowers you to follow Him, causing you to grow in Him. It stops your flesh from ruling your life. His grace empowers you to make good decisions. What if God were to remove His hand of grace in areas of our lives? What if He did it to reveal a deeper revelation of who He is to us because of His great love for us? I can't help but think of the story of King David and Bathsheba in Second Samuel 11–12. King David had a relationship with God since he was a young boy. He walked with God, and yet David fell into sin that was evil in the sight of the Lord.

We can talk about all of David's faults that got him into this situation, but there is something much deeper going on. David did not know the depth of God's mercy and grace. God revealed that grace and mercy to David by allowing him to walk after his flesh. When God removed His hand of grace, David did what the flesh does and made decisions contrary to the nature of God. David fell into sin, but it was in this journey of sin where David discovered God's grace and mercy like he had never experienced in the past. God loved him so much that He allowed him to fall in order to more fully reveal Himself. *God did not cause David to sin; in fact, God does not cause anyone to sin. When God leaves us to ourselves, we make the decision to sin. That is the nature of the flesh.*

Think about Jesus's words to Peter in Luke 22:31-32: "Simon, Simon, behold, satan has demanded permission to sift you like wheat; but I have prayed for you, that your faith may not fail; and you, once you have turned again, strengthen your brothers." Jesus calls Peter Simon because it is indicative of his flesh. Satan couldn't do anything to Peter without permission from God first. Even though satan was going to test Peter, Jesus prayed for Peter that his faith would not fail. He was talking about the faith that came when God gave him a RHEMA regarding who Jesus is. He said to him, "Once you turn again," revealing that Peter will fall but will also turn to Christ again; and when he does so, he is to encourage his brothers. God allows circumstances to happen for His greater purposes. He sees the whole picture. This is why we need a RHEMA from God and need to stop telling God how we think things should be done.

Before we were born, God knew what we would do. He knew every step we would and would not take. He knew every decision we would and are still going to make. Can He stop the uncomfortable situations from happening in our lives? Darn straight, He can—He's God. He doesn't stop those uncomfortable situations, however, because they are the method by which He reveals Himself to us. Every situation is an opportunity to get to know God in a way we did not know Him before.

In the Bible, God repeatedly tells Israel how things should be done and how they should live their lives. Israel continually demonstrates their desire to do what they want. When that happens, God lets them do what they want, and then they suffer the consequences of their actions. While walking through those consequences, it is then that they realize that God is right and they need Him. We don't know the value of the light until we've walked in the darkness.

A Canaanite woman cries to Jesus in Matthew 15:22, saying, "Have mercy on me, O Lord, Thou son of David; my daughter is grievously vexed with a devil" (KJV). This woman is a native of Gentile Palestine, and when she presents her request to Jesus, He refuses to answer her. She continues to make a fuss, and His disciples want Him to send her away. She is an outsider, not somebody they would typically talk too. But Jesus's response is deliberate. He states her cultural and social status and then tells her that He was only sent to "the lost sheep of the house of Israel." Instead of walking away, however, the woman begins to worship Him, begging Him for help. She agrees yet argues that "the dogs eat of the crumbs which fall from their master's table" (Matthew 15:27 KJV). Jesus relents: "O woman," He says, "great is thy faith: be it unto thee even as thou wilt" (Matthew 15:28 KJV). And her daughter was instantly healed!

Jesus told her that she had great faith. But where did her faith come from? She had a word from God that produced faith in her heart. Faith comes by hearing, and hearing by a RHEMA of God. How bizarre was that whole conversation. Jesus states what society thinks of her—she is not chosen and has the value of a dog—and yet she's had a revelation from God! How powerful this is! This Gentile woman has the kind of faith that comes from hearing God. And Jesus demonstrated to everyone present that God will speak to anyone regardless of their culture or social status.

In Second Corinthians 1:3-8, Paul describes the tribulations he has endured to the point where he and his companions "despaired even of life." This man of faith has been honest about what he has just gone through. How contrary that is to some of what we say in church where people don't want to confess what's really going on. Yet Paul says, "Look, we wanted to die." That's how bad his situation was. But despite his "sentence of death," they did not trust in themselves "but in God who raised the dead." Paul and his friends needed to convince themselves to trust. The Greek word he uses here is *peitho*, which means "to convince." Crazed by their torments, trials, and tribulations, they wanted to die. They had to look to God, the author and finisher of their faith, because they could hardly go on. What were they trusting God for? For getting through that situation. That trust is different from faith.

Here's another illustration from Luke 18:35-43. Jesus and His entourage are walking along the road approaching Jericho when a blind beggar calls out to Him from the side of the road. "Jesus, son of David, have mercy on me!" the beggar says. The leaders of the procession try to shush him, but the blind beggar keeps crying out even louder, "Son of David, have mercy on me." Jesus stopped and told them to bring the beggar to Him. When the beggar got to Him, Jesus asks him what he wants. When the beggar asks for his sight, Jesus responds by saying, "Receive your sight, for your faith has made you well."

Faith comes by hearing a RHEMA from God. The pattern continues: God speaks to the beggar, and faith has been imparted to be made well. He moved from having a need to regaining his sight and following Jesus, glorifying God. Faith has come by hearing, and hearing by an utterance or a RHEMA of God.

Paul writes more on this subject in First Timothy 4:10: "For therefore we both labour and suffer reproach, because we trust in the living God, who is the Saviour of all men, especially of those that believe" (KJV). Again, the Greek word for *trust* means to expect or confide. And again Paul is talking about long-term persevering. He's giving us a big picture. God wants us to have a walk of trust that enables us to be content whether we are laboring or suffering reproach. That's what trust is all about.

God wants us to know Him in the context of Him solving our circumstances. It's the difference between walking in the Spirit and walking in the flesh. Jesus said that a person does not live by bread alone but by every RHEMA that proceeds out of the mouth of God (see Matthew 4:4). To be embraced by the fullness of God is to have the RHEMA as well as the LOGOS. The sword of the Spirit is two-edged—it's RHEMA as well as LOGOS. It is spirit and it is truth. He who worships God must worship Him in spirit and in truth.

God designed us to walk in the fullness of who He is, which doesn't necessarily mean everybody will go on the journey. Our responsibility is to not be critical or judgmental of those who don't make that journey; our responsibility is to encourage others to discover new things about

God. We demonstrate this by experiencing a life of discovery in our walk with Him. But we need to recognize that some people will just be where they are, and it is God who will cause them to grow. Romans 12:4-6 says there are many members of the body, but not all have the same function. We are one body in Christ and members of one another. We have gifts according to the grace that was given to us. No one is less important than anyone else; it only means we are at different places in the journey.

In Romans 1:16-17, Paul declares he's not ashamed of the gospel because of its power to save everyone, both Jew and Gentile, and that God's righteousness is revealed "from faith to faith." Since faith comes by hearing, and hearing by a RHEMA, we can more clearly see what faith is. It is hearing God in each situation as we travel through life, allowing Him to impart the necessary faith to see His promises come to pass. Our lives should be filled with stories of God speaking and doing what we had no power in ourselves to do, "for therein is the righteousness of God revealed from faith to faith." One revelation at a time.

Look at your life as a Christian. Is it not different than it was fifteen years ago? Hasn't your revelation of God changed and grown since you were first born again? "As it is written," writes Paul, "the just shall live by faith" (Romans 1:17 NKJV). Justified Christians live by a conviction that is imparted from a loving God who speaks to them. Faith is an impartation from God regarding a current circumstance, while trust is continuing with God regardless of the current circumstance in which you find yourself. Faith comes from hearing God, but trust comes from knowing God.

Notes

1. Craig D. Lounsbrough, *An Intimate Collision: Encounters with Life and Jesus* (Belfast, Northern Ireland, UK: Ambassador Books, 2013).
2. Samuel Chadwick, *The Path of Prayer* (Sheffield, UK: Cliff College Publishing, 1801), 65.

POWER THOUGHTS FOR *Chapter 7*

We cannot of ourselves produce any of the experiences of the Christian life. We cannot regenerate ourselves, for we are born again not of the will of the flesh but of God (John 1:13). We cannot confess Jesus as Lord but by the Holy Spirit (1 Corinthians 12:3). We cannot understand the Bible but by the Holy Spirit (John 14:26). We cannot live the Christian life—Christ lives in us (Philippians 1:21; Galatians 2:20). The natural man cannot receive the things of the Spirit of God (1 Corinthians 2:14). We can consent and cooperate, but this is a supernatural work of God from start to finish.

—Vance Havner[1]

Words create worlds. Releasing what you think is God's word with your faith is presumption. This practice creates your world with your words. Hearing God's Rhema word, infused with God's faith, accomplishes His purposes, and creates His world, His way.

—Dave Lake and Ed Delph

If it's flesh-based, it's erased, 'cause it's not graced.

—Ed Delph

Chapter 7

NO DOUBT ABOUT IT

The fact is that not everyone receives RHEMA. This concept is quite the religion-buster because people have a certain perception about how God operates. As He continues to give us a greater understanding of who He is and how He operates, it becomes obvious how small our perception of God truly is. Yesterday's revelations are only a small glimpse of the character of God. We are on a journey to know the fullness of His character.

In Matthew 13, Jesus is sitting by the sea. Because of a large crowd pressing in close to Him, He gets into a boat where He starts to speak to them in parables. In verse 10, Jesus's disciples come to Him and ask Him why He teaches them parables. In response, Jesus tells them that they have been granted to "know the mysteries of the kingdom of heaven, but to them it has not been granted." *Granted* here means "to give." Notice that some people are given the ability to know the mysteries of the kingdom, while other people have not been given that ability. In verse 12, Jesus says, "Whoever has, to him shall more be given and he will have an abundance, but whoever does not have, even what he has shall be taken away from him."

Jesus is telling His disciples that they have been given an ability to know and will have an "abundance" of knowledge. He also points out that a person who does not have that ability to know, "even what he has shall be taken away from him." Each of us have talked to these types of people. They're individuals who don't get it, no matter what you do and how hard you try to explain it. Why? It is because there's not a divine interaction occurring within their hearts.

Though Christ has placed in our hearts a yearning for all to be saved, He never told us we had the ability to make that happen. Rather, Jesus says in John 6:44, "No one can come to Me unless the Father who sent Me draws him; and I will raise him up on the last day" (NKJV). We preach the Word as the Holy Spirit leads, we sow seed as the Holy Spirit leads, and we water that seed as the Holy Spirit leads. But only God is responsible for the growth. Christians need to stop manipulating people to get them to decide for Christ. Rather, God has asked us to show them Jesus by our love, and then they will come to Christ as the Holy Spirit draws them. When God tells us to speak, pray, or give, we only have to respond by doing it. Then we move on. If He really has spoken a RHEMA, it will accomplish what is pleasing to Him and prosper in the thing for which He has sent it. Jesus is telling the disciples that they have received RHEMA and will receive even more RHEMA.

You are His disciple, so it has been granted to you to know the mysteries of the kingdom of Heaven. And God is going to show you more of the mysteries of the kingdom. Those who are not of His kingdom "while seeing they do not see, and while hearing they do not hear, nor do they understand" (Matthew 13:13). Rejoice in the reality of the privileges He's given us as His children.

When I was first exposed to a charismatic church, my wife and I were in church when a local prophet came to speak. We usually don't get picked out of the crowd and prophesied over, but this guy called us from the crowd and started praying over us. He said to me, "You will be a man who walks the world." All I could think about was how we lived paycheck to paycheck with four young children. Money went out the door just as fast as it came in.

Yet, since 1993, I've walked the world. And I've watched God do what He said He was going to do. It is His proclamation over our lives that brings His purposes to pass. It was RHEMA and His impartation of faith that allowed me to do what I had no belief that I could do. *God spoke, and so there was no possibility of it not happening.* As God has caused our relationship to grow, and He continues to reveal Himself to me, I look forward to the tasks He has ahead. Every time God tells me to do something, I look forward to the journey. He makes things happen and brings situations in line as only He can do. I take no credit, nor do I deserve credit.

While Jesus is talking to His disciples about speaking to the crowds in parables, He declares that the prophecy of Isaiah 6 is fulfilled:

> *Hearing you will hear and shall not understand, And seeing you will see and not perceive; For the hearts of this people have grown dull. Their ears are hard of hearing, And their eyes they have closed, Lest they should see with their eyes and hear with their ears, Lest they should understand with their hearts and turn, So that I should heal them* (Matthew 13:14-15 NKJV).

This is what God sent Isaiah to do when Isaiah responded and said, "Send me!" (see Isaiah 6:9). The point is that God gives understanding to whom He desires to give understanding, He gives sight to whom He desires to give sight, and He gives hearing to whom He desires to hear. God is the revealer of all mysteries!

"But," He tells His disciples, "blessed are your eyes for they see, and your ears for they hear; for assuredly I tell you that many prophets and righteous men desired to see what you see, and did not see it, and to hear what you hear, and did not hear it" (Matthew 13:16-17 NKJV). Do not think highly of yourself when He reveals His secrets to you, for God speaks to those who hear what He has shown them. Just as He gave you RHEMA regarding a particular situation, so He will also give others RHEMA. But this happens only in His timing—you can't make it happen. God has to speak to them.

There will be times and seasons when you speak and God uses you as that person to give others revelation. Preachers, teachers, prophets, apostles, and pastors deliver revelations as God has shown them, then they walk away with the understanding that God must reveal it to the people. I could speak a message to a crowd of people, and if God doesn't open their ears, then they won't hear a thing. It's okay because it is His responsibility. He knows what He is doing.

The other day I was in the bank to take care of some things for my business. As I was walking out, the banker who was reviewing my account stopped me and asked me the secret of the business's success. I told him the amazing things God had been doing in my business. And I told him about God running a business. That's it. I have no experience building a business or running a business; I don't know anything about this stuff, but I've watched God give me wisdom, open doors for me, and give me knowledge and understanding for what I had never thought about before.

A couple years ago, as I flew home from a Philippines missions trip, God began speaking to me about growing the business. I had been content with how the business was going. In fact, God had taken us from nothing in 2008 to a thriving business in 2014. We had a couple of employees and a showroom. I was happy with what God had done. But then God spoke to my heart Matthew 13:31-32: "The kingdom of heaven is like a mustard seed, which a man took and sowed in his field, which is indeed the least of all seeds; but when it is grown it is greater than the herbs and becomes a tree, so that the birds of the air come and nest in its branches" (NKJV). God then said, "That is what a kingdom business is to be. And the business I placed you in is a kingdom business."

I had no idea where to start to make the business grow. So I spent the next year asking God how to make the business grow. The following year on another return trip from the Philippines, God spoke clearly, "Now." When I got home, we opened another showroom on the other side of town and put more people on payroll. My business vision moved from the attitude of "what we have is enough" to "God wants this business to grow." The business is showing signs of growing another 50 to 70 percent. I don't know how much it will grow or how long the process will take, but I am standing back and watching God do what He does. Because He spoke it to my heart, there is no possibility of it not coming to pass.

Knowing God

I used to teach a class called "Knowing God." Participants could ask any question about God they wanted and we would search Scripture for the answer. People could bring their preconceived ideas to the class, but they had to be able to scripturally substantiate their beliefs. We had many lively discussions, and we also discovered that many ideas that we had embraced as scriptural were really the traditions of others.

One of our discussions involved the idea of getting more faith. We had heard of people "praying for more faith," and we had heard preachers ask us to "extend our faith." Not only that, but we'd heard teachings on "sowing seeds of faith," and people were accused of not "having enough faith" when situations did not change following prayer. When I asked the class how to increase faith, or how we could believe harder for something, no one offered an answer.

Luke 17 addresses this issue. In verse 5, the apostles said to the Lord, "Increase our faith." Jesus's response is a bit unexpected. "If you had faith like a mustard seed," He tells them, "you would say to this mulberry tree, 'Be uprooted and be planted in the sea,' and it would obey you" (Luke 17:6). Jesus was telling them this is what faith looks like, and they did not have it.

He goes on to tell them how bondservants operate: namely, they do what they are told. The master does not thank the servant for doing what he is told to do. Then Jesus sums up His point in verse 10: "So likewise you, when you have done all those things which you are commanded, say, 'We are unprofitable servants. We have done what was our duty to do'" (NKJV). This is His answer to their request for more faith.

As servants of God, we do what He tells us to do. When He tells us to do something, He imparts the faith to do it. And so we can't take credit for the faith or the actually doing that is the result of faith.

You see, Jesus changed the disciples' perspective. They were taking faith as a spiritual status. Don't we do that today? And Jesus said, "Wait a minute, let Me give you a new perspective. Here's what faith really looks like, and I've not seen any of you do that. In fact, let Me break it down a little bit more: you're a bondservant; I tell you what to do and I empower you to do it. How can you take any credit for that?" We are bondservants of God; a bondservant does simply what he is told to do.

The next story in Luke 17 tells us that while Jesus was on His way to Jerusalem, He passed between Samaria and Galilee. And as He entered a village, ten lepers standing at a distance called out to Him, "Master, have mercy on us!" And after He asked them what they wanted from Him, He told them to go and show themselves to the priests. As they were going, they were cleansed of their leprosy. Only one of them, when he saw that he was healed, turned back, glorifying God with a loud voice. This single cleansed leper fell on his face at Jesus's feet. And Jesus said to him, "Didn't I cleanse ten of you? Where's everybody else? Is this foreigner the only one who came back to give glory to God?" Jesus said to him, "Stand up and go, for your faith has made you well."

How many of the ten were healed because of faith? Only one of them. How did the other nine get healed then? It was by God's mercy. You see, God causes the rain to fall on the righteous and the unrighteous alike. Nine lepers got healed out of mercy, but one of them was healed by faith. We know that faith comes by hearing an utterance from God, so of the ten healed lepers only the Samaritan was credited with possessing faith. This means he was the only one who heard the utterance from God. He was the only one who heard Jesus say, "Your faith has healed you."

What does faith look like? It looks like one man out of ten who came to Jesus and humbly fell at Jesus's feet and gave glory to God.

That's the fruit of faith. Not everybody out of that group had a RHEMA from God; only one of them did. Though ten were healed only one was pleasing to God, the one with faith.

In Matthew 16:13-19, Jesus asks His disciples who people think He is. The disciples give Jesus the gossip about Him they've heard going around the town: "Some say John the Baptist, some Elijah, and others a prophet." But what Jesus really wants to know is, "Who do *you* say that I am?" And it is here where Simon Peter blurts out his famous revelation, "You are the Christ, the Son of the living God." And Jesus tells him, "Blessed are you, Simon Bar-Jonah, for flesh and blood has not revealed this to you, but My Father who is in heaven" (Matthew 16:17 NKJV).

Who revealed Jesus's identity to Simon? This revelation came only from the Father in Heaven. Jesus addresses Peter as Simon Bar-Jonah. Do you know why Jesus used this name? It was because Simon Bar-Jonah is who he was before Christ renamed him. This is significant because the Father spoke to Simon before Simon came to Christ! But after this RHEMA, Simon had a revelation that Jesus is the Son of God, and Jesus renamed him Peter: "I also say to you that you are Peter, and on this rock I will build My church" (Matthew 16:18 NKJV). Jesus is not talking here about building His church upon Peter, but upon the revelation that Jesus is the Son of God. Jesus continues, "... on this rock I will build My church, and the gates of Hades shall not prevail against it" (Matthew 16:18 NKJV). The only thing that the gates of hell doesn't overpower is Christ the Rock! Then He tells them He'll give them the keys of the kingdom of Heaven, and whatever they bind on earth will be bound in Heaven, and whatever they loose on earth will be loosed in Heaven.

What are the keys to the kingdom of Heaven? What is Jesus talking about? Jesus is talking about revelation; He's talking about RHEMA. One of our problems is that we bind and loose what we think we should be binding and loosing with no RHEMA regarding what should be bound or loosed. Jesus puts it in perspective when He says,

"Whatever you bind on earth you *shall have been* bound in heaven." Why? Because God gives you a RHEMA regarding what He has already bound and loosed.

After Jesus tells Peter about binding and loosing, the first thing He does is warn them that they were to tell no one that He was the Christ (see Matthew 16:20). As a human being, what would be your first reaction to learning all this revelation? Wouldn't you go preach the gospel? Why did Jesus tell them not to tell anyone else? It was because He was setting the foundational value of doing what He said, not just acting on what He had told them about a circumstance. You see, God gave them revelation, but He had no desire for them to declare that revelation until He said it was time for it to be declared. Obedience is most important regardless of revelation!

From then on, Jesus began telling His disciples about what lay ahead of Him in Jerusalem—suffering abuse from the elders, chief priests, and scribes, and being killed and then raised up on the third day. Peter took Jesus aside and began contradicting Him. "God forbid it, Lord," he said. "This shall never happen to you!" Was that the Spirit of God speaking through him? No, it was the flesh because Jesus was already telling them what had to happen.

I often ask people, "When you're praying for all the stuff that's happening, are you praying because God wants it to happen or are you praying because you want it to happen?" If world events get worse, then should we be praying that the world gets better? Or should we pray for Jesus to come back, knowing full well what the world has to look like before He returns? Peter was contradicting God's will when he was opposing Jesus.

Jesus tells him, "Listen to Me; I'm going to suffer a bunch of things. They're going to hang Me on a cross. They're going to beat Me. They're going to do all this bad stuff to Me." And Peter, in all his righteousness, stands up and says, "No! It won't happen to You. Let it not happen." And what did Jesus say to him? "Get behind Me, satan!

You are a stumbling block to Me; for you are not setting your mind on God's interests but man's" (Matthew 16:23).

When we put this in the context of the chapter, we can see how it all comes together. We can't separate the different scenes from the whole story. Jesus is talking about revelation, then He gives a RHEMA, then He verifies that what's most important is what He tells us to do, not what we think we should do. In fact, in verse 24-26, He says it this way: "If anyone wishes to come after Me, he must deny himself, and take up his cross and follow Me. For whoever wishes to save his life will lose it; but whoever loses his life for My sake will find it. For what will it profit a man if he gains the whole world and forfeits his soul? Or what will a man give in exchange for his soul?" Jesus is telling us that the most important things that we will ever do in our lives are what God utters to us, and in the timing that He tells us to do them.

Peter walked right through this. First, Jesus tells him, "Simon Bar-Jonah, My Father in Heaven showed you the revelation that I am His Son. He gives you the keys to the kingdom of Heaven by the revelations you're going to get from Me. Now don't go telling anybody about Me yet. And here is what's going to happen: this world's going to get worse and worse." Yes, this world's going to get worse. Are you concerned about what people want to do? Or are you more concerned about what God wants to do? If you're going to be a follower of Christ, then you must take up your cross, deny yourself—your emotions and your feelings—and walk by what God said about how this world should be.

As you mature in God, you need to remember to walk by His voice more than by the voice of the world. We must decrease so that He might increase. Walk by the Spirit more every day. "For the Son of Man is going to come in the glory of His Father with His angels, and will then repay every man according to his deeds" (Matthew 16:27). Jesus tells His disciples this to assure them that God has it covered: "Truly I say to you, there are some of those who are standing here who will not taste death until they see the Son of Man coming in the kingdom"

(Matthew 16:28). Remember that the underlying foundation of this chapter is RHEMA; life is all about hearing from God.

Note

1. Vance Havner, *Pepper 'n' Salt* (Grand Rapids, MI: Fleming H. Revell Company, 1966).

POWER THOUGHTS FOR *Chapter 8*

Ears that hear and eyes that see—we get our basic equipment from God.

—Proverbs 20:12 MSG

Wise men and women are always learning, always listening for fresh insights.

—Proverbs 18:15 MSG

God has no use for the prayers of the people who won't listen to Him.

—Proverbs 28:9 MSG

If people can't see what God is doing, they'll stumble all over themselves. But when they attend to what He reveals, they are most blessed.

—Proverbs 29:18 MSG

The very steps we take come from God; otherwise how would we know where we're going?

—Proverbs 20:24 MSG

Put God in charge of your work, then what you've planned will take place.

—Proverbs 16:3 MSG

Chapter 8

ADVENTURES AND MISADVENTURES IN FAITH

People often declare by faith what they want God to do instead of what God has said He is going to do in and through them. These people take hold of a specific scripture—LOGOS—and they begin declaring or "trying to pull down from Heaven" or speaking into existence what that scripture promises. All these means only end up being self-motivated. Satan did the same thing when tempting Jesus in the wilderness. Satan quoted LOGOS to manipulate Jesus. Jesus rebuttals by emphasizing RHEMA. Faith is not taking a Bible verse we've found and attempting to apply it to our circumstances to acquire our desired results—that's trust. That is not to say the Lord does not impart faith when we read His LOGOS (written Word) but don't recognize RHEMA (Him speaking). Early in our spiritual growth, we do not recognize His voice.

Jesus says in John 6:44-45 that only people who are drawn by the Father, have heard from the Father and have learned from the Father, can come to Him. What must happen before somebody can come to Jesus? He or she must first be taught of the Father. Here's the thing: we often take credit for coming to Jesus. "I realized I needed God," we say, "so I decided to follow Him." The only things we've known till that point of our lives are the decisions made by what we think. When the

Holy Spirit speaks through our minds, however, we have no discernment between what is us and what is Him. Paul said in Ephesians 4:23 that we are to be "renewed in the spirit of [our] mind" and in Romans 12:2 that we are to be "transformed by the renewing of [our] mind." A characteristic of a renewed mind is the ability to discern what is His voice and what is our own voice.

"It is written in the prophets," Jesus says in John 6:45, "'and they shall all be taught of God.' Everyone who has heard and learned from the Father, comes to Me." And do you know where Jesus takes those who hear from the Father? He takes them back to the Father; Jesus always takes us back to the Father. In John 5:19, Jesus says, "Truly, truly I say to you, the Son can do nothing of Himself, unless it is something He sees the Father doing...." Jesus does only what He sees His Father doing. He does not add to or give suggestions to the Father about how something should be done. Since we are Christians, we are to be like Jesus. This means we are to look to the Lord and become imitators of what He does and when He does it. Faith comes from hearing a word from God. In fact, God designed us to reflect Him in this world, which is how He is glorified. We should hear from God and reflect the Father, just as Jesus did.

A little further along, in John 5:30, Jesus says, "I can do nothing on My own initiative. As I hear, I judge; and My judgment is just, because I do not seek my own will, but the will of Him who sent Me." Jesus's actions have everything to do with hearing God, with doing what God wants to do.

For example, just before His arrest and crucifixion, Jesus was praying with His dozing disciples for the second time. "My Father," He prayed, "if this cannot pass away unless I drink it, Your will be done" (Matthew 26:42). We need to stop assuming. We need to hear what God wants us to do.

In His "vine and branches" dissertation in John 15, Jesus says, "I am the true vine and My Father is the vinedresser" (John 15:1). Unfruitful branches will be removed from the vine, and fruitful branches will be pruned so they can bear more fruit. Then He tells His disciples that they are already "clean" or pruned "because of the word [LOGOS] which I have spoken to you." He warns them of the importance of abiding in Him, because apart from Him they cannot bear fruit, but in Him they'll be fruitful. "If you abide in Me, and My words [RHEMA] abide in you, ask whatever you wish, and it will be done for you" (John 15:7). Notice how Jesus emphasizes the importance of abiding in Him and His RHEMA abiding in us. As His RHEMA abides in us, we can ask what we wish and it is given to us because we are asking what He tells us to ask for.

Jesus continues in verse 15, telling His disciples that they are not slaves but friends. A master doesn't have to give reasons for his actions to a slave or let a slave in on his plans. But, Jesus says, "I have called you friends, for all things that I have heard from my Father I have made known to you" (John 15:15). God has chosen and appointed Jesus's disciples to go and bear fruit that remains "so that whatever you ask of the Father in My name He may give to you" (John 15:16). Again, Jesus is telling them that the Father's positive response has everything to do with hearing and being about His business.

Moving on to Hebrews 4, the writer tells us about the Sabbath rest God has for His people. God wants His people to rest from their own works, just as God rested from His. God wants believers to be diligent to enter His rest and not fall short of it, following Israel's example of disobedience. At that time in history, Israel had failed to enter God's rest: "But the word they heard did not profit them, because it was not united by faith in those who heard" (Hebrews 4:2).

Israel did not enter God's rest because the LOGOS was not mixed with faith (which is imparted by hearing a RHEMA from God). They thought they could please God by doing works; therefore, they could not enter His rest. If you are doing works instead of allowing works to come as a result of faith that is imparted by God, then you cannot enter His rest. Hebrews 4:10 says, "For the one who has entered His rest has himself also rested from his works, as God did from His."

God is revealing Himself to His people. How many believers who've been Christians for thirty years or more are still worried about their circumstances if something doesn't go perfectly? They've never moved on to realize that God's bigger than those things, and, as Hebrews says, they have failed to "enter His rest." One of the biggest indicators that the corporate church does not know God is our lack of ability to enter His rest.

The truth is that nobody enjoys the journey; many fail to understand that God is who God is and He will do what He says He will do. This isn't about having more money or comforts on earth. We are to set our hearts on what is in Heaven. We are not to love the world or the things that are in the world; we are not about doing everything the way we think they should be done. We should hear the "now words" for the "now times." Faith is God-centered, because faith comes from Him. Faith is not about our ability to accomplish what God says He will do; it is about us resting in what He has spoken to us.

Notice in Second Corinthians 12 how Paul approaches God regarding this. To keep Paul from thinking too highly of himself due to his tremendous spiritual revelations, God has given him "a thorn in the flesh, a messenger of satan," some overwhelming weakness that keeps him humble. He has "implored the Lord three times that it might leave," but God has replied that His grace is sufficient for Paul and His power is perfected in Paul's weakness. I love how Paul responds to what God tells him, because the reality of who Paul knows God to be surpasses everything else that is taking place in his life. He declares, "I will rather boast about my weakness so that the power of Christ may dwell in me. Therefore I am well content with weaknesses, with insults, with distresses, with persecutions, with difficulties for Christ's sake; for when I am weak, then I am strong" (2 Corinthians 12:9-10).

Does that sound like anything that we hear much about these days? Being content in weaknesses? Yet Paul had a reality of who God is and he took this problem to God on three separate occasions. And

God said, "I've been talking to you about this, Paul. When you are weak, I'm strong."

Paul was then able to say, "I get it now. I will be glad when I'm weak. I will glory in those things." Yet what message do we hear in our churches today? *A better life! No pain! No discomfort.* This message is contrary to what the Scriptures say. It's contrary to Paul's attitude. It's contrary to what the message of the cross is all about. Again, this message has everything to do with hearing God. Faith is God-centered because faith comes from Him. It's not about our ability to accomplish what God says He will do.

Back in the 1990s, when the Toronto Blessing was going on, I had a unique RHEMA moment. At that time in my life, our church was heavily involved in the deliverance ministry. I loved seeing the power of God put the devil in his place. I was part of a small team called DET, the Demon-Expulsion Team. I was beginning to understand spiritual warfare and discernment, and I took great pleasure in "knowing" who was demonically oppressed or possessed. I would be in church looking for "spiritual darkness" that was trying to invade our congregation. No demon was coming into church to create disorder on my watch!

At that time, our church sent a pastor to Toronto to find out what was going on up there. He came back and proceeded to give us a full report of what he'd seen. The church service that day was about six hundred people. I was sitting somewhere in the middle of the sanctuary. Most of the time we kept the lights low and the stage lit up so the people could more clearly see the speaker, but from the stage it was hard to recognize faces in the audience. While the pastor was reporting about the movement of the Spirit in Toronto, suddenly the Holy Spirit came upon me and God clearly said to me, "Roar!" A crisis of faith happened in my mind! I sat there thinking, "No way. This cannot be God. There's no way this could happen." The Holy Spirit came upon me again and I began to shake.

There I was, sitting in church, shaking next to my wife (my poor wife...I've written her up for sainthood), going through every reason in my mind why this wasn't from God. He said to me again, "Roar!" The pastor was walking back and forth on the church platform. He couldn't see me, but he stopped in the middle of his talk, looked out at the crowd, and said, "Somebody here, God is telling you to do something, and He says you are not doing it."

I began to cry. And I began wondering when the proper time to roar in church would be. By this point, I was a weeping, shaking mess. The pastor began speaking again, and in the middle of his sentence I stood up and roared at the top of my lungs. Not once, but twice! I was sobbing uncontrollably. It was a powerful moment, but please take note, I did not develop the ministry of the roar after that. It was a RHEMA moment. As I wept in that service, the pastor said, "You need to come up here and pray for people." I had never prayed over people with the power of God on me like I did that day. And I didn't even have to pray for them. I would just lay hands on them and the power of God was so strong that people were falling over, crying or roaring. God was powerfully moving.

I'm not sure how long the anointing rested on me that day, but I do know that God touched a bunch of folks. The experience was so far out of my comfort zone that it had to be from God. It was a RHEMA from God to do that which I did not have in me to do. God spoke and imparted something in me to minister to people the way He wanted to minister to them. He not only touched lives in church that day, but He also began to reveal to me what was going on in the life of our church. It took several months to understand much of what He did that day. One of those revelations was how "religious" we had become. We had LOGOS but were missing RHEMA. We substituted working hard for God's approval instead of bearing the fruit that comes from hearing God.

This was one of the most powerful seasons I ever walked through. To this day, no one has ever asked me what happened during that experience, but it was God-centered. *Nobody in his or her right mind stands up in church and roars!*

The Flesh Is Death

The flesh has been death from day one. Additionally, the flesh has certain other characteristics to it too. Jesus said in John 3:6, "That which is born of the flesh is flesh." Flesh does not produce Spirit. In Romans 7:18, Paul writes, "For I know that nothing good dwells in me, that is, in my flesh." And in Romans 8, he demonstrates the reality of this principle. He starts out by saying that those of us in Christ Jesus are not condemned by our sin but are set free from the law of sin and death by the Spirit of life in Christ. Because our flesh is so weak, there is no way for us to achieve righteousness by keeping the law, so God sent His Son as the perfect sacrifice, completely fulfilling the law's requirements in us "who do not walk according to the flesh but according to the Spirit" (Romans 8:4).

Paul then goes on to contrast the difference between a life lived according to the flesh and one lived in the Spirit. The mind-set of the flesh thinks about fleshly things and is hostile toward God, it cannot please God, it does not have the Spirit of God, it does not belong to God, and it is ultimately dead. But people who set their minds on the Spirit have life and peace; they have the Spirit of God dwelling within them, giving eternal life to their mortal bodies. We can see the characteristics of the flesh, and none of them have anything to do with spiritual life.

In First Corinthians 15:50, Paul makes the point that flesh "cannot inherit the kingdom of God," while in Second Corinthians 7:1, he warns believers to cleanse themselves "from the filthiness of the flesh" (NKJV). The Scriptures make it clear that we all must deal with the flesh.

What is the flesh? It's the tent we live in here on earth. But this earthly tent in which we live is subject to our five senses, because that's how we interact with the world. We make lots of decisions, and a lot of the time we walk by the flesh, not by faith. And what does the flesh do? It does what feels good and it fails to do what doesn't feel good. That's the flesh.

There's an interesting story in Second Chronicles 18. The godly king Jehoshaphat of Judah has allied himself through marriage with the wicked king Ahab of Israel. And he goes to visit Ahab at Samaria. Ahab put on a huge feast for Jehoshaphat and his entourage, thus enticing them to fight with him against Ramoth-Gilead. Jehoshaphat agrees on the condition that Ahab gets counsel from the Lord. So King Ahab assembles four hundred prophets and says to them, "Shall we go against Ramoth-Gilead to battle, or shall I refrain?" And they say, "Go up, for God will give it into the hand of the king."

But Jehoshaphat asks, "Is there not yet a prophet of the Lord here that we may inquire of him?" Interestingly, even though Jehoshaphat is listening to four hundred people prophesy great and wonderful things about their future, he hears something inside that says, "Wait a minute. Isn't there somebody else here? God's saying something else." And Ahab says to Jehoshaphat, "There is yet one man by whom we may inquire of the Lord, but I hate him because he never prophesies good concerning me but always evil. He is Micaiah, son of Imla."

Both kings in their royal robes are sitting on their thrones, and four hundred prophets are telling them to go ahead and fight because they'll be victorious against Ramoth-Gilead. And the messenger who goes to summon Micaiah begs the prophet to agree with the other four hundred prophets. But Micaiah says, "As the Lord lives, what my God says, that I will speak." But when the king asks him if they should go up against their enemy, Micaiah at first says what he knows the king wants to hear: "Go up, succeed, for they will be given into your hand." But the king knows—even this wicked king knows—there is something more.

The king presses Micaiah until he finally gives him the truth: "I saw all Israel scattered on the mountains like sheep which have no shepherd. And the Lord said, 'These have no master. Let each of them return to his house in peace.'" Ahab then asked Jehoshaphat, "Didn't I tell you that he's not going to prophesy good concerning me but evil?" And Micaiah says:

> *Therefore, hear the word of the Lord. I saw the Lord sitting on His throne, and all the host of heaven standing on His right and on His left. And the Lord said, "Who will entice Ahab, the king of Israel, to go up and fall at Ramoth-Gilead?" And one said this while another said that. Then a spirit came forward and stood before the Lord and said, "I will entice him." And the Lord said to him, "How?" He said, "I will go and be a deceiving spirit in the mouth of all of his prophets." Then He said, "You are to entice him and prevail also. Go and do so"* (2 Chronicles 18:18-21).

Did God give permission for a deceiving spirit to go and speak through the prophets? Yes, He did. Is that a characteristic of God? Yes, it seems to be one of His characteristics. Is this possible today? Yes, it is. Hence, this shows the importance of being in the habit of hearing from God.

I preach and teach quite often. And do you know what I tell people almost every time I preach? I tell them to go home and open the Bible and ask God if what I said was true. We can clearly see that God opens the realm of Heaven to show this prophet exactly what happened in that instance. God had a purpose in allowing the four hundred prophets to be deceived. But speaking the truth to the king isn't without its consequences for Micaiah. First, the deceived prophet Zedekiah slaps him across the face, and then King Ahab orders Micaiah to be sent to prison and fed bread and water until he returns safely from battle. Micaiah replies, "If you indeed return safely, then the Lord has not spoken by me."

When these kings go into battle, wily Ahab tells Jehoshaphat, "I'll disguise myself to go to battle, but you put on your royal robes." But his ploy doesn't work because the other army had been commanded to target only the king of Israel. And when they see Jehoshaphat in his royal robes, they set their sights on him, but *"Jehoshaphat cried out to the Lord. And the Lord helped him, and diverted them from him."* Jehoshaphat knew when he heard those four hundred prophets prophesying that it wasn't a word from God, and still his flesh did what he wanted to do. The mercy of God is clear here. God redeemed him anyway because he was His child.

The enemy stopped chasing Jehoshaphat, and then an archer randomly shoots an arrow that happens to strike the disguised king Ahab in a joint of his armor. After being hit, Ahab has his chariot driver take him off the battlefield, and the king props himself up in his chariot and watches the battle in plain sight of his enemy until he dies at sunset. God, who was seeking something against wicked King Ahab, purposed this whole situation. And even the godly king Jehoshaphat didn't heed God's voice because the flesh doesn't have the ability to obey God apart from the grace of God, despite hearing God. There was no RHEMA.

In Second Chronicles 19, Jehoshaphat returns home to Jerusalem, and Jehu, another prophet, confronts him. Jehu says, "Should you help the wicked and love those who hate the Lord, and so bring wrath on yourself from the Lord? But there is some good in you, for you have removed the Asheroth from the land and you have set your heart to seek God." God cares for Jehoshaphat enough to give him an explanation of what happened. His flesh, even though it heard God's word, did not obey because there was no faith imparted from a RHEMA.

My final point comes from Genesis 3. The crafty serpent demonstrates the flesh's inability to obey the commandment of God without a RHEMA by sowing doubt in the mind of the woman by asking, "Indeed, has God really said, 'You shall not eat from any tree of the garden?'" The woman replies, "From the fruit of the trees of the garden we may eat; but from the fruit of the tree which is in the middle of the garden, God has said, 'You shall not eat from it or touch it, or you will die.'" Did the woman hear God? She sure did. Was her flesh able to do anything to obey the law? No, it wasn't, because she ended up eating from the tree.

Church teaching tends toward a mentality that flesh didn't enter the picture until after the man and woman ate the forbidden fruit.

Somewhere we have come to believe that there is good in the flesh. Consider the following. Woman was uniquely created in the garden. Man was formed from dust and God breathed into him, but woman was not created out of the dust and God did not breathe into her as He did with Adam. She was created from Adam. He took a rib from Adam, closed up his flesh and fashioned woman. Woman was a part of man. This does not make Eve less important than Adam. This means she is different than Adam. God made her that way for His purpose. "Having then gifts differing according to the grace given to us..." (Romans 12:6 NKJV). She was pure flesh because she came out of Adam. In fact, God didn't name her; it was Adam who named her. He called her Woman because she was taken out of man. The difference between Adam and Eve's creation is the difference between Adam and Eve's ability to resist the temptation of the enemy. Before Eve, Adam's flesh was subject to the Divine Spirit in him. First John 3:9 tells us, "Whosoever is born of God doth not commit sin; for His seed remaineth in him: and he cannot sin because he is born of God" (KJV). Remember, though she is taken from man the two are still one flesh. Eve was Adam's flesh magnified. Why did Satan tempt Eve? What is the only way Satan has access to you? The flesh. Eve is the flesh of man. What does the flesh do? According to Scripture, does flesh ever produce life? No. Eve had the law; she knew the law. She told the serpent the law that she had heard.

She had a verse and yet she did what was contrary to the nature of God. Understand that this isn't about man or woman (male or female) because in Heaven gender is not an issue. But in this context regarding the fall, we see that the flesh knew the law but was unable to follow it. She didn't get a RHEMA; rather, she only had LOGOS. God demonstrated the flesh's inability to obey the law though it knows the law. The flesh needs a RHEMA to be saved. Now before this sounds like a woman-bashing session, let's bring this picture full circle. God reintroduces His Divine Spirit back into humanity by the virgin birth. The Holy Spirit overshadows Mary and she becomes pregnant with the Son of God! Just as God's Spirit created life in Mary so His Spirit creates life in one that is born again! It blows my mind that from the beginning, God wanted us to listen to Him. And from the beginning, we only demonstrated our inability to hear Him.

Ed and I have written this book to show the need of hearing from God. There is a tremendous need in receiving RHEMA from the Lord, showing the true value that faith comes from God and manifests through humans. God could have avoided the whole incident in the garden. He knew what Adam and Eve were going to do. He could have gotten rid of the tree and then we would have no issues at all. He could have not given them the law, "Don't eat from the tree." But God still put the tree in garden even though He knew what was going to happen. He still put the law there so that humanity would understand from day one that the flesh could not obey the law of God. By doing this, God demonstrated our need for His grace, thus showing His great love for us by extending grace regardless of our "fleshly" condition. It is the experience of spiritual darkness where the realization of our need for God is magnified.

If we are going to declare something by faith, then we must be sure we have received a RHEMA word from the Lord first, because what He declares He will also perform.

Section III

THE COOPERATION AND OPERATION OF LOGOS AND RHEMA

by Ed Delph

POWER THOUGHTS FOR *Chapter 9*

An Exhortation from a True Intercessor

When God speaks, we have an obligation to hear and comply. According to Merriam-Webster's Learner's Dictionary, to comply means "to do what you have been asked or ordered to do." First Samuel 15:22 says, "Obedience is better than sacrifice."

In Song of Solomon 5:2-3, the bride is in bed asleep with the door latched when she hears a voice cry, "Open to me." It is the bridegroom. She hears but she says, "I have washed my feet; how can I dirty them again?" She won't be inconvenienced, which leads to separation and then torment.

In John 13:7-8, Jesus is washing the disciples' feet when Peter questions His self-debasing action. Jesus responds, "What you do not realize now, but you will understand hereafter." Peter reacts with, "Never shall you wash my feet!" Peter doesn't hear.

In Revelation 3:19-20, the lukewarm Laodicean church is told to repent. Jesus says to them, "Behold, I stand at the door and knock; if anyone hears my voice and opens the door, I will come in to him."

In all three passages of Scripture, God is saying to hear and (be) open to Him.

The LOGOS of God, the two-edged sword of Hebrews 4:12, is the written Word of God. The sword of the Spirit, which is the RHEMA of God (see Ephesians 6:17), is the utterance from God. We need both sides for balance through fullness.

—JANE CHERNEY

Chapter 9

Two Swords from the Lord for Every Believer: Logos and Rhema

It's one thing to have a sword. It's quite another to use the sword correctly and accurately.
—Ed Delph

Did you know that every believer has two swords? If you remove the "s" from the word *sword*, what do you get? You get *word*. The Word of God and a sword of the Lord have very similar functions. Let's look at the following verses in the Bible:

> *For the word* [LOGOS] *of God is living and active and sharper than any two-edged sword, and piercing as far as the division of soul and spirit, of both joints and marrow, and able to judge the thoughts and intentions of the heart* (Hebrews 4:12).
>
> *And take the helmet of salvation, and the sword of the Spirit, which is the word* [RHEMA] *of God* (Ephesians 6:17).

The first verse informs us about LOGOS, while the second informs us about RHEMA. LOGOS is the Bible, the written Word of God—the solid, unchangeable, complete Word of God. LOGOS is strong and amazing; it is for everybody. LOGOS is what and how God thinks about life. LOGOS is one of the swords that each believer is to be equipped with. But God decided that believers, pastors, and marketplace ministers need another sword too—RHEMA.

As we have learned, RHEMA is *a faith-infused utterance from God, providing the recipient with illumination, wisdom, or direction.* RHEMA is God speaking presently and biblically to a person for a specific reason. God speaks to a person or through a person *a now word, for a now time, in a now circumstance.* RHEMA is for somebody who needs to hear it at that moment. In fact, RHEMA is a powerful sword too! The two swords work in harmony with each other. We need both swords to achieve balance through fullness. One sword without the other sword is not biblical. In fact, it's a violation of LOGOS.

This chapter investigates three different angles of rediscovering, redefining, and refining RHEMA. Let's move from seeing it "like a tree" to seeing it clearly. The first is a look at LOGOS and RHEMA—their operation and cooperation. I created a comparison chart and included detailed definitions to clarify your understanding of LOGOS and RHEMA. Special thanks to Reverend Nadine Drayton-Keen for her help in the definition portion of this chapter. I gleaned great understanding and clarity from an article she wrote in her blog called "*Gone Fishin.*"[1]

Second, the verses below contain most of the references to RHEMA in the Bible (about seventy different verses). We have substituted the word RHEMA in place of the English *word* in each example to allow you to feel the intent and impact of its usage. Our desire is to enhance your comprehension of RHEMA.

Third, we also inserted our definition of RHEMA into the faith hall of fame in Hebrews 11:3-40. Since faith comes by hearing a RHEMA from God, we can see how ordinary people accomplished incredible feats. Looking at the faith hall of fame in this way clarifies why

Abraham did what he did, and why God inducted him into the faith hall of fame for it. Faith came by hearing a present word from God!

Take your time, read, grow, learn, and appropriate. Our birthright is two swords of the Lord, especially for such a time as this.

Logos and Rhema: Their Operation and Cooperation

The Bible utilizes two Greek terms to refer to the Word of God: LOGOS and RHEMA. Both are biblical and important to understanding the whole counsel of God. Delving into the Greek, which is a more precise language than English, leads us to a fuller understanding of the Trinity. David has correctly and accurately presented revelation on the meanings and nuances of these words. Both are necessary, both are good, and both reveal the nature of God. To function at the level at which God wants us to operate requires both light and truth. That is what Paul means by "the fullness of all in all" (Ephesians 4:13). Let's explore LOGOS and RHEMA more fully to recognize how they operate together and what the implications are for your life, marriage, business, education, children, and future.

Logos

LOGOS refers to that which gives general knowledge, understanding, and wisdom about God. It's unchangeable, eternal, immortal, and never passes away. LOGOS is the Word that God has "said" or has "spoken." LOGOS is Jesus the Christ, who is the living LOGOS (living Word). LOGOS also refers to the entire spoken Word of God, which is the mind of God, as revealed in the God-breathed, God-inspired holy Bible (both Old and New Testaments). The apostle John supports these definitions of LOGOS when he writes:

> *In the beginning was the Word* [LOGOS], *and the Word* [LOGOS] *was with God, and the Word [LOGOS]was God....And the Word* [LOGOS] *was made flesh, and dwelt among us, (and we beheld His glory, the glory as of the*

> *only begotten of the Father,) full of grace and truth* (John 1:1,14 KJV).

LOGOS, the written Word of God, is a comprehensive survey, in that in every book of the holy Bible, from Genesis to Revelation, readers are provided basic information about God and the Word (Jesus Christ). LOGOS is given to everybody, to anyone who will read or listen to the preached LOGOS. Simply said, LOGOS is what and how God thinks about many things. It's His person, His mind, His will, His nature, His laws, and His ways that apply to everyone.

Rhema

While LOGOS is what God "*has said*" or "*has spoken*," RHEMA is what God "*is speaking*" or "*is saying*" right now. When God is speaking to an individual's present situation, the God-spoken Word—LOGOS—becomes RHEMA. RHEMA *is a faith-infused utterance from God that is a specific, relevant revelation delivered via the Holy Spirit to a person for salvation, direction, illumination, clarity, insight, or guidance. LOGOS is about the implications of the written Word, while RHEMA is about the application of the written Word.*

LOGOS, having been broadcast to the nation of Israel and through Israel to the world, does not have faith attached to it. RHEMA does. RHEMA comes with faith attached to it for fulfillment. According to Romans 10:17, faith comes by hearing an utterance from God concerning something. It should be clear to the person receiving it that God-given faith comes from hearing RHEMA.

RHEMA is taken from the totality of LOGOS, but not given equal status with LOGOS. LOGOS has a higher status and standing than RHEMA. RHEMA is personal but not general. It's the spoken, present word of God for such a time as this; it is personal and may or may not be shared with others. RHEMA will never contradict LOGOS and works within the boundaries of LOGOS. It is what causes a verse or a portion of LOGOS to become an aha. The Holy Spirit quickens or illuminates LOGOS and it becomes RHEMA. Next, the Holy Spirit applies that verse or larger portion of LOGOS to that believer's current circumstances or to his or her need for direction or clarity.

Jesus Christ's incarnated life supports the definition of RHEMA when He says, "It is written, Man shall not live on bread alone, but on every word [RHEMA] that proceeds out of the mouth of God" (Matthew 4:4). The Lord is saying that RHEMA is every word that God is presently speaking, either directly or indirectly, to someone. RHEMA is spiritual food, a specific word spoken to a specific person who is in a specific situation, much like Jesus was when He was in the wilderness and the devil was tempting Him.

The Holy Spirit, then, can not only burn that RHEMA into that believer's soul (make that RHEMA indelible, impossible to remove, unforgettable), but He is also able to help that believer know that this RHEMA unequivocally applies to his or her specific situation. When God gives RHEMA for His body to act upon, He often confirms that RHEMA by providing a second RHEMA. The apostle Paul supports this last statement when he writes that "by the mouth of two or three witnesses every word [RHEMA] shall be established" (2 Corinthians 13:1 NKJV; see also Deuteronomy 17:6; 19:15; Matthew 18:16).

Comparing LOGOS and RHEMA

LOGOS	RHEMA
Written Word of God: God has spoken	An utterance from God: God is speaking
General: written for everyone	Personal: spoken to you or someone you are speaking to
Is written and never passes away	Is spoken in every generation for the time and occasion
Is the general Word of God for everyone	An utterance from God that may not be for everyone
The whole truth	Illumination of a specific truth for clarity and direction
The whole	The part

Comparing LOGOS and RHEMA	
LOGOS	RHEMA
Truth	Truth with light
Unchangeable, immortal, eternal status	Temporal: for such a time as this
The Master	The servant the Master sends for clarity and guidance
Transcendent: high and lifted up	Imminent: Abba Father, our Daddy
Mental assent	Faith
Does not come with faith attached to it	Comes with faith attached to it
You find faith	Faith finds you
Knowledge	Understanding
Information	Revelation that creates transformation
Impression	Expression
What	Why the what
Communication	Illumination
First touch: possible to see like a "tree"	Second touch: seeing clearly
Touch	Change
Oversight	Insight
RHEMA comes from LOGOS	LOGOS does not come from RHEMA
Implications of the written Word	Application of the written Word
General guidance	Specific guidance
General timing	Specific timing
General truth about marriage	"Whom should I marry?"
General truth about business	"Should I start a business? If so, what, when, and how?"
Knowing the Word of God	Hearing the word of God
The Word uses the sword of the Spirit	The Spirit uses the sword of the Word
Is not subject to others' opinions	Can be validated and substantiated by others
Tells facts about past, present, and future	Gives understanding of the past, present, and future

Let me simplify Logos and [RHEMA] in a way that makes these two words clear and simple.

LOGOS is the entire Mind and Word of God, as revealed in the God-breathed, God-inspired Holy Bible. LOGOS is truth. While LOGOS is what God has "said" or has "spoken," [RHEMA] is what God is speaking or saying to us and to others presently, illuminating and applying LOGOS in our daily lives. [RHEMA] is truth illuminated by God's Spirit in a way that is Biblically correct and spiritually accurate.

For example, LOGOS is God's general wisdom concerning marriage. RHEMA is God saying, "Marry this person." LOGOS is God's general wisdom and knowledge on business. RHEMA is God saying, "Buy this business, start this business, make this decision."

Learning to Grasp a Second Sword

Most of the Bible's seventy references to RHEMA are listed below. Note the impact of the concepts when you substitute RHEMA for the "word" in the verses. We are defining RHEMA here as an "utterance from God." For example, consider John 15:7, which is a familiar Bible verse to many people, with RHEMA inserted into the verse, and keeping in mind our definition "utterances from God."

> *If you abide in Me, and My* [RHEMA] *abides in you, ask whatever you wish, and it will be done for you* (John 15:7).

Why will it be done for you? It is because you heard from God and asked for what God said to ask for. Many have tried to use this verse for their own desires but it hasn't worked. Why? Because it was not RHEMA. Let's look at the verses:

> *But He answered and said, "It is written, 'Man shall not live on bread alone, but on every* [RHEMA] *that proceeds out of the mouth of God'"* (Matthew 4:4).

But I tell you that every careless [RHEMA] *that people speak, they shall give an accounting for it in the day of judgment* (Matthew 12:36).

But if he does not listen to you, take one or two more with you, so that by the [RHEMA] *of two or three witnesses every fact may be confirmed* (Matthew 18:16).

And Peter remembered the [RHEMA] *Jesus had said, "Before a rooster crows, you will deny Me three times." And he went out and wept bitterly* (Matthew 26:75).

And He did not answer him with regard to even a single [RHEMA], *so the governor was quite amazed* (Matthew 27:14).

But [the disciples] did not understand this [RHEMA], *and they were afraid to ask Him* (Mark 9:32).

Immediately a rooster crowed a second time. And Peter remembered how Jesus had made the [RHEMA] *to him, "Before a rooster crows twice, you will deny Me three times." And he began to weep* (Mark 14:72).

For [no RHEMA] *will be impossible with God. And Mary said, "Behold, the bondslave of the Lord, may it be done according to your* [RHEMA]*." And the angel departed from her* (Luke 1:37-38).

When the angels had gone away from them into heaven, the shepherds began saying to one another, "Let us go straight to Bethlehem then, and see this [RHEMA] *that has happened which the Lord has made known to us"* (Luke 2:15).

But Mary treasured all these [RHEMAS], *pondering them in her heart* (Luke 2:19).

Now Lord, You are releasing Your bond-servant to depart in peace, according to Your [RHEMA] (Luke 2:29).

But [the disciples] *did not understand the* [RHEMA] *which He had made to them. And He went down with them and came to Nazareth, and He continued in subjection to them; and His mother treasured all these [RHEMAS] in her heart* (Luke 2:50-51).

In the high priesthood of Annas and Caiaphas, the [RHEMA] *of God came to John, the son of Zacharias, in the wilderness* (Luke 3:2).

Simon answered and said, "Master, we worked hard all night and caught nothing, but will do as You [RHEMA] *and let down the nets"* (Luke 5:5).

When He had completed all His [RHEMAS] *in the hearing of the people, He went to Capernaum* (Luke 7:1).

But they did not understand the [RHEMA], *and it was concealed from them so that they would not perceive it, and they were afraid to ask Him about this statement* (Luke 9:45).

But the disciples understood none of these things, and the [RHEMA] *of this statement was hidden from them, and they did not comprehend the things that were said* (Luke 18:34).

And they were unable to catch Him in a [RHEMA] *in the presence of the people; and being amazed at His answer, they became silent* (Luke 20:26).

And they remembered His [RHEMA] (Luke 24:8).

But these [RHEMAS] *appeared to them as nonsense, and they would not believe them* (Luke 24:11).

For He whom God has sent speaks the [RHEMA] *of God; for He gives the Spirit without measure* (John 3:34).

But if you do not believe his writings, how will you believe My [RHEMA]*?* (John 5:47)

It is the Spirit who gives life; the flesh profits nothing; the [RHEMA] *that I have spoken to you are spirit and are life* (John 6:63).

Simon Peter answered Him, "Lord, to whom shall we go? You have [RHEMA] *of eternal life"* (John 6:68).

These [RHEMAS] *He spoke in the treasury, as He taught in the temple; and no one seized Him, because His hour had not yet come* (John 8:20).

He who is of God hears the [RHEMAS] *from God; for this reason you do not hear them, because you are not of God* (John 8:47).

Others were saying, "These are not the [RHEMAS] *of one demon-possessed. A demon cannot open the eyes of the blind, can he?"* (John 10:21)

If anyone hears My [RHEMAS] *and does not keep them, I do not judge him; for I did not come to judge the world, but to save the world. He who rejects Me and does not receive My* [RHEMAS] *has one who judges him; the* [LOGOS] *I spoke is what will judge him at the last day* (John 12:47-48).

Do you not believe that I am in the Father, and the Father is in Me? The [RHEMAS] *that I say to you I do not speak on My own initiative, but the Father abiding in Me does His works* (John 14:10).

If you abide in Me, and My [RHEMAS] *abide in you, ask whatever you wish, and it will be done for you* (John 15:7).

For the [RHEMAS] *which You gave Me I have given to them; and they received them and truly understood that I came forth from You, and they believed that You sent Me* (John 17:8).

But Peter, taking his stand with the eleven, raised his voice and declared to them: "Men of Judea and all you who live in Jerusalem, let this be known to you and give heed to my [RHEMA] *for you"* (Acts 2:14).

Go, stand and speak to the people in the temple the [RHEMA] *for the recipients of this Life* (Acts 5:20).

And we are witnesses of these [RHEMAS]; *and so is the Holy Spirit, whom God has given to those who obey Him* (Acts 5:32).

Then they secretly induced men to say, "We have heard him speak blasphemous [RHEMA] *against Moses and against God"* (Acts 6:11).

They said, "Cornelius, a centurion, a righteous and God-fearing man well spoken of by the entire nation of the Jews, was divinely directed by a holy angel to send for you to come to his house and hear [RHEMA] *from you"* (Acts 10:22).

You yourselves know the [RHEMA] *which took place throughout all Judea, starting from Galilee, after the baptism which John proclaimed* (Acts 10:37).

While Peter was still speaking these [RHEMAS], *the Holy Spirit fell upon all those who were listening to the* [LOGOS] (Acts 10:44).

And he will speak [RHEMA] *to you by which you will be saved, you and all your household* (Acts 11:14).

And I remembered the [RHEMA] *of the Lord, how He used to say, "John baptized with water, but you will be baptized with the Holy Spirit"* (Acts 11:16).

As Paul and Barnabas were going out, the people kept begging that [RHEMA] *might be spoken to them the next Sabbath* (Acts 13:42).

The policemen reported these [RHEMAS] *to the chief magistrates. They were afraid when they heard that they were Roman* (Acts 16:38).

But Paul said, "I am not out of my mind, most excellent Festus, but I utter [RHEMAS] *of sober truth"* (Acts 26:25).

And when they did not agree with one another, they began leaving after Paul had spoken one parting [RHEMA], *"The Holy Spirit rightly spoke through Isaiah the prophet to your fathers"* (Acts 28:25).

But what does it say? "The [RHEMA] *is near you, in your mouth and in your heart"—that is, the* [RHEMA] *which we are preaching* (Romans 10:8).

So faith comes from hearing, and hearing by the [RHEMA] *of Christ. But I say, surely they have never heard, have they? Indeed they have; "Their voice has gone out into all the earth, and their* [RHEMA] *to the ends of the world"* (Romans 10:17-18).

[I] *was caught up into Paradise and heard inexpressible* [RHEMA], *which a man is not permitted to speak* (2 Corinthians 12:4).

This is the third time I am coming to you. Every [RHEMA] *is to be confirmed by the testimony of two or three witnesses* (2 Corinthians 13:1).

So that He might sanctify her, having cleansed her by the washing of water with the [RHEMA] (Ephesians 5:26).

And take the helmet of salvation, and the sword of the Spirit, which is the [RHEMA] *of God* (Ephesians 6:17).

And He is the radiance of His glory and the exact representation of His nature, and upholds all things by the [RHEMA] *of His power. When He had made purification of sins, He sat down at the right hand of the Majesty on high* (Hebrews 1:3).

By faith we understand that the worlds were prepared by the [RHEMA] *of God, so that what is seen was not made out of things which are visible* (Hebrews 11:3).

And to the blast of a trumpet and the sound of [RHEMA] *which sound was such that those who heard begged that no further* [LOGOS] *be spoken to them* (Hebrews 12:19).

"But the [RHEMA] *of the Lord endures forever." And this is the* [RHEMA] *which was preached to you* (1 Peter 1:25).

That you should remember the [RHEMA] *spoken beforehand by the holy prophets and the commandment of the Lord and Savior spoken by your apostles* (2 Peter 3:2).

But you, beloved, ought to remember the [RHEMAS] *that were spoken beforehand by the apostles of our Lord Jesus Christ* (Jude 17).

For God has put it in their hearts to execute His purpose by having a common purpose, and by giving their kingdom to the beast, until [RHEMA] *of God should be fulfilled* (Revelation 17:17).

Rhema and the Faith Hall of Fame: Embracing and Using the Sword of Rhema

Do you remember the faith hall of fame in Hebrews 11? Where did these Old Testament saints get the faith to do what they did? Hebrews 11:3 has the answer: "By faith we understand that the worlds were prepared by the [RHEMA] of God, so that what is seen was not made out of things which are visible."

How does faith come to a person? It comes from hearing a RHEMA or utterance from God concerning something. When these hall of famers heard an utterance from God, faith came attached to it. This means they did what they had heard. It was finished the moment they started. God supplied more than enough faith to them for what He wanted them to do. No RHEMA spoken by God will not happen. With RHEMA, faith finds you—you don't have to find faith.

Remember our definition of RHEMA? It is a *faith-infused utterance from God providing illumination, clarity, wisdom, or direction to the recipient.* Since faith for the Hebrews 11 saints involved hearing an utterance from God concerning something that God wanted done, we have replaced the word "faith" with our definition of RHEMA to enhance the verses below. Notice that the recipients of God's RHEMA heard before they spoke or acted. Faith comes by hearing an utterance of God.

> *By* ***hearing a faith-infused utterance from God providing illumination [regarding Genesis],*** *we understand that the worlds were prepared by God's faith-infused utterances so that what is seen was not made out of things which are visible* (see Hebrews 11:3).
>
> *By* ***hearing a faith-infused utterance from God providing illumination and direction [what to sacrifice],*** *Abel offered to God a better sacrifice than Cain, through which he obtained the testimony that he was righteous,*

God testifying about his gifts, and through faith, though he is dead, he still speaks (see Hebrews 11:4).

By ***hearing a faith-infused utterance from God providing illumination and wisdom [how to please God],*** *Enoch was taken up so that he would not see death; and he was not found because God took him up; for he obtained the witness that before his being taken up he was pleasing to God* (see Hebrews 11:5).

And without ***hearing a faith-infused utterance from God providing illumination, clarity, or direction [to believe in God]*** *it is impossible to please Him, for he who comes to God must believe that He is and that He is a rewarder of those who seek Him* (see Hebrews 11:6).

By ***hearing a faith-infused utterance from God providing direction [to build an ark],*** *Noah, being warned by God about things not yet seen, in reverence prepared an ark for the salvation of his household, by which he condemned the world, and became an heir of the righteousness which is according to* ***acting on hearing a faith-infused utterance from God providing illumination, clarity, or direction*** (see Hebrews 11:7).

By ***hearing a faith-infused utterance from God providing direction [to leave Ur and go to the Promised Land],*** *Abraham, when he was called, obeyed by going out to a place which he was to receive for an inheritance; and he went out, not knowing where he was going* (see Hebrews 11:8).

By ***hearing and acting on a faith-infused utterance from God providing direction [to wait for God to give him the Promised Land],*** *he lived as an alien in the land of promise, as in a foreign land, dwelling in tents* *with Isaac and Jacob, fellow heirs of the same promise; for he was looking for the city which has foundations, whose architect and builder is God* (see Hebrews 11:9-10).

*By **hearing a faith-infused utterance from God providing illumination [for an eighty-year-old woman to become pregnant]**, even Sarah herself received ability to conceive, even beyond the proper time of life, since she considered Him faithful who had promised* (see Hebrews 11:11).

*By **hearing and acting on a faith-infused utterance from God providing direction [to sacrifice his son and heir]**, Abraham, when he was tested, offered up Isaac, and he who had received the promises was offering up his only begotten son* (see Hebrews 11:17).

By hearing a faith-infused utterance from God providing illumination [in prophetic blessing], Isaac blessed Jacob and Esau, even regarding things to come (see Hebrews 11:20).

*By **hearing a faith-infused utterance from God providing illumination [in prophetic blessing]**, Jacob, as he was dying, blessed each of the sons of Joseph, and worshiped, leaning on the top of his staff* (see Hebrews 11:21).

*By **hearing a faith-infused utterance from God providing direction [for a future return to the Promised Land]**, Joseph, when he was dying, made mention of the exodus of the sons of Israel, and gave orders concerning his bones* (see Hebrews 11:22).

*By **hearing a faith-infused utterance from God providing direction [to hide Moses in a basket in the bulrushes]**, Moses, when he was born, was hidden for three months by his parents, because they saw he was a beautiful child; and they were not afraid of the king's edict* (see Hebrews 11:23).

By ***hearing a faith-infused utterance from God providing direction [to identify with Israel],*** *Moses, when he had grown up, refused to be called the son of Pharaoh's daughter, choosing rather to endure ill-treatment with the people of God than to enjoy the passing pleasures of sin* (see Hebrews 11:24-25).

By ***hearing a faith-infused utterance from God providing direction [to flee Egypt],*** *he left Egypt, not fearing the wrath of the king; for he endured, as seeing Him who is unseen* (see Hebrews 11:27).

By hearing a faith-infused utterance from God providing direction [to have Israelites sprinkle the blood of lamb on their doorposts], he kept the Passover and the sprinkling of the blood, so that he who destroyed the firstborn would not touch them (see Hebrews 11:28).

By ***hearing a faith-infused utterance from God providing direction [guidance to cross Red Sea],*** *they passed through the Red Sea as though they were passing through dry land; and the Egyptians, when they attempted it, were drowned* (see Hebrews 11:29).

By ***hearing a faith-infused utterance from God providing illumination, with clear direction [to march around the city, priests blow trumpets, etc.],*** *the walls of Jericho fell down after they had been encircled for seven days* (see Hebrews 11:30).

By ***hearing a faith-infused utterance from God providing direction [to hide the Israelite spies and misdirect their enemies],*** *Rahab the harlot did not perish along with those who were disobedient, after she had welcomed the spies in peace* (see Hebrews 11:31).

And what more shall I say? For time will fail me if I tell of Gideon, Barak, Samson, Jephthah, of David and Samuel and the prophets, who by ***hearing a faith-infused utterance from God providing illumination, clarity, and direction [to perform the following feats]*** *conquered kingdoms, performed acts of righteousness, obtained promises, shut the mouths of lions, quenched the power of fire, escaped the edge of the sword, from weakness were made strong, became mighty in war, put foreign armies to flight. Women received back their dead by resurrection; and others were tortured, not accepting their release, so that they might obtain a better resurrection; and others experienced mockings and scourgings, yes, also chains and imprisonment. They were stoned, they were sawn in two, they were tempted, they were put to death with the sword; they went about in sheepskins, in goatskins, being destitute, afflicted, ill-treated (men of whom the world was not worthy), wandering in deserts and mountains and caves and holes in the ground. And all these, having gained approval through their* ***hearing a faith-infused utterance from God providing illumination, clarity, and direction,*** *did not receive what was promised, because God had provided something better for us, so that apart from us they would not be made perfect* (see Hebrews 11:32-40).

Creation Started with Logos but Ends with Logos Speaking Rhema

Here is another amazing truth concerning LOGOS and RHEMA and how the two work together. As you know, John 1:1-3 is a restatement of Genesis 1:1-2. Our world and all creation starts with LOGOS:

In the beginning was the Word [LOGOS], *and the Word* [LOGOS] *was with God, and the Word* [LOGOS] *was God. He was in the beginning with God. All things came into*

> *being through Him, and apart from Him nothing came into being that has come into being. In Him was life, and the life was the Light of men* (John 1:1-4).

But notice how the world ends in Revelation 19:13-16:

> [Jesus] *is clothed with a robe dipped in blood, and His name is called The Word* [LOGOS] *of God. And the armies which are in heaven, clothed in fine linen, white and clean, were following Him on white horses. From His mouth comes a sharp sword, so that with it He may strike down the nations, and He will rule them with a rod of iron; and He treads the wine press of the fierce wrath of God, the Almighty. And on His robe and on His thigh He has a name written, "KING OF KINGS, AND LORD OF LORDS."*

Here we have the LOGOS riding on a horse and He speaks. The scripture says, "From His mouth comes a sharp sword." It is a specific spoken word from the LOGOS to a specific people at a specific time for a specific reason. It is like a sword giving truth and light. If we compare this with Ephesians 6:17, we see exactly how the process of RHEMA works: "... and take up the sword of the Spirit, which is the word [RHEMA] of God." Notice that RHEMA comes right out of the mouth of LOGOS and is like a sharp sword. This is not a coincidence. This also correlates with Jesus's admonition to satan in Matthew 4:4: "Man shall not live by bread alone, but by every word [RHEMA] that proceeds out of the mouth of God." This is also a picture of Jesus showing us how He "upholds all things by the word [RHEMA] of His power" (Hebrews 1:3).

You see, RHEMA comes from LOGOS, so it never contradicts it. God speaks RHEMA from LOGOS, not the other way around. In the realm of God's kingdom, light comes from truth, not truth from light. Illumination needs an object for it to reveal. Understanding how the two swords work together peels back layer upon layer of spiritual revelation. This process started the world and it will finish the world. And we get to be among those to whom and then through whom the LOGOS speaks RHEMA!

In fact, Joshua Churchyard notes that the type of sword used in Hebrews 4:12 and the reference to "two-edged" in the Hebrew means "the mouth of God and the mouth of man." Just think of the power of this concept—Jesus's mind and then His mouth speaking through man's mind and then mouth when LOGOS is used truthfully, accurately, and correctly.

Redefining Rhema: Turning the Telescope Around

I will conclude this chapter with a bit of a midcourse correction regarding the misuse of RHEMA, which has hurt the church and many people in it. In fact, much teaching on this subject has caused a lot of confusion. As a result, the church is weaker, resulting in weakened communities and culture. Here's a word of wisdom on using the sword of RHEMA correctly from an apostolic perspective.

In the past, many have used RHEMA to their own end. Most books and messages on the subject of RHEMA were written from the perspective of what RHEMA personally does for a believer. It can make one rich; it can give one faith to get stuff. It can give one status as a Holy Spirit person in the church. One can be perceived by others as "spiritual" or even "mystical." It produces a newfound identity or becomes a source of significance and security. One may be respected or even feared. In other words, *it's all about me.*

But what is the real reason God gives us RHEMA? RHEMA is given for God's purposes, not our purposes. RHEMA is God giving us the privilege as well as the responsibility to "bind" on earth what has already been bound in Heaven. God gives us the privilege as well as the responsibility of "loosing" on earth what God has already been loosed in Heaven. RHEMA is God presently speaking, giving us clarity, illumination, guidance, and direction for His purposes, not ours. God speaks to us and even through us, positioning us for His utmost and our highest. RHEMA is God saying again, "Let there be light!"

Picture yourself looking though a telescope at a full moon. When you look in the small end and out through the large magnifying end, the moon looks big, as indeed it truly is. But if you look at the moon through the big end, then the moon looks small. Many have had this mistaken perspective of RHEMA. When they look in the wrong end, they may see RHEMA mightily at work—but, like that diminished view of a full moon, God's purposes at the other end appear small.

In writing this book, David and I have turned the telescope around. We want you to see God's purposes at the big end, magnified, like observing the full moon through the proper end of a telescope. One's need for self-aggrandizement should be small. That is the only way to correctly use RHEMA. We don't seek first the kingdom of God for our sake; we don't seek God's kingdom to get rich, to be the center of attention, or to gain status. We seek the kingdom of God for God's sake alone. Then we receive those extra blessings as a reward. God is a rewarder when faith from RHEMA is used correctly and accurately (see Hebrews 11:6). It's time to turn the telescope around for God's sake, our sake, and the community's sake. Don't you agree?

Thank You, God, for entrusting us with Your two swords. Thank You for clarity in times of ambiguity. Thank You for caring enough to cause us to hear first and speak second. Thank You for allowing us to be part of Your kingdom come, Your will be done, on earth as it is in Heaven. Amen.

Section

IV

Implications and Applications of Rhema in Salvation, the Church, and the Kingdom

by Ed Delph

POWER THOUGHTS FOR *Chapter 10*

Whatever you don't recognize, you don't appreciate. Whatever you don't appreciate, you don't celebrate. Whatever you don't celebrate may eventually exit your life.

—Mike Murdock[1]

It's not what you look at that matters, it's what you see.

—Henry David Thoreau

The best way to make your dreams come true is to wake up.

—attributed to Paul Valery[2]

We rarely see what we are not looking for.

—Unknown

The opportunity of a lifetime must be seized within the lifetime of the opportunity.

—Leonard Ravenhill

Can an egg fly? Yes...after it's transformed.

—Unknown

Some see the light by revelation; others just see the light when they open the refrigerator door in the middle of the night.

—Unknown

Chapter 10

Three Revelations Every Christian Needs to Illuminate Nations

One of the most captivating chapters in the New Testament is Matthew 16. It starts off with Jesus asking His disciples who the pundits in the local Gentile community thought He, the Son of Man, was. None of them were getting it right. Then He asks His disciples, "But who do you think I am?" Peter blurted out something that probably surprised himself as well as Jesus. Peter declared, "Thou art the Christ [the Messiah], the Son of the living God" (Matthew 16:16 KJV). Jesus was looking for something big in this short exchange. There is a story here, but let's look at the story that is behind the story. What is God saying? What is really going on?

Flesh and Blood Can't Save You

Notice what Jesus said to Peter after Peter spoke what God illuminated to him: "Blessed are you, Simon Barjona, because flesh and blood did not reveal this to you, but My Father who is in heaven" (Matthew 16:17). Notice the words *blessed* and *reveal.*

I like the word *blessed* in this passage. In Hebrew, *blessed* means "to kneel down to and give or bestow a gift." Jesus recognized that God had knelt to Peter and given him a gift, the gift of salvation. Only God can do that. Flesh and blood can't do that. It takes an illumination from God for that to happen. Salvation is a free gift of God. Believe it or not, God knelt to you through Jesus and gave you this gift. This happened not because you were good, not because you were perfect, and not because you prayed enough. God gave you salvation just because. He chose you; you didn't choose Him.

Peter had a revelation of who Jesus really was. And God did everything to give him that revelation. God blessed Peter and He blessed you and me with salvation. How? He did this through speaking to us, shedding light on Jesus, and then we heard the truth, that Jesus is Lord.

Stage One: Rhema of Salvation

The first revelation that you and I have is the revelation that Jesus is Lord. He is the Son of God. Peter believed in his heart and confessed with his lips that this was true. He heard first and spoke second. The speaking was physical evidence of what took place in his heart. God open the eyes of his heart, and then Peter opened the lips of his mouth. It was on earth as it was in Heaven. Peter experienced the RHEMA of salvation.

The first place every Christian starts is with the RHEMA of salvation. Many people say they have never had a RHEMA from God. Yes, all Christians have had a RHEMA from God if they are indeed Christians. The first RHEMA that you will ever have is the one given to you at salvation. Notice that it was God who did everything. You can't work your way into Heaven; rather, you "hear and agree with God" your way into Heaven.

I like to compare Christian growth and maturity to a three-stage rocket. The first stage is the illumination and revelation of *salvation*. This stage gets you started on your journey. Stage one is big horsepower. Your salvation cost God a lot—the price of His beloved Son. Salvation boosts you from ground to liftoff and gets you started on your heavenly journey. But liftoff is not the mission. Liftoff gets you to Heaven but it doesn't get you to your assignment on earth.

After salvation, your destiny is to go to Heaven but your responsibility is to bring Heaven to earth. And notice that there are more stages to the rocket than just the first one. The reason for the launch is in the third stage of the rocket, for that is the purpose for which the rocket was launched. RHEMA of salvation is the alpha but not the omega—it is the beginning but it is not the end. Your salvation is secure, but your purpose or assignment is still waiting to be fulfilled.

Stage Two: The Rhema of Church

After the first stage gets you up and going (it took heaps of horsepower to get me going; I had a slow start with lots of corrections and adjustments), then the second stage kicks in. Let's read the second revelation we will all need to fulfill our purposes on earth. It is called the RHEMA of *church*, which is found in Matthew 16:18. Right after the RHEMA of salvation in Matthew 16:17, Jesus went on to tell Peter, "I also say to you that you are Peter, and upon this rock I will build My church; and the gates of Hades will not overpower it" (Matthew 16:18).

There are many interpretations of what *rock* means in this passage. But one thing is for sure: Jesus was impressed with the fact that Peter heard from God first before he ever spoke. Jesus wasn't used to that from Peter; usually, it was the other way around. My personal conviction is that Jesus meant more than just physical rocks or that Peter would be a rock in the church. Both interpretations have valid arguments, but I'm convinced that Peter heard from God that the rock of revelation that He would use to build His church is "Jesus is the Christ, the Messiah," and "Jesus is Lord." Jesus was going to build His church through the knowledge of LOGOS and the revelation of RHEMA. He was going to build His church through knowledge (LOGOS) and, from time to time, give us revelation (RHEMA) and faith when and where we needed.

Before He even considered the church, Jesus talked to Peter. "Listen, Peter, you are going to be speaking RHEMA soon, and you just took your first step into the process of building My church. You just experienced a RHEMA on RHEMA." Jesus said, "I will build My church" through people who know how to hear first and speak and do second, especially through leaders in the church as well as in neighborhoods and communities.

Notice that Jesus said that there are gates in Hades. Hearing first and speaking second is a potentially stronger weapon than an onslaught from the gates of Hades. But what does a gate require? To open a gate, a person must use a key. And not just a key, but a key turned the right way. What good is a key if we don't know how to use it or turn it the correct way? We need to remember the keys.

After you have the revelation of salvation, God wants you to get involved in His body called "church." The church is designed to equip you to do the work of your ministry for which you were prepared from before the foundations of the earth. Church equips you for life, not just "church life." In the second stage, you get going much faster than you did in the initial launch. Church is a means to an end, not the end itself. The mission is in the third stage.

In the first stage of salvation, God does everything; all you do is believe and confess what you heard God say: "Jesus is Lord." God puts the faith in you to agree that yes, Jesus was raised from the dead. Now, in the second stage of church, Jesus does everything. He, not you, will build His church—not your pastor, not the elders, not the board of directors, not the seminaries, not the prophets and apostles with more degrees than a thermometer, and certainly not the government. *Jesus does everything by us hearing first and speaking second.*

Stage Three: Use the Keys of the Kingdom

The second stage prepares us for our mission here on earth as it is in Heaven. Without a doubt, whatever your mission is here on the earth, it will involve a component of making things on earth the way they are in Heaven. Where do we get the keys to do that? Jesus said that we get those keys in the kingdom of God. Let's consider Matthew

16:19: "I will give you the keys of the kingdom of heaven; and whatever you shall bind on earth shall have been bound in heaven, and whatever you shall loose on earth shall have been loosed in heaven."

In salvation, *God* does everything; in the church, *Jesus* does everything; and in the kingdom, *you (and the Holy Spirit)* do everything. You have the keys. What are the keys for? The keys are to open the gates of Hades. That is the modus operandi of how what we pray in the Lord's Prayer: "Thy kingdom come, Thy will be done, on earth as it is in heaven."

Jesus gives us the keys to the kingdom as we are born again and become a citizen of His kingdom. The keys of God's kingdom are simply the process of doing what God tells us to do: "Whatever you bind on earth shall have been bound in heaven." The language is crucial here. God will tell us to bind something on earth only when it has already been bound in Heaven. If God tells us to "loose" something on earth, it is only because it has already been loosed in Heaven. When you are in the kingdom, you had better hear first and speak second, for only then are you "loosing" God's kingdom to come and His will (not our wills) to be done on earth as it is in Heaven. Everything starts in Heaven and manifests itself on earth.

Many Christians have tried to bind whatever they don't like or whatever they want to do, but it is not in Jesus's name. Rather, it is done in their name. It's not a RHEMA; it's a wish-dream. It's not maturity. The church should have prepared them better. Because their second stage was not competent, it affected their third stage of growth. *If it's flesh-based, it's erased because it's not graced.* As one worship song says, we touch Heaven by hearing from heaven and then changing earth. We seek first His kingdom.

Baby, You Can Drive My Car

When I turned sixteen, the first thing I wanted to do was drive a car. I asked my parents, "Can I have the keys, please?" I had gone through the birth stage; I had gone through the preparation stage and maturing stage; I even took classes on how to safely drive. I was ready to drive the car. I had spent sixteen years getting to the point of receiving the keys. And so I assumed I was mature enough to turn the keys the right way and drive the car. I had the education, but I just needed the experience.

If we want to live according to God's kingdom, then we had better live according to His revelation. Otherwise, we will be dangerous. Our misuses affect others. The keys are not for us; the keys are for the gates. God will let us know how to close the gates of hell by His revelation, not by our information. Using the key correctly requires the maturity that salvation and the church should bring to us so that when we get to the purpose for which we were created, we have the maturity to handle it. In other words, if you want to drive God's car, you had better be going where He is going.

Purpose and Destiny "Still Births"

As a pastor since 1980, I have noticed a phenomenon which often occurs among Christians. Returning to our three-stage rocket idea, one phenomenon is that the first stage of the rocket works but the second stage is never activated. Many people watch television evangelists, go to crusades, and get saved—they confess that Jesus is Lord, they prayed the prayer and they meant it—but they never got involved in a church, the body of Christ. They were never healed from the effects of sin. They never learned how to understand the LOGOS and RHEMA of God. They were never equipped for the work of their ministry. They never bound or loosed. They never got to drive the car—they never got the keys. They had the potential, but they just never realized their potential.

If the first stage of the rocket works and the person is launched, but they never enter the second stage, then the whole rocket (and its mission) falls back to Earth. First-stage-only people are going to Heaven, but the purpose for which they were created is never realized. The same holds true when Christians have a salvation experience then go to church but never get involved in the kingdom of God. They are like a three-stage rocket getting through the first and second stages but never activating the third stage. Like the first-stage-only rocket, it falls back to the earth and makes an even bigger splash, with wreckage spread across a larger area. God invests all that preparation in them, but they can't escape the strong inward gravitational pull of the church.

Many churched people don't understand that they were created for such a time as this—for their community, for their mountain, and for God's purposes. Sitting in a chair and singing songs never changed a culture. *Two thirds of G-o-d is G-o!* When Christians abandon the culture, they allow the world to determine the culture.

It's time to stop this roll-over-and-play-dead pattern. The Bible says in Revelation 1:6 that Christians are a nation of kings and priests. Israel was also called the church (*ekklesia*) in the wilderness (see Acts 7:38). Applying this principle in terms of church structure, we see that one tribe or one-twelfth of the nation of Israel was called to ministry inside the temple and synagogue walls—they were called priests or Levites—while the other eleven tribes made their living outside the synagogue walls. These are whom Revelation 1:6 calls kings.

The kings were eleven tribes of the nation, while the priests were only one tribe out of the nation. However, it was the whole nation, both kings and priests, who were appointed by God to be a blessing to all the nations in the world. The kings and priests were all in full-time ministry to the nations—the whole nation was blessed to be a blessing. In fact, the priests anointed the kings for their role in the nation.

In the church today, every Christian is in full-time ministry in some capacity in various places. The priests' role (one-twelfth of the church body) is to minister within the church walls, whereas the kings' role (eleven-twelfths of the church body) is to minister outside the church walls. They both have equal status but different roles.

Pastors and church leaders take note: equipping the saints to do the work of the ministry is seen in how Old Testament prophets and priests anointed kings to do the work of their kingly ministry outside the temple. Pastors, let's equip the saints to do the work of *their* ministry, not your ministry. Eleven-twelfths of the church is destined for the throne, outside the church walls. Marketplace ministers serve at church, but their ministry is outside church walls. That is a key. Now drive the car.

An Argentine Illumination

A few years ago, Pastor Hugo Weiss of San Nicolas, Argentina, invited me to be the main speaker at a conference his church, El Rey Jesus, hosts each year. The theme of the conference is called *Extiende*, or Reach Out. I was sitting in a hotel having breakfast before the conference when I heard first and wrote second. It was like a download straight from Heaven. I was thinking of the three successive revelations when I started writing what clarifies the stages. Here is what God gave me.

Three Successive Levels of Revelation that Every Christian Needs to Illuminate Nations		
SALVATION (MATTHEW 16:16-17)	CHURCH (MATTHEW 16:18)	KINGDOM (MATTHEW 16:19)
God—Stage 1	Jesus—Stage 2	You and the Holy Spirit—Stage 3
Surrender	Serve	Subdue
Identity	Integrity	Influence
Sit (see Ephesians 2:6)	Walk (see Ephesians 4:1)	Stand (see Ephesians 6:14)
Christ in you	Christ in the church	Christ in the community
Personal blessing (Genesis 12:2b)	National blessing (Genesis 12:2a)	International blessing (Genesis 12:3c)

Three Successive Levels of Revelation that Every Christian Needs to Illuminate Nations		
SALVATION (MATTHEW 16:16-17)	**CHURCH (MATTHEW 16:18)**	**KINGDOM (MATTHEW 16:19)**
Reach the lost	Disciple the found	Release the ready
"Try-outs"	Regular season	Playoffs
Deny yourself (see Matthew 16:24)	Take up the cross	Follow me
Passion for God	Passion for people and service	Passion for cities and nations
King	King's palace	King's kingdom
Out of Egypt	Wilderness	Canaan

Most of this chart will instantly make sense to you based on what I have written above. You recognize the three stages of the rocket. In fact, you should recognize the *salvation*, *church*, and *kingdom* revelations. Salvation is where we learn to surrender, the church is where we learn to serve, and the kingdom is where we subdue the garden and bring it into alignment with God, like Adam and Eve were supposed to do in the garden of Eden.

Salvation is where we learn our identity in Christ, church is where we learn integrity, and the kingdom is where we are secure in our identity and integrity so we can influence a runaway culture back to God. The Ephesians model of sit, walk, and stand works perfectly here. Salvation is where we learn that we are seated with Christ in heavenly places, the church is where we learn to walk in a manner worthy of our calling, and the kingdom is where we, having done all, stand. Salvation is Christ in us, the church is Christ in the church, and the kingdom is Christ in the community and the seven mountains of culture. If we use the Abrahamic covenant as a model, salvation is where we are personally blessed, the church is where Israel (or the church, spiritual Israel) is blessed, and the kingdom is where there is an international blessing. We were blessed and the church or Israel was blessed in order to be a blessing to all the nations.

Salvation is where we reach the lost. Church is where we disciple the found. The Kingdom is where we release the ready to go out to minister in the marketplace or wherever they are called by God.

I like the sports-team analogy. Salvation is where you make the team. You have to make the team in order to play. Church is the regular season where everyone learns to play together and as a team. The kingdom is like the playoffs. The kingdom is what you spent the whole season trying to get to. It's where you win the Super Bowl of the culture. But it is the regular season that prepares you for the mission.

Salvation is where you deny yourself, the church is where you take up Jesus's cross and die to yourself, and the kingdom is where you follow Jesus into the community. Earth wasn't going to Heaven, so Heaven had to come to earth to show the way. Now His ways have become your ways.

Salvation is where you get a passion for God. Have you ever seen someone who has just accepted Christ? Their newfound life is usually all they can talk about. Church is where you get a passion for service and people, while the kingdom is where you get a passion for cities and nations. If we use the feudal idea of kingdom, it works this way: Salvation is where you meet the King, the church is the King's palace, and the King is in residence there. The King's kingdom is outside the city or palace. Every king wants to expand his influence and jurisdiction. The kingdom is what is outside the church walls. It is the King's: "The earth is the Lord's and the fulness thereof" (Psalm 24:1 KJV). God wants us to fill it and subdue the whole world for His glory. He wants us to cry out for His will to be on Earth as it is in Heaven.

The final metaphor is this: in salvation, the Israelites escaped from Egypt, but the church is the wilderness time where the people of Israel learned to trust God daily. Remember, when the Israelites left Egypt, they were the lowest-tech people in the world. They were called children. They needed a place to grow up. They needed food. They needed care and inspiration. But most of all, they needed God's Word. By the time they were ready to go into Canaan (the Promised Land), they were the highest-tech people in the world. The young people who survived the old ones knew God's Word. They knew God's ways. They were ready to go in and fulfill their destiny. They were ready to take the mountains. Each person was ready to not only take his or her land, but also to occupy it.

Which of These Three Columns or "Mindskins" Can Illuminate a Nation?

Look at the salvation column on the chart. Could a Christian or a church illumine a nation with these attributes? They know God only, which is the first stage of the rocket—they are saved, they have surrendered, they know their identity, Christ is in them, they are personally blessed, they reach the lost, they've made the team but haven't played in a game, they have denied themselves, they have a passion for God, they know the King, and they have just come out of Egypt. Could this person transform a nation or change the culture? No, probably not. They have started but are nowhere near finishing. They are only partially ready.

Let's look at the characteristics of the next column, the church. These characteristics reflect where most churches are today. They know the Father and Jesus. They have mastered stage one and two of the rocket. They have a revelation of salvation and the church. They surrender and serve. They know their identity and integrity. The sit and walk. They know Christ in them and Christ in the church. They are personally blessed and their church is blessed. They reach the lost and disciple the found. They have made the team and are playing in the regular season. They have denied themselves and taken up the cross. They have a passion for God and people and service inside the church. They have met the King and regularly attend the inside of the palace. They've made it out of Egypt and are in the wilderness eating quail, milk, and honey. But they are still not ready to change a culture.

The first column is good; the second column is better. However, without the keys of the kingdom, they are not going to open many gates or influence the culture in which they live.

An Apostolic Paradigm: Embracing the Fullness of All in All

Let's look at all three of the columns combined. Can this "mind-skin," which creates a wineskin, illuminate a nation? Absolutely. This is the "fullness of all in all...growing up into all aspects" that Ephesians 4:13-15 talks about. This equipping is so that the "man of God may be adequate, equipped for every good work" (2 Timothy 3:17). This person knows God, Jesus, and Holy Spirit. He has all three stages launched, separated, and in orbit, doing what the satellite was created to do.

He is aware of the specialness of salvation, church, and kingdom. He has surrendered, is serving, and is subduing and filling his space with the presence of Jesus just by being there. He knows his identity, has integrity, and has influence because of his example. He has gone through the sit, walk, and stand revelations. Christ is in him, he is in church, and he is involved in the community and his mountain. He is personally blessed, his church is blessed, and he is a blessing outside the walls of the church. He understands the importance of salvation, he understands the necessity of discipleship, and he is ready to be released into the kingdom.

The man of God who has been adequately equipped has made it through the tryouts and the regular season and is now playing to win the culture back to Jesus. He knows to deny himself, has taken up Jesus's cross, and he is following Jesus into the community. He has a passion for God, a passion for people and service, and a passion for cities and nations. He knows the King, he knows the King's palace, and he is involved in expanding the King's kingdom. He has come out of Egypt, Egypt has come out of him during his time in the wilderness, and he is taking and holding ground in the land of milk and honey.

You may be saying, "Impossible! Only Jesus could do all this." No, these are progressive revelations that take us on to maturity. We never get rid of any of the attributes of salvation and church, as if we must discard what we have previously learned in order to progress into the next stage. Rather, we take them into the kingdom, which is where the culture is won. Priests change the church, kings change the world, but both working together change the culture.

Notes

1. Mike Murdock, *The Law of Recognition* (Ft. Worth, TX: Wisdom International, 1999).
2. Paul Valery, http://thinkexist.com/quotes/paul_valery/, accessed March 27, 2017.

POWER THOUGHTS ON *Chapter 11*

When we have an encounter with the Holy Spirit, it should make us more missional, not mystical.

—Steve Murrell[1]

The best tact for community transformation is contact.

—Unknown

We don't become culturally relevant when we become like the culture, but rather when we model what the culture hungers to become.

—Bill Johnson

Our destiny is to go to Heaven. Our responsibility is to bring Heaven.

—Bill Johnson

There will be no transformation without incarnation, without becoming present among people. That is the way of the gospel. That was the way of Jesus who entered our frail humanity to save us—not from a distance, but from the position of a participant, a fellow human being.

—Pastor Alan Platt[2]

Every saint has a past and every sinner has a future.

—Oscar Wilde

Chapter 11

Rhema in Salvation: Saving Peter, Paul and...Mr. Banks

We need to evangelize to civilize.
—Joseph Mattera[3]

You have probably heard of the movie *Saving Mr. Banks.* The movie was based on P. L. Travers' famous book, *Mary Poppins.* Mr. Banks was the rich banker and the father of two children who was driven by his work. He had no time for the children. He needed to be saved from his obsession. He could be your boss, your neighbor, your best friend's dad, or anyone else that has not been saved by accepting and receiving Jesus Christ. This chapter is about the Apostle Peter and Paul's salvation experience and process. Even though he had been with Jesus for a few years, he had not yet accepted Christ as the Messiah, the Christ. You will see why in a moment. But before we explore further, here are our guiding verses for this chapter:

> *He said to them, "But who do you say that I am?" Simon Peter answered, "You are the Christ, the Son of the living God." And Jesus said to him, "Blessed are you, Simon*

> *Barjona, because flesh and blood did not reveal this to you, but My Father who is in heaven"* (Matthew 16:15-17).

The historical account of Peter's salvation experience is significant. First, it was prophetic in that Peter would become the apostle to the Jews, and the Bible's kingdom order is that the gospel must go "first to the Jew, then to the Gentile" (Romans 1:16 NIV). Peter would experience the first real New Testament conversion. He would be the first Messianic Jewish believer who would go on to be their apostle and pastor.

Second, the place where Peter was to experience this first New Testament conversion (Caesarea Philippi) was in a Gentile area amid all kinds of people and all sorts of secular hedonism of which no proper Jew would approve. It was home to an altar to the god Pan, who was a demon god who gave the people power. In fact, proper Jews would walk completely around this Gentile area so they could avoid it. Of course, it was no accident that Jesus and His disciples were here. God was showing Peter that all people need to have the gospel preached to them. All people need to be given an opportunity to go to Heaven. God was revealing to Peter that a person's soul is more important than his or her behavior at a given moment. Peter needed an aha moment to show him that God could even be in places like Caesarea Philippi. He needed to understand there could even be a gate of Heaven, a place of revelation from Heaven, in Caesarea Philippi.

Third, Peter needed to *experience* the first New Testament salvation so he could *preach* New Testament salvation. What he was about to experience would be a key to the kingdom of God. In order to use the key, however, he would first need to be able to obtain the key. Peter needed to be unbound so that others could be unbound too. Peter, as a Jew, needed to be genuinely converted and saved so that other Jews could be genuinely converted and saved too. He needed to be introduced to kingdom revelation so that others could be introduced to kingdom revelation. *This was going to be a new deal, so Peter needed to speak from it, not just about it.*

Last, Peter would need to know the difference between Old Testament legislation and New Testament revelation. In the Old Testament, the synagogues gave knowledge; but in the New Testament, the church would give understanding. In the Old Testament, God spoke *at* people; but in the New Testament, God speaks *to* people. This event would change everything.

Let's look at this Holy Spirit appointment that would change the world as they knew it then. It's in Matthew 16:13-26. Get ready for an aha moment. We're going to do a bit of deep diving on the concept of hear first and speak second.

Who Do People Say the Son of Man Is?

> *Now when Jesus came into the district of Caesarea Philippi, He began asking His disciples, saying, "Who do people say that the Son of Man is?" And they said, "Some say John the Baptist; and others, Elijah; but still others, Jeremiah, or one of the prophets"* (Matthew 16:13-14).

Here are Jesus and His disciples in a Gentile area, and Jesus asked the disciples what His public-relations image was in that area. Did He have a good reputation? Did people recognize Him? Did they know who He was? What are the media moguls saying about Him? What were the newspapers and universities saying about Him?

Notice that Jesus calls Himself the Son of Man. He appealed to their head knowledge. He did this because He was going to make a distinction to Peter and the disciples later. Jesus knows that the natural person does not accept the things of the Spirit of God (see 1 Corinthians 2:14). He knows their answer will be incorrect because their ears have been plugged so their speech would be impeded. They are spiritually deaf, so they will be spiritually dumb. They "speak with difficulty." They see Jesus "like a tree." The disciples have *knowledge of Jesus but not a revelation of Jesus.*

The disciples answer His question. Let me put this in contemporary terms: "Well, CNN says You are John the Baptist; BBC says You are Elijah; *The New York Times* suggests Jeremiah, and a religion professor at Harvard says You are one of the prophets." Notice, not one of pundits got it right. Their villages have a voice, and they listen to that voice, so their ears have been plugged. But Jesus wasn't interested in what people said about Him at that moment; He was interested in what His disciples said about Him.

He said to them, "But who do *you* say that I am?" (Matthew 16:15). He was expecting the people in a Gentile community to answer incorrectly. But what was His disciples' take on this question? They should have a more accurate definition of Jesus than the area locals. They've walked and talked with Him, eaten with Him, healed with Him, and listened and prayed with Him. They've seen Him perform miracles; they've seen Him engage other people in extraordinary ways. They know Him up close and personal, not just by reputation or through the media. God has manifested Himself to them. The Word has become flesh in front of them. The unseen has become the seen. Something is up. They can feel it. Is it possible that, much like the Gentile pundits, they could know Him but not *know* Him?

Telling by Showing

Think about this: Jesus gave the Father a voice and a face in this forbidden, forgotten land, to a people who were aware of gods but not of God. Jesus came to make God known by His voice and by His presence (see John 17:26). The whole countryside was aware of Jesus after the Word became flesh. God showed up on their turf, in a way they could understand and relate to. Do you know that is what we do when we go into the community? We have a voice and a presence. We are living epistles distributing living words within the community. Armed with God's Word and His image, we become flesh and blood within the community. We connect the message and the audience. We are a more accurate definition of Jesus and therefore of God than what the pundits are reporting. Like Jesus, we are sent into the communities, cities, and nations to make God known. *If they can't see us, then they won't be us.*

If we hide and don't represent God in word and in deed, then the city will continue to listen to the voice of the village. The pundits will make God into their own image and broadcast their opinions as truth. Do you see God's strategy here? A real person, a living word, who is a carrier and a courier of God's voice and image is a stronger definition of who Jesus is than a pundit's opinion. Consider a friend who works with you and knows that you are a Christian. Then that friend hears the voice of someone in the media define what all Christians are like. If the media reports an inaccurate definition, then your friend who hears this inaccurate report didn't know you or have a Christian friend, then his definitions of God, Jesus, the church, and Christians would not be accurate. This is because the natural man doesn't understand the Spirit of God. As a result, that person will live by and form opinions from the voices he or she hears in the village. If you put garbage in, then you will get garbage out.

Jesus knew the only way to redefine Himself, God, the church, and Christians was for Christians—at work, in media, and in all the seven mountains of society—to incarnate God's presence into the world. The Word had to become flesh outside of Heaven and the church walls.

Your friend knows you. He's been with you. He's heard wisdom from you. He's seen a bit of Jesus in you. He's heard a different voice than what the pundits are saying. When the pundit inaccurately says something about all Christians, your friend knows it is not true because he knows you and has been with you. That's how we redefine God for the culture in which we live. We are a personal touch from God to the culture around us. We are a more accurate picture of God. That sets people free. Right input creates a right outcome. That's why it is so important to hear first and speak second. The definitions people live by determine their beliefs, which determine their actions, which determine their outcome.

God wants us to be the definers of God to the world around us. If they have heard us, then they have heard Christ; if they have heard Christ, then they have heard from God; and if they have heard from God, then they could be connected to God. If they have seen us, they have seen Christ; if they have seen Christ, then they have seen God; and if they have seen God, the earth has been filled with the knowledge of the glory of the Lord just as the waters cover the sea.

The First New Testament Salvation

Jesus asked His disciples a compelling question:

> *"But who do you say I am?" Simon Peter answered, "You are the Christ, the Son of the living God." And Jesus said to him, "Blessed are you, Simon Barjona, because flesh and blood did not reveal this to you, but My Father who is in heaven"* (Matthew 16:15-17).

Do you hear what I hear? Peter heard something. He heard an utterance from God that was personal, specific, timely, and appropriate for the occasion. And the message came infused with saving faith. Peter heard an utterance from God concerning Christ—the message was loud and clear. Jesus is the Christ, the Messiah, the Son of the living God. Peter heard what the Spirit always says, "Jesus is Lord" (1 Corinthians 12:3).

Peter moved from *information about Christ* to the *revelation of Christ*. He moved from the LOGOS to the RHEMA. Peter had an aha moment, an epiphany. And for the first time, saving faith came from hearing an utterance from God. Jesus acknowledged this when he told Peter that this revelation only came from the Father. To say it in modern vernacular, "Wow! CNN, NBC, your university professor, and the city newspaper did not reveal this to you, Peter. My Father in Heaven did. You heard directly from Heaven. You heard from God what was unheard by others. You got past the voices of the village. Your ears now hear another voice, the voice of God."

Notice that Peter heard first then spoke second. What did he hear? He heard that Jesus is the Messiah, his Lord and Savior. And then he confessed that Jesus is Lord. Where did he get the faith to do that? He received faith to do this by hearing an utterance from God concerning Jesus that was faith-infused, personal, specific, clear, and for such a time as this. He heard a "now" word from God. There's a difference between believing *in* Jesus and *believing Jesus*. Peter moved from believing in Jesus as a Messiah to come one day to believing Jesus as His Lord and Savior had already come. He moved from Jesus as the Son of Man to Jesus as the Son of God. Peter moved from the Old Testament to the New Testament, from the Holy Spirit *on* him to the Holy Spirit *in* him.

What sense enabled this transformation to happen? Hearing. Peter had seen Jesus do plenty of miracles. He had seen Jesus (like a tree), but he hadn't seen Jesus clearly. Before he could see Jesus clearly, before he could get the second touch, Peter had to hear an utterance from God concerning Christ. Hearing God changes the heart so that person can see what the Spirit tells him or her: Jesus is Lord. With the heart a person believes, and with the mouth a person speaks what he or she believes. Hear first, speak second.

The Process of Salvation

Paul, an apostle, starts off in Romans 10:1 by saying his heart and his prayers for the Jewish people are for their salvation. Then he goes on to explain the process of salvation in Romans 10:17—faith for salvation comes by hearing an utterance from God concerning who Christ is. This RHEMA from God concerning Christ comes with faith attached to it. For each believer, that hearing is clear enough for us to take a step forward into Christ.

Even though you don't know everything about Christ, even though you may have questions about Him, there are no more doubts in your mind once you are born again. There are no more arguments, debating, or waiting. Now is the time for salvation. That's called faith.

Where did it come from? God spoke to your heart, just like He did with Peter. Flesh and blood did not reveal it to you but your Father in Heaven did. How? By personally and clearly speaking to your heart. You didn't initiate the process; God did. You didn't choose God; God chose you (see John 15:16). You just responded to the invitation that God uttered to you. God spoke, you responded, and then God gave you the faith to receive Christ. Even the faith for salvation comes from God. But what does it say?

> *"The* [RHEMA] *is near you, in your mouth and in your heart"—that is, the* [RHEMA] *of faith which we are preaching, that if you confess with your mouth Jesus as Lord, and believe in your heart that God raised Him from the dead, you will be saved; for with the heart a person believes, resulting in righteousness, and with the mouth he confesses, resulting is salvation* (Romans 10:8-10).

Paul is saying that his and his contemporaries' preaching contained RHEMAS or *utterances from God concerning Jesus that were faith-infused, personal, specific, clear, and for such a time as theirs.* Some of the people had ears to hear these utterances that were infused with faith for salvation. They heard from God concerning Jesus, they believed in Jesus, and then confessed with their mouths. Then Paul concludes the process: "So faith [for salvation] comes from hearing, and hearing by the word [RHEMA or utterance] of Christ" (Romans 10:17).

Did you do anything to receive your salvation? Did you initiate it? Did you choose God? Did you have to get baptized? Did you have to get confirmed? Did you have to pump yourself up with faith and say, "Look at me; I'm cool; I have faith; I'm powerful; I fasted; I prayed; I'm a women or man of faith; I worked hard to have this kind of faith"? The answer to all this, of course, is no. All you had to do was hear an utterance from God concerning Christ. All you had to do was hear what the Spirit said. All you had to do was wait, be quiet, and listen for a RHEMA from God. All you had to do was receive the faith that God infused into the words He spoke to you. Then all you had to do was confess, "Jesus is Lord." All you had to do was hear first, then speak second. Illumination, then communication.

If you have received Christ as Lord, then you have heard an utterance from God. You heard the voice of God in your heart. In fact, you have received a RHEMA from God. God said, "Let there be light" within you, and there was light! God is light, so He created light both naturally and spiritually. Every Christian has heard the word, an utterance from God with faith attached to it, which is near them and in their heart. That's extraordinary light. *Spiritual sight needs spiritual light.*

"Let Him Who Has an Ear" Implies Some Can't Hear

In my opinion, Acts 11:19-21 is one of the most hard-hitting accounts in the book of Acts. It comes and goes so quickly that it's easy to miss. I wrote about Peter and the first New Testament-style of conversion. How would Peter pass this experience on to others? How would he duplicate in others' lives what happened to him? How would he multiply his life-changing faith? Good news must be spread around. *God gives it to us so God can get it through us.* What good is seed in a bag? Spread the seed around. Let there be light, and to some, there was light.

> *So then those who were scattered because of the persecution that occurred in connection to Stephen made their way to Phoenicia and Cyprus and Antioch, speaking the* [LOGOS] *to no one except to Jews alone. But there were some of them, men of Cyprus and Cyrene, who came to Antioch and began speaking to the Greeks also, preaching the Lord Jesus. And the hand of the Lord was with them, and a large number who believed turned to the Lord* (Acts 11:19-21).

Here was a "microsynagogue" that fled into three cities. They had heard about Jesus, and so they wanted to share about Jesus. But their mission was twofold: they were to speak to Jews only and share the LOGOS or Torah of God with their audience. As you know, the LOGOS is the written Word of God. It contains what and how God thinks. It is the whole general truth of God's Word that will never pass away. It's what Peter knew before His conversion with God. There are no conversions here—LOGOS doesn't come with faith attached to it like RHEMA does.

There was a smaller group who came out of the Jewish microsynagogue. These were Greek-speaking Jews who came from Cyprus and Cyrene. They enlarged their religious borders by speaking to the Greeks. They were preaching the Lord Jesus. Don't miss this: Greek-speaking Jews were preaching the Lord Jesus. These Greek-speaking Jews also had a salvation encounter like Peter's. They moved from speaking about the written Word of God, the LOGOS of God, the dead liturgy of the time, to speaking about Jesus. They moved from "Torah is Lord" to "Jesus is Lord," just like Peter had done. They shifted from *speaking* about the *written Word of God* to *knowing* the *living Word of God*. They moved from a microsynagogue to a microchurch that Jesus was building. They heard a personal utterance from God attached with the faith for salvation concerning Christ. That's a RHEMA; they had an aha.

They heard from the God channel. God is always broadcasting; however, some tune in to the God channel while others tune in to other channels. They heard the right voice. Just like Peter, they heard God's voice. Flesh and blood didn't reveal this to them—God did. They were preaching what the Spirit always says: "Jesus is Lord." They had an ear to hear what the Spirit said to the churches. What happened when they preached "the Lord Jesus"? The hand of the Lord was with them and large numbers of them believed and turned to the Lord.

Notice the differences here between the microsynagogue and the microchurch. The microsynagogue had output, whereas the microchurch had outcome. What made the difference? It was RHEMA! They heard first and spoke second. Saving faith comes by hearing, and hearing comes by an utterance from God. Please don't see this example as demeaning the LOGOS or the written Word of God. LOGOS is crucial, but so is RHEMA. We aren't taking anything away from LOGOS; we are only emphasizing the necessity of RHEMA to the necessity of LOGOS. RHEMA *is the interpretive key to LOGOS. RHEMA takes the written Word of God and moves it to the living Word of God.* RHEMA is not the Word of God, but it is a word *from* God. RHEMA is light and truth.

Saving Apostle Paul

Let's look at the salvation experience of the apostle Paul. It's important to understand that the apostle Paul had to go through a conversion similar to Peter's so they both would understand the process of seeing someone come to Christ. Peter needed the experience so he could minister to the people group he was called to, primarily the Jews, while Paul needed to experience the process of salvation so that he could minister to the people group he was called to, primarily the Gentiles.

You will remember that before his conversion, Paul was a persecutor of the church. He was in "hearty agreement" with the stoning of Stephen (see Acts 8:1). Paul began "ravaging the church, entering house after house, and dragging off men and women...[putting] them in prison" (Acts 8:3). He was totally sold out to God through Judaism, but he was not a friend of God. He knew *about* God but *didn't know God.* But God saw his heart. Jesus was not going to allow Paul to stay this way. Paul, after all, was chosen for "such a time as this."

Let's look at his conversion experience in Acts 9:3-20. Paul's (initially Saul's) conversion happened while he was on the way to Damascus to look for followers of Jesus he could arrest and bring back to Jerusalem for imprisonment. Even though many of us know this story, let's look at it again through the process of hearing first, illumination second, and speaking third.

As he was traveling, it happened that he was approaching Damascus, and suddenly a light from heaven flashed around him; and he fell to the ground and heard a voice saying to him, "Saul, Saul, why are you persecuting Me?" And he said, "Who are You, Lord?" And He said, "I am Jesus whom you are persecuting, but get up and enter the city, and it will be told you what you must do." The men who traveled with him stood speechless, hearing the voice but seeing no one. Saul got up from the ground, and though his eyes were open, he could see nothing; and leading him by the hand, they brought him into Damascus. And he was three days without sight, and neither ate nor drank.

Now there was a disciple at Damascus named Ananias; and the Lord said to him in a vision, "Ananias." And he said, "Here I am, Lord." And the Lord said to him, "Get up and go to the street called Straight, and inquire at the house of Judas for a man from Tarsus named Saul, for he is praying, and he has seen in a vision a man named Ananias come in and lay his hands on him, so that he might regain his sight." But Ananias answered, "Lord, I have heard from many about this man, how much harm he did to Your saints at Jerusalem; and here he has authority from the chief priests to bind all who call on Your name." But the Lord said to him, "Go, for he is a chosen instrument of Mine, to bear My name before the Gentiles and kings and the sons of Israel; for I will show him how much he must suffer for My name's sake." So Ananias departed and entered the house, and after laying his hands on him said, "Brother Saul, the Lord Jesus, who appeared to you on the road by which you were coming, has sent me so that you may regain your sight and be filled with the Holy Spirit." And immediately there fell from his eyes something like scales, and he regained his sight, and he got up and was baptized; and he took food and was strengthened.

Now for several days he was with the disciples who were at Damascus, and immediately he began to proclaim Jesus in the synagogues, saying, "He is the Son of God" (Acts 9:3-20).

God Found Saul, *Then* Saul Found God

As we read this account of Paul's conversion, notice some key words we have been exploring. "Suddenly, a *light* from heaven flashed around him..." (vs. 3). That calls to mind the account in Genesis 1: "Let there be light." Then he "fell to the ground, and *heard a voice* saying to him, 'Saul, Saul, why are you persecuting Me?'" (vs. 4). There's God's voice getting ready to create something. God spoke, then there was illumination, both naturally and spiritually. Notice Saul's reply: "Who are you, Lord?" Saul was God-aware but not God-illuminated. Jesus's response was, "*I am Jesus* whom you are persecuting, but rise and enter the city, and *it shall be told you what you must do*" (vs. 5).

As one who speaks on community and city transformation, I like the idea of "rise and enter the city." It was only then that he would be "told what [he] must do." God had Saul's attention. And his hearing came before seeing—Saul was still blinded by the light at this point. Even though he heard the voice of Jesus speaking to him and saw Him, the others who stood by only heard a sound: "And the men who traveled with him stood speechless, hearing the voice [the actual word is sound], but seeing no one" (Acts 9:7). If you can't hear God's voice, then you will not be able to see what is going on. You can hear something but not *hear* it, you can see something but not *see* it, and you can know something but not *know* it.

When Saul got up from the ground, he had no light—he went three days without seeing. His eyes were covered with scales. In both the natural and the spiritual, sight requires light to see. God appointed a man who knew God's voice to give Saul illumination so he could regain his sight. This man's name was Ananias. God spoke to Ananias in a vision, "Ananias." And he said, "Behold, here I am, Lord" (vs. 10). Do you see the difference here? Saul said, "Who are You, Lord?" and Ananias said, "Here I am, Lord."

Saul, at this point, had heard about God; Ananias heard God. Knowing God's voice is the first step in the process of salvation. Then God gave Ananias illumination, revelation, and instruction on what to do next. At the same time, after speaking to Saul, God gave him illumination also. God told him that a man named Ananias was going to lay hands on him that he might regain his sight. So both Ananias and Saul, the saved and the unsaved, had the same experience—they heard God first and then God gave them illumination. Even though Saul didn't yet have natural sight, he was beginning to have spiritual sight. God was preparing the religious zealot Saul for a God-encounter like Peter's.

Initially, Ananias was concerned because he had heard how Saul persecuted the saints of Jesus and had authority from the chief priests to arrest every Christian he found. Then God gave Ananias more insight: "Go, for he is a chosen instrument of Mine, to bear My name before the Gentiles and kings and sons of Israel" (vs. 15). After God told him to go, Ananias went to Saul, laid his hands on him, and told Saul how Jesus sent him so that Saul would regain his sight and be filled with the Spirit. As soon as Ananias said this, the scales fell from Saul's eyes, and he could suddenly see. Paul had an epiphany. He would never be the same again: "and immediately he began to proclaim Jesus in the synagogues, saying, 'He is the Son of God'" (Acts 9:20).

Paul believed in his heart and confessed with his tongue "Jesus is Lord" (see Romans 10:9). Saving faith came by hearing a RHEMA. Let me say it another way: Saving faith came by Saul hearing a faith-infused utterance from God giving him the revelation that Jesus is Lord. No one can say "Jesus is Lord" except by the Holy Spirit (see 1 Corinthians 12:3).

Notice the new-creation account of two apostles, Peter and Paul. God spoke, God gave illumination concerning Christ, and they both said in essence, "Thou are the Christ, the Son of the Living God." God said, "Let there be light," the Holy Spirit gave illumination about who Jesus was, and then they both confessed with their mouths, "Jesus is Lord." Hear first what God spoke, which is truth, then light or illumination comes after hearing the truth.

Flesh and blood does not reveal this to us. Rather, it is our Father in Heaven who starts the process; the Holy Spirit continues the process in giving illumination to what God said, which imparted to Peter and Paul the faith to say, "Jesus is Lord." Notice the parties involved here: God the Father, the Holy Spirit, the recipient, and then Jesus.

Illumination Illumined the Two Nations: Jew and Gentile

The processes in saving the apostle Peter and saving the apostle Paul are significant. At that time, in a Jewish person's mind, there were only two main people groups on the earth: Jew and Gentile. Both groups were called nations; God wanted both nations to be reconciled to Him. He loved both nations; Jesus died for both nations. In fact, both Jew and Gentle were made in His image, they both had access to the Father through Jesus Christ, and they both had equal status but different roles.

The Jewish nation was first on the scene. However, they were blessed to be a blessing to all the others nations of the earth. But the Jewish nation thought they alone were God's chosen people, not the Gentile nations of the world. The Jewish nation became exclusive. Anyone other than a Jewish person was called a dog. Jesus, as a Jewish man, came to show the Jewish nation that He was the example for other Jewish men, to be a light (there's that word again) to the Gentiles also.

In the Bible, Simeon quotes from the Old Testament when he saw the child Jesus:

> *Now Lord, You are releasing Your bond-servant to depart in peace, according to Your word; for my eyes have seen Your salvation, which You have prepared in the presence of all peoples, a Light of revelation to the Gentiles, and the glory of Your people Israel* (Luke 2:29-32).

We need to take note of two interesting words here. First, when Simeon says, "according to Your word," he uses the word RHEMA. God spoke to him what He had spoken to Isaiah (see Isaiah 42:6). In other words, Isaiah (hundreds of years earlier) and Simeon both heard a faith-infused utterance from God concerning Jesus.

The second word is *revelation*, which means "fire." The verse could be translated like this: "A light of fire to the Gentiles." Jesus came to set on fire a movement that would bring salvation to the Gentiles and then send others to do the same. A candle loses nothing by lighting another candle. Jesus was coming to build His church to do just that—light other candles and so make its light even brighter.

The God-Impartial Ministries of Peter and Paul

Since the Jews thought they had the upper hand and were superior to the Gentiles, God was going to have to speak to them in a way that would capture their attention. He would have to change the Jewish "mindskin" to create a new wineskin—a wineskin that contains both Jew and Gentile. To make a new wineskin requires a new "mindskin." God was going to have to speak and let the Holy Spirit illuminate so the Jews could hear and see what the Spirit was doing.

Throughout the New Testament, God equates Paul's ministry to Peter's ministry. Peter was accepted and endorsed by the church in Jerusalem. He was the apostle. He was the man! Peter was the apostle to the Jews (see Galatians 2:7). On the other hand, Paul was the apostle to the Gentiles (see Romans 11:13). Both Peter and Paul were Jews—Peter was born in Bethsaida in Galilee, and Paul was born in the Roman colony of Tarsus in Cilicia. No believing Jew could refute

Paul's testimony by comparing it with Peter's if they were factual. The facts below demand that Jewish believers accepted God's concern for the Gentiles also. Look at the chart and let there be light.

	PETER	PAUL
1. Heard God speak revelation for salvation.	Matthew 16:7	Acts 9:17-20
2. Received illumination/light concerning Jesus.	Matthew 16:7	Acts 9:18
3. Spoke what he heard from God confessing Jesus as Lord.	Matthew 16:16	Acts 9:20
4. An apostle.	Galatians 2:7	Romans 11:13
5. Both were given a new name after coming to faith in Christ.	Matthew 16:17	Acts 13:9
6. Was filled with the Holy Spirit.	Acts 2:1-4	Acts 9:17-18
7. Both spoke in tongues.	Acts 2:4	1 Corinthians 14:18
8. Laid hands on people and they received the Holy Spirit.	Acts 8:17	Acts 19:6
9. Operated in a word of knowledge.	Acts 5:3	Acts 27:34
10. Saw a vision.	Acts 10:17	Acts 16:9
11. Cast out demons.	Acts 5:16	Acts 16:18
12. Healed.	Acts 9:34	Acts 14:10
13. Raised the dead.	Acts 9:40	Acts 20:12
14. Preached salvation by faith.	Acts 2:38	Acts 13:38-39
15. Released from jail by miracle.	Acts 12:7	Acts 16:26
16. Angelic visitation.	Acts 5:19	Acts 27:23
17. Peter's shadow fell on people and they were healed.	Acts 5:15	
18. Paul's handkerchief and apron cured people.		Acts 19:11-12

Where did both Peter's and Paul's salvation start? God spoke, the Holy Spirit illuminated, and then they spoke their confession that Jesus was Lord. And all of that came from a RHEMA. They heard a faith-infused utterance from God concerning the revelation of Christ. This is how RHEMA works in salvation.

Notes

1. Steve Murrell, http://victory.org.ph/audio-message/steve-murrell-the-power-to-preach-the-gospel/.
2. Used by permission of Alan Platt.
3. This is used by permission of Joseph Mattera.

POWER THOUGHTS FOR *Chapter 12*

How do you like the subtitle of this chapter: Between Exodus and Genesis Is Revelation? The title might be confusing to you, so let me explain. The book of Exodus is about how Israel came out of bondage, which was a type of salvation. Genesis is about beginnings and a new start. Genesis in this instance means the start of a new nation or a new beginning. Between the Israelites' exodus from slavery and the genesis of a real and tangible nation called Israel was the wilderness. God took them out into the wilderness to give them a revelation of the laws and ways of the new Israel. The wilderness is a place where God speaks revelation to His people and gets them ready for what He has ready for them. It's true for us too. Between exodus and genesis there is revelation.

—Ed Delph

Sometimes religious services are announced "as usual." Maybe that's what's wrong with them! Nothing else is "as usual" these days. We are living ordinary lives in extraordinary times. The emergency requires urgency. We are passing resolutions when we should be promoting revolutions—the Acts of the Apostles kind.

—Vance Havner[1]

Talk about revolutions and reformations! The Great Reformation started when Martin Luther received a RHEMA on LOGOS. He received the revelation in the wilderness of the Dark Ages. That RHEMA transformed the church forever—that's called the Reformation—but it also transformed the community—that's called the Renaissance. Reformation had to do with the church mountain, but the Renaissance had to do with the other six mountains.

—Ed Delph

The world is separated but acts as one. The church is one but acts as if separated. Stop the circular firing squad.

—Lance Wallnau[2]

Chapter 12

Rhema in the Church: Between Exodus and Genesis Is Revelation

Jesus did not give a mission to His church;
He formed a church for His mission.
—Christopher Wright[3]

After the RHEMA of salvation occurs within the heart of the believer, the next successive and progressive revelation is the revelation of the church. It's the second stage of the rocket that we discussed earlier. And who is the one who builds the church? Jesus. Let's look at the guiding verse for RHEMA in church: "I also say to you that you are Peter, and upon this rock I will build My church; and the gates of Hades will not overpower it" (Matthew 16:18).

I like churches and I love the body of Christ. Churches do heaps of "God things" and good things both inside and outside of the church walls. Churches give people hope, inspiration, and knowledge, and they teach people to worship the Lord. Churches provide stability. People make friends at church. People come to Christ. Church is family. It's familiar. Churches have Sunday school for children and youth programs for teens. People seek God's presence there. Believers develop and grow in character as they attend church. People learn how to deal with problems rather than let problems deal with them. Churches are pillars of truth. Love, mercy, forgiveness, and grace are all found there.

Pastors of churches become part of people's families for special occasions like births and marriages. Churches are there for sad occasions like funerals too. They introduce people to the Word of God, the Bible, and help guide them in what it means to apply it to their lives. People sick in body, soul, and spirit get well in churches. Many people mature spiritually in churches. Churches move members from relationship with God to fellowship with God and others. Church is a special community within the community. It is a light set on a hill.

But (you knew I was building up to something, didn't you?) I am concerned about a crucial aspect of churches that I have consistently noticed worldwide. As someone who is more apostolic by nature, I always look for what is lacking, wanting, and in need of building up in the body of Christ. Somewhere along the way, we have lost our way in equipping the saints for real life. I'm not saying we should get rid of all the good things about church. But can we add something important and strategic to all those good things?

Here's what I'm not seeing very often. I don't see teams of pastors or prophets or teachers or evangelists or apostles equipping the saints on how to discern and use RHEMA, the sword of the Spirit, correctly, accurately, and fully. Church should be a garden of LOGOS and RHEMA where God walks with us and talks to us and tells us that we are His own. There's corporate anointing there that can be found only when two or three are gathered together in His name. Church was designed to be a place of revelation and illumination to both the lost and the found. It should be a place where truth with understanding—not just information—is dispensed.

When I do come across teaching on RHEMA or hearing from God, it is in the "Spirit" side of the church. I see it used but not used wisely. It usually ends up with some wonderful people who have a great heart thinking what they are speaking is God speaking through them.

They use the sword, but there is little skill in how they wield it. They are generally absorbed with whatever emphasis their church or they individually are seeking. Because of the misuses and abuses of this tendency, the other side of the church, the "truth" side, is afraid to even mention a spooky word like RHEMA. Because of this, these churches generally turn into LOGOS studies. Anything other than knowledge accumulation is generally discarded.

Remember, Jesus will build His church and He will build it in His way. Jesus means it when He says, "But an hour is coming, and now is, when the true worshipers will worship the Father in spirit and in truth; for such people the Father seeks to be His worshipers. God is spirit [the original language says that 'God is a Spirit'] and those who worship Him must worship in spirit and truth" (John 4:23-24). Both sides have what the other needs. Just think what could happen if the two swords could be used together. That key will open gates!

John 4:25-26 highlights Jesus's conversation with the woman at the well as follows: "The woman said to Him, 'I know the Messiah is coming (He who is called the Christ); when that One comes, He will declare all things to us.' Jesus said to her, 'I who speak to you am He.'" Notice that Jesus speaks and will declare *all* things, not just a few things. He desires that when He speaks, we listen, learn, speak, and act on what He says. He builds His church by giving His church the whole counsel of God's general LOGOS and specific RHEMA.

If all we have is truth without light, then we will underachieve in all that God has for us. The Jews had LOGOS but were in complete darkness. Saul, who became Paul, had his doctorate in the Torah but was in complete and utter darkness. Saul was imprisoning believers when he had only the LOGOS. He had the truth without light. But when he saw the light, he saw the whole truth clearly. Saul became Paul after he experienced a RHEMA.

Until we have truth with light, the gates will remain closed. Remember that the gates are in the church realm. God wants to walk with us and talk to us like Adam and Eve in the garden of LOGOS and

RHEMA. We have access to His heart. We have His identity. We have been given an assignment. Jesus builds His church by declaring to us all things that we need for our present circumstance—when He is ready and we are ready.

A Time of Preparation: From Egypt to the Wilderness

Recall that in the three successive revelations in Chapter 11, I mentioned that salvation is where we get out of Egypt and that the church is a type of wilderness. In salvation we get out of bondage (flesh), but in the church bondage gets out of us. In salvation we get out of Egypt (world), but in church Egypt gets out of us. Salvation is where we got out of hell (the devil's domain), by God's revelation and Christ's sacrifice, but church is the place where Jesus gets hell out of us by conforming us into His likeness and image.

If I add the kingdom stage to this idea, I can say it this way: in salvation, we get out of hell; in church, Jesus gets the hell out of us; and in the kingdom, we use the keys to unlock the gates of Hades so others can get out of hell and then go to church to get the hell out of them and enter kingdom ministry to release others to unlock the gates. Get the idea? That's called New Testament ministry. The enemy loves it when believers get stuck in the second stage and stay in the church. This is because they never get to the Promised Land.

The church is a type of wilderness. This is not a denunciation of church. When the Israelites escaped Egypt, they were the lowest-tech people in the world. For years, they had been in captivity. All they knew was making bricks without straw. Pharaohs and malevolent dictators do that to you.

The future nation of Israel was in a frustrating position. They were on their way but, if not given knowledge and wisdom from God in all areas of His Word, they were going to be in the way. They had the capacity but lacked the competency to govern themselves, much less the nation called and chosen to be a blessing to all the nations. They were raw, uneducated, and unprepared. They were called "the children of Israel" in the wilderness. They were going to have to grow up and get equipped for the work of their future ministry. They were going to have to learn how to work with God. They were going to have a new "mindskin" to have a new wineskin. A transformation was going to have to take place. Living in a place like Canaan or the Promised Land requires it. You don't give the keys to the car to a two-year-old child. That's not wise.

What was God's plan? God did what He usually does with His people under construction. He took them into the wilderness. There weren't many restaurants or cell phones or Starbucks out there like there would be in Canaan. There was nothing to steal in the wilderness. God needed a quiet place where they would be protected and grow up in all aspects into His ways. They didn't know it, but for the next forty years they were going to "reform" school. These wilderness years would be a time of reformation, preceding another reformation that would take place several thousand years later. Why did God do this? Because God walks with and talks to people in the wilderness. He gives His people His Word while they are in the wilderness. Between the exodus from our old nature to the genesis of our new nature, there must be revelation of God's Word—the two swords of the Lord.

The Church in the Wilderness

There are some incredible verses in Acts 7:35-38 that are confirmed in Acts 3:22-26. Take a moment to read these passages because these concepts are important. Get ready to enter the revelation zone:

> *This Moses whom they disowned, saying, "Who made you a ruler and a judge?" is the one whom God sent to be both a ruler and a deliverer with the help of the angel who appeared to him in the thorn bush. This man led them out, performing wonders and signs in the land of Egypt and in the Red Sea and in the wilderness for forty years. This is the Moses who said to the sons of Israel, "God will raise up*

> *for you a prophet like me from your brethren." This is the one who was in the congregation in the wilderness together with the angel who was speaking to him on Mount Sinai, and who was with our fathers; and he received living oracles to pass on to you* (Acts 7:35-38).
>
> *Moses said, "The Lord God will raise up for you a prophet like me from your brethren; to Him you shall give heed to everything He says to you. And it will be that every soul that does not heed that prophet shall be utterly destroyed from among the people." And likewise, all the prophets who have spoken, from Samuel and his successors onward, also announced these days. It is you who are the sons of the prophets and of the covenant which God made with your fathers, saying to Abraham, "And in your seed all the families of the earth shall be blessed." For you first, God raised up His Servant and sent Him to bless you by turning every one of you from your wicked ways* (Acts 3:22-26).

Look at Acts 7:38. Stephen, who is speaking what he just heard from the Holy Spirit, calls Israel the congregation (or church) in the wilderness. The Greek word he uses here is *ekklesia*, which is the New Testament word for church. The words *ekklesiazien* and *sunagogein* were often used in the Old Testament, which church and synagogue are obviously derived from.[4]

We have established the church or wilderness idea. But who is the one who builds the church? Who does everything within the church? It is Jesus. Stephen quotes what Moses said to the church in the wilderness, and then Peter gives us further insight into who this "man" was. He starts off by quoting the Old Testament: "The Lord God shall raise up for you a prophet like me from among you. Listen to this prophet. All prophets before and after him will be speaking of him" (see Deuteronomy 18:15).[5]

Do you realize it was Jesus who did everything in the wilderness for the Israelites, the church in the wilderness? Jesus was there in Egypt, He was there during the parting of the Red Sea, and He was there in the wilderness. The Rock was rolling with them and was of them (Jesus was a Jew), with them, and for them. In Acts 3:26, we see that Jesus did this for the Jews first! Now it's our turn! Paul went on to write about how this was an example for us:

> *For I do not want you to be unaware, brethren, that our fathers were all under the cloud and all passed through the sea; and all were baptized into Moses in the cloud and in the sea; and all ate the same spiritual food; and all drank the same spiritual drink, for they were drinking from a spiritual rock which followed them; and the rock was Christ* (1 Corinthians 10:1-4).

The rock was Christ (the Messiah). Jesus was building the church in the wilderness. Moses knew who the Rock was; it is no wonder Moses got stuck on the wrong side of the Jordan. But he eventually got over to the Promised Land—he was at the Mount of Transfiguration with Jesus. This is encouraging.

God is forming us and filling us—getting us well and fit for duty. He is showing us that we are totally dependent on Him. We can't do it on our own. He is taking us right into where He wants us. It's a Promised Land, and the architect and builder of it is God. God is also forming us so that we can be part of "Thy kingdom come, Thy will be done." The church (or the body of Christ) is a great place to prepare for that coming kingdom. He is the greatest body builder of all time—and He does it in the wilderness. The wilderness is the space and time between being set free to fulfill your purpose and the fulfillment of that purpose.

God Uses Wilderness Experiences in His People and His Church

One of my closest ministry friends is a man by the name of Joshua Churchyard. He pastors a church, Church of the Way, in Benoni, Johannesburg, South Africa. He is prophetic and loves to think about the in-depth meanings of Hebrew terms in the Bible. He wrote the following exhortation for us to see not only the what but also the why of God's pattern of using wilderness experiences in our lives:

> The country of Israel is known as the land of milk and honey. Bees in the northern area of Galilee produce delicious honey. Shepherds and their milk-producing flocks of goats live in the desert regions.
>
> The image of milk and honey symbolizes the fertile land and the desert/wilderness area. The desert is important in hearing first and then obeying or speaking what the Lord gives us.
>
> The word for *wilderness* in Hebrew is MDBR (*midbar*) and the root of that Hebrew word is DBR. דָּבָר (*dbar*), which is pronounced dah-bawr, means word or speech. מִדְבָּר (*midbar*), which is pronounced mid-bawr, means a wilderness that is a place of Word or a place of speech.
>
> *Bamidbar* is the Hebrew name for the book of Numbers. It means "in the wilderness" and is the first word in Numbers. The setting for the book is in the desert. Numbers 1:1 says, "The Lord spoke to Moses in the wilderness of Sinai, in the tent of meeting, on the first day of the second month, in the second year after they had come out of the land of Egypt, saying...."
>
> The desert is a place in which God speaks His words to us. The ancient Hebrew people could be called people of the desert. Many of their journeys and significant

encounters with God in which they heard Him speak took place in the desert.

Abraham was a desert person, Moses could be called a desert person, and David spent many of his years in the wilderness. Even Jesus was led by the Spirit into the desert. There will be times when God leads us into the desert in the same way that He led the Israelites into the desert. Why? To speak to us.

It was in the desert that God spoke the Ten Commandments and the law to Moses. And the desert/wilderness is where the Spirit led Jesus after His baptism to be tempted by satan. Jesus then left the desert in the power of the Holy Spirit.

John tells us grace and truth came through Jesus. As this incident is described in Matthew 4, Jesus refers to the LOGOS and RHEMA. In the desert, Jesus heard the Father speak RHEMA to Him. When He came out of the wilderness, grace and truth were released in power to accomplish His divine plan. He lived by the bread of RHEMA in the wilderness, and He returned from the wilderness to do His ministry in power.

In the desert, flocks of sheep and goats depend on their shepherd for their survival and existence. If they do not hear first and obey second, they will die in the wilderness. They depend on the shepherd for water, food, shelter, and protection.

In today's tumultuous world, we find ourselves in the wilderness. However, the wilderness is the place where God speaks to us and leads us through the storms the wilderness brings, if only we will hear first and speak and obey second. In these desert places, believers need two swords—LOGOS (see Hebrews 4:12) and RHEMA (see Ephesians 6:17). Look at what Jesus said in response to a half-truth pulled from God's LOGOS and spoken by the devil: "But [Jesus] answered and said, 'It is written [LOGOS], Man shall not live on bread alone, but on every word [RHEMA] that proceeds out of the mouth of God'" (hearing, speaking, and doing what God just uttered). Jesus understood what happens in the desert.

In the desert, we learn to become totally dependent on God for our existence. If we don't trust Him and follow Him, we will not survive. In John 10:27, Jesus said, "My sheep hear My voice" and follow. This is another picture of the wilderness where the sheep listen to the voice of the Shepherd and follow Him wherever He leads. The Lord provides manna and water for every journey and revelation He sets in His sheep's path.

If they continue to not listen and to not follow Him, they will miss God's provision, protection, and destination. Sheep in the desert are totally dependent on their Shepherd to lead them in paths of righteousness. Tracks made in the desert lead to protective shade in the heat of the day.

Hosea 2:14 says, "Therefore, behold, I will allure her, and bring her into the wilderness, and speak tenderly to her" (ESV). It's in God's heart to speak to us in the desert for that is where we recognize the necessity of listening to Him. Those who want to hear first and speak second need an epiphany of the wilderness as a place of God speaking.

Abraham, the father of our faith, was a desert person. Moses was a desert person. David was a desert person. Paul spent thirteen years in the desert of Arabia. They were all trained to hear first, then speak or act second.

> Our journey of life leads us to and through deserts where we get to hear God with clarity and exactness. He will lead us on paths of righteousness by RHEMA, faith-infused utterances from God for illumination, clarity, or direction concerning how to thrive in wilderness times and in times of ambiguity. Remember, let the Word speak to you a word before you speak a word.

As someone once said in a conversation we were having, "If you can live in the desert, you can live anywhere." Moses said to the people of Israel, "If you can't make it through what's happening now, wait until you see what will happen in the future. You need to be prepared. Otherwise, the Promised Land will chew you up and spit you out." The Word was journeying with the Israelites as they went on to their future. The Word was training them to reign through His word. Just read Deuteronomy 8. God didn't merely lecture them; God went on the journey with them. The Word not only gave them the word but also showed them how to use the word. He moved them from "It is written" to "It is written and here's how to apply it." That's true discipleship. They started as the lowest-tech people in the world and came out the highest-tech people in the world. They moved from the early wilderness stage of "Why me?" to the mission-accomplished third stage of "What's next?"

Most of the old crew didn't make it. They sang that old song to God, "I'm stuck in the middle with You!" They couldn't go forward and they couldn't go backward, so they just went in circles. To use church vernacular, they could have been a forty-year-old Christian, but instead they ended up being a one-year-old Christian forty times. It was the younger ones who made it to the other side. There are still heaps of Calebs out there. The millennials would be smart to listen to them. Why? Because if they made it this far, they probably listen to God. Age doesn't matter when it comes to spiritual maturity.

Between Exodus and Genesis Is Revelation

What caused the Israelites to grow up in the wilderness? It was the LOGOS and the RHEMA of God. It was both swords—light on one side and truth on the other—that sustained, nourished, journeyed with, protected, and delivered them. In those forty years, they moved from members to ministers. The Rock followed them—He never left or forsook them even when they wanted to forsake Him. They had ups and downs and all arounds. Jesus was LOGOS to them in the beginning, light to them in the middle, and RHEMA to them in the end. They were delivered from Egypt in the exodus, but they were delivered to their Promised Land in the genesis of their nation. In between those two times, there was a slow revelation taking place.

Here is my concern for our own day: if church people don't have both knowledge and understanding of the Word of God, then how will they be able to have wisdom? How will they know the implications of what they are doing and why they are doing it? For example, if people don't know why they worship by singing from the Word of God, then their experience will most likely be just a good feeling or perceived as a concert.

Jesus, facing starvation in His wilderness experience, quoted Deuteronomy 8:3, saying, "It is written [LOGOS] that man shall not live by bread alone but on every RHEMA that proceeds from the mouth of God" (see Matthew 4:4). As the Son of Man, Jesus needed RHEMA to stop the tempter—and so do we!

Shouldn't we as the church be making sure that our people know the ways of God by knowing both the LOGOS and the RHEMA of God? Isn't that what was required by God in Deuteronomy 8 in the Israelites' wilderness experience? "Learn My ways by learning My word." Otherwise, we just have dead orthodoxy or misguided enthusiasm. No wonder so many today are sick and dying. They don't have the manna (daily bread) on their journey from exodus to the genesis of what they were created for via revelation. The devil quoted LOGOS to Jesus in

Matthew 4:6, but Jesus, who is the LOGOS of God, responded with RHEMA in Matthew 4:7. He had both swords and He used both.

Pastors, are your people equipped to handle that type of assault, especially when we have a runaway culture like our current one? LOGOS and half-truths taken out of context are everywhere. Are your people equipped to hear the real voice of God through any other vehicle besides preaching or reading (but not understanding) the Bible? Do they know how to position themselves to hear God? Do they know how to make the invisible visible by making the inaudible audible? When you are in the Land of Promise, these things become important. Your spiritual life and physical life depend on them.

When people initially receive Christ, they are like the children of Israel after they escaped Egypt. They are what the Bible calls babies in Christ. They will need some care if they are to grow up. How are they going to grow up in a spiritual sense? They will not be nourished by loud music, a million-dollar sound system, or fog coming up from the stage. That's nice gravy, but it is not the meat. The meat is the combination of LOGOS and RHEMA. Do you know who said that? Jesus, who is the Rock that rolls with us as we grow in the church: "In the beginning was the [LOGOS], and the [LOGOS] was with God, and the [LOGOS] was God. He was in the beginning with God" (John 1:1-2).

Skillful Swordsmanship Learned Through Experienced "Wordsmanship"

We can hear God through many different ways. We can hear Him through listening to preaching and reading the Bible, or even through receiving a prophecy from others. God or other believers might speak a word of knowledge or a word of wisdom to us. We might receive wisdom through counselors or mentors. And God even speaks through His creation. Just look at stars on a clear night from atop a mountain—those stars are proclaiming, "Look what God created!" You might hear God through your conscience. You might hear God as you meditate or through a still, small voice. Sometimes God speaks through natural disasters or events. God speaks through angels, and sometimes God can even speak through a donkey, as in the case of Balaam.

God can communicate through almost anything. The form is not necessarily what is important; the function—listening, perceiving, sensing, and hearing a faith-infused utterance of God that provides illumination, clarity, and direction is what is important. But always validate RHEMA with the Bible. RHEMA will *never* contradict LOGOS. The two swords validate each other—they always work together.

God can and does use RHEMA when people don't know the LOGOS. This is often seen with people who start seeking God. They don't know anything about God, but suddenly they have faith for finding Him. They know they need to go to church and get saved. They are compelled to do it and do it now. But after they receive Christ, God will bring in LOGOS so they can add knowledge to their experience. And we can see RHEMA in action in Christians who know in their spirit they are supposed to do something or not do something. Then, months or years later, they're reading the Bible and they see it written about what they did or didn't do. That's positive reinforcement from Heaven.

How does a person, whether saved or not, know something is true even when they have never heard it from the Bible? Remember the verse in Matthew 16:17? "Blessed are you...*because flesh and blood did not reveal [that Jesus is Lord] to you, but My Father who is in heaven [did].*" Sometimes the Father says, "Let there be light," while at other times Jesus is the Light, appearing as in the case of Saul of Tarsus in blinding light. But most often in this age, the Holy Spirit does the work. He guides. He illuminates our way. He helps us find the way so that we can know the truth and thus experience His life. The important thing to remember is that this activity doesn't start from Earth; rather, it starts from Heaven and then comes to Earth.

We Have the Advantage

When Jesus was about ready to leave the earth, He made an incredible statement to His sorrowful followers:

> *But I tell you the truth, it is to your advantage that I go away; for if I do not go away, the Helper shall not come to you; but if I go, I will send Him to you.*
>
> *But when He, the Spirit of truth, comes, He will guide you into all the truth; for He will not speak on His own initiative, but whatever He hears, He will speak; and He will disclose to you what is to come. He will glorify Me, for He will take of Mine and will disclose it to you. All things that the Father has are Mine; therefore I said that He takes of Mine and will disclose it to you* (John 16:7,13-15).

Jesus is saying to His disciples and to us, "You have the advantage. You aren't slaves any longer. You are My friends. Friends know what the Father and the Son are doing. The Holy Spirit will disclose it to you. You have a Guide; therefore, you have guidance. You have light and truth. Just like in the creation of the world, the Spirit will hear first and then create what God spoke. He will inform you of everything pertaining to life and godliness." Jesus wanted His disciples to get used to the idea of being led by the Spirit of God. This was a new deal. In the Old Testament, the Spirit came upon people of God's choosing for God's appointed purposes, but in the New Testament, the Spirit is in all believers, empowering them for action.

I want to make a definite distinction between a RHEMA and a "prophetic" prompting or sense or feeling. A prophetic prompting is what we think God is saying to us or through us to another. It may be God or it may not be God. Most people go by a prophetic prompting or a sense that what they think they are hearing is from the Lord. This is fine because many times these types of promptings are true and a blessing.

The difference between a RHEMA and what I just described is faith. RHEMA has faith attached to it. It's a faith-infused utterance from God that will resonate with you. When God speaks to you or when someone else does, faith for the utterance will come with it. The most important indicator is not whether the other person has faith for what he or she is saying, but whether the receiver of the word has faith for what is spoken. You have heard from God through the deliverer of the message. The message didn't originate with the messenger. God, speaking through him or her, validates the message by an impartation of faith for illumination, clarity, confirmation, or direction.

The Holy Spirit Guides You into Truth with Light

Have you noticed when receiving a prophecy, a word of knowledge, or a word of wisdom that some parts may resonate with you and other parts don't? Perhaps it is because the one giving the message may know in part and prophesy in part. Some parts are for you and some parts aren't. Listen for the parts that have a revelation or a "that's it; that is what I needed" element to them. That is probably the RHEMA part of the word given to you.

Or perhaps you are reading along in your Bible and the Holy Spirit gives you an aha of the verse. Suddenly, you have clarity and understanding that you didn't have before. You have so much understanding that you start to do what the verse says. You are convinced and you now have faith to apply it when you didn't have it before. You say to yourself, "Yes, this is God. I'm doing it." That is a RHEMA, and you need to know it is a RHEMA that has come from God because it has faith attached to it. That is what we live by, especially in the wilderness.

How do you know a voice is God's voice speaking to you personally or corporately? Ask yourself, "Does it sound like God? Is it biblical? Is it wise? Do people who love me and love God agree with it? Is faith attached to it? Do I have confidence that this is God? Do I have peace? Does it benefit others? Is it a blessing?" Answering these questions will help in discerning the voice of God.

Two Practical Examples of Receiving Rhema

Here's another practical example of receiving RHEMA that comes from the beginning of Jesus's ministry. The multitude was pressing around Jesus "listening to the LOGOS of God." Jesus decided to get into a boat belonging to one of the fishermen named Simon Peter, and He told him to go out a bit from the shore so everyone could hear Him while He taught. When Jesus finished speaking, He said to Simon Peter, "Put out into the deep water and let your nets down for a catch."

Peter (the professional fisherman) said to Jesus (who was carpenter), "Master, we worked hard all night and caught nothing, but at Your RHEMA [bidding] I will let down the nets." Peter sounded a bit skeptical, but he recognized something. He sensed something. He did it despite his training and experience as a fisherman. He obeyed Jesus's words because he had a faith impartation, maybe not a huge faith impartation, but enough to respond to the Lord with action.

Sensing when faith is being imparted is a big deal. People called to kingdom ministry need to know when that happens, and church is the place to learn it, they learn how to handle it and let it be part of building Jesus's church. Mature believers in the church provide guidance so young newbies don't get spooked when the Spirit starts moving.

We read on that Peter won the fishing tournament. He called over his business partners and they also caught a huge haul. A RHEMA spoken by Jesus to Peter affected and blessed others. Peter heard first and spoke and acted second. But he would have missed the whole experience if it wasn't for LOGOS and for RHEMA. Why did Jesus tell Peter to cast out the net on the other side? Because God told Him to. RHEMAS can be for practical purposes too.

Here's the final example, which provides insight into what and how to ask from God. People in the church need to know this for good swordsmanship. Good swordsmanship is not using God's Word as a vehicle to ask for anything our flesh wants; in other words, don't walk after the flesh and ask amiss. Remember, God watches over *His* Word to perform it; He doesn't watch over *our* word to perform it.

Jesus said, "If you abide in Me, and My RHEMA [faith-infused utterance from God] abides in you, ask whatever you wish, and it shall be done for you" (John 15:7 paraphrased). In other words, as we remain or abide in Christ, just like a branch of the vine abides in the vine, our desires become His desires. We are to pray for His will to be done on the earth just as it is done in Heaven. Our job is to bind whatever has been already bound in Heaven and loose whatever has already been loosed on earth. When Heaven communicates what to bind and loose, that is a RHEMA. Faith is attached to it as we hear first and then speak second.

Many Christians take John 15:7 out of context, thinking it is a free ticket to whatever they want. But that is us speaking first and then trying to make God hear second. Nimrod did that. He went *before* God. Other Christians never loose what God wants on earth as it is in Heaven because they are afraid of asking amiss. It's a message of sorts, but not if we listen to God's message. This is normal. This is the way God's kingdom works.

How a Large Church Gauges Heaven-Inspired Prayer and Rhema

I would like to introduce you to Pastor Dan Steffen of Pure Heart Church in Glendale, Arizona. We were recently talking over coffee, discussing the ideas in this book. Dan got excited because Pure Heart has set up a way to measure or gauge the ahas that happen during messages or sermons. I thought this might be helpful to many of you pastors, leaders, and intercessors, so I asked Dan to explain their method.

> As the senior pastor of Pure Heart Church in Phoenix, I am committed to helping people respond to the voice of God. I am convinced that our loving heavenly Father longs for us to hear His voice. As a good Father, His heart is to impart not only His truth but also His wisdom and direction into our hearts and minds.

I was having coffee with my friend Ed Delph at a local Starbucks, and he was downloading to me all his latest adventures (I love these moments with Ed). He started to unpack a book idea he was working on dealing with the idea of recovering RHEMA. I was intrigued. I am forty-seven years old, so I am old enough to remember when the power and blessing of RHEMA was derailed by many abuses in the church (so much more to say there, but this isn't the place). Needless to say, I was fired up to hear that Ed was going to reintroduce this life-changing experience with God to today's generation.

I told him that as Pure Heart has grown from hundreds to now thousands, it has become more and more impractical to make room in our four weekend services to share individual Pure Heart family members' RHEMA moments during the service. It was then I told Ed about a RHEMA idea we recently put into practice.

We have tapped into the power of communicating a RHEMA word from God in real time by utilizing the technology of the smartphone and launching the "text a prayer" program during each weekend service. I tell our people, "God is speaking to us all the time, and oftentimes during the teaching or worship, we have an aha moment. It's at that moment of our awareness of His voice that transformation begins. The aha moment may be the conviction to change a behavior, seek reconciliation, begin to serve, or receive an insight into our relationship with God. Maybe you are reminded of someone you love who is hurting and the Holy Spirit prompts you to pray right now."

For this reason, we have put a phone number in the weekend teaching notes that provides immediate access to the intercessory prayer team by text. People can

> reach out and have others join them in responding to the Holy Spirit.
>
> The first text our team received confirmed God was going to use this idea to help us experience RHEMA together. The first text prayer request simply read, "Pray for my uncle who is in the hospital." That was *all* the details given! The team started praying and before long the intercessor receiving that text had her own RHEMA moment. She heard, "The health issue with the uncle is related to his heart." The team began to pray specifically for this man's heart. After the team finished praying, the person who sent the original text sent another text: "So sorry I didn't give you more detail. My uncle is in the hospital with a heart condition." Our team went crazy—high fives all around.
>
> Each text is responded to with this reply: "We are praying Now! We invite you to come to the front of the stage after service for additional prayer with our prayer team. If you would like to have further contact with our prayer team, please e-mail us at the following e-mail...."

Maybe this will get us started on what the Lord would lead us to do in making sure that we are accessing light and truth within church. Marketplace ministers could do this in the mountain to which they have been assigned.

What to Do When You Don't Know What to Do

When Israel came out of Egypt into the wilderness, they had no idea where to go and what to do. Until they matured, they needed to follow God's leader as God's leader followed God and the Rock that rolled on in front of them. They were in way over their heads, and most of them knew it. The wilderness was the place where God showed them how dependent they were on hearing Him. They needed guidance and a guide. God was about to lead them through the wilderness to a place they had never seen. Their lives were in His hands.

That sounds like a new Christian to me. When I first received Jesus, I was lost in the wilderness. I needed guidance as well as a guide. I am grateful I made it to a church and met some really committed young Christian adults in a Jesus-music band. They led me as they followed Jesus. The church experience initially seemed strange, but it grew on me. I had arrived in the second stage. I could hear God's voice in others, in the pastor, and in my thoughts. But I had to learn something I had never learned before: I had to learn how to dance. An article from my column "The Church-Community Connection" for the northwest Phoenix newspaper, *The Glendale Star*, explains. I think it says all I need to say here about guidance:

> One of my favorite and least favorite things to do is dance. I'm not a natural at dancing but, of course, I married the dancing queen. Man, can Becky dance! She was trained by her father. She has more natural rhythm than Ricky Ricardo. Go figure!
>
> In my teenage years, I was onstage all over Phoenix, Arizona, playing guitar in a rock-and-roll band, so I never learned to dance. When Becky and I dance, we're like a Yugo dancing with a Ferrari. It's not fair! Mind you, I'm an expert at the hold-me-close, sway-back-and-forth, and slow-side-step stuff. But that works for one or two slow dances and then I can't fake it anymore. When you marry the dancing queen, two slow dances are not enough. Becky likes that infomercial that says, "But wait...there's more!"
>
> I'm thinking about giving in and, torture of all tortures, taking dancing lessons. I'm going to become vulnerable, teachable, and a follower for the sake of the dancing queen. I probably will like it. Don't tell Becky.

I've started thinking about dancing. I think it's incredible that even though Becky can dance circles around me, she follows me. I'm amazed that when I move my hand forward or backward, she follows. When I step on her foot accidentally, she says it's her fault because it's her job to follow. That is her role and responsibility on the dance floor. If I step on her foot anywhere else, I'm toast!

Let's consider this thought: Dancing is a type or shadow of the way we follow or abide in God. We are free beings under divine guidance! A number of years ago, before the days of social media, this idea circulated through the cyber world via a forwarded e-mail message. When I meditated on the word *guidance*, I kept seeing -dance at the end of the word. I remembered reading that doing God's will is a lot like dancing.

When two people try to lead, nothing feels right. The movement doesn't flow with the music, and everything is quite uncomfortable and jerky. When one person realizes that and lets the other lead, both bodies begin to flow with the music. One leads with gentle cues, perhaps with a nudge to the back or by pressing lightly in one direction or another. Then it's as if two become one body, moving beautifully. The dance takes surrender, willingness, and attentiveness from one person and gentle guidance and skill from the other.

My eyes drew back to the word *guidance*. When I saw "g," I thought of God, followed by "u" and "i." "God," "u" and "i" "dance." God, you, and I dance. To receive God's guidance, we must become willing to trust that the Lord of the Dance is gently leading, still proceeding, guiding us in and to His perfect light! It reminds me of God's role as leader in my life. I listen. I follow

> God's hand movements. When God speaks, I hear. What God speaks, I speak. What God sees, I see. What God does, I do to the best of my ability. God, you and I dance.
>
> That's the picture of the Hebrew word *mahanaim* in the Bible. The story is in Song of Songs 6:13. Solomon and his no-longer-swarthy wife/helpmate dance the whirlwind dance of two companies. That dance is a prophetic picture of God and humankind in sync—Christ and His body flowing together. That's a picture of the two becoming one with a leader who leads from love. As I choose to follow the Lord of my own free will, we dance!
>
> Like I said earlier, I'm starting to enjoy dancing. As I lead, Becky follows me of her own free will. I have the privilege as well as the responsibility of leading her, not driving her, in the dance of this life. We are both free beings under divine guidance with equal status but different roles. And we dance. I hope you dance.

The Israelites who learned to dance and be led by God according to this analogy made it to the Promised Land. Between the exodus and the genesis, there is always revelation.

Notes

1. Vance Havner, *Pepper 'n' Salt* (Grand Rapids, MI: Fleming H. Revell Company, 1966).
2. Used by permission of Lance Wallnau.
3. Quoted in J. D. Greear, *Gaining By Losing: Why the Future Belongs to Churches that Send* (Grand Rapids, MI: Zondervan, 2015).
4. This information is taken from http://www.pickle-publishing.com/papers/church-in-old-testament.htm, accessed March 27, 2017.

5. Remember the verse that says, *"The spirit of prophesy is the testimony or testifying of Jesus"* (Revelation 19:10). Now look at Acts 3:26*: "For you first, God raised up His Servant* (the actual word is Child, with a capital C) *and sent Him to bless you...."*

POWER THOUGHTS ON *Chapter 13*

Let's think about binding and loosing in Matthew 16:19: It says, "Whatever you bind and whatever you loose shall have already been bound and loosed in Heaven." In other words, hear what God says and then bind or loose it, not the other way around. Many people have the key but don't know how to use it. Having a key and using it correctly are two different things.

—Ed Delph

As a marketplace minister, if you are in marketing, you're not marketing; you're manifesting. If you're in managing, you're not managing; you're manifesting. You're a living epistle. Your life is a living example of the language God has spoken to you.

—Unknown

God raised us up in order to mess things up.

—Joseph Garlington[1]

Jabez had everything against him. But God wanted to turn Jabez's mess into a message. God told Jabez what to pray; Jabez prayed what God asked him to pray and then God watched over His word to perform it. That's why he was more honorable than his brothers. They made him the mayor of the city because he heard first, then spoke second.

—Ed Delph

Doing God's business is doing what God just spoke to you about your business.

—David Lake

If you don't have a check in your spirit, don't invent one.

—Unknown

As a marketplace minister, you have in your mouth what God has in His heart.

—Ed Delph

Joseph's name in Egyptian meant "God speaks through him." Pharaoh and the Egyptians recognized Joseph and named him accordingly. Not only did Joseph climb the government mountain, but he also had something to say when he got there. God spoke to Joseph and God spoke through Joseph.

—Ed Delph

The Purpose of a Boat and Fishing Business. "Sitting there, using the boat (vehicle of commerce) for a pulpit (place to speak for God), Jesus taught the crowd." (see Luke 5:3). Jesus used Peter's fishing business as a vehicle to teach and influence those outside of the church. Jesus was fishing for men. Your career is vehicle for influencing commerce...a place and space assigned to you by God to bring His presence into. Your ministry is your career and your career is your ministry.

—Drew Neal and Ed Delph

Follow the Holy Spirit's example: Wait, listen, hear, speak then do. Then the worlds we create are God's worlds and not human created worlds. God is raising up a movement of 'God U and I Dance' listeners who hear first then speak and do.

—Ed Delph

Chapter 13

Rhema in the Kingdom: Go Tell It on the Mountains—All Seven of Them

As the Son of God, Jesus is an example ***for*** *us; as the Son of Man, Jesus is an example* ***of*** *us.*
—Joshua Churchyard[2]

The Three Kings and Their Kingdoms

Jesus schooled Peter about salvation, the church, and the kingdom, and the former fisherman knew he was saved to build the church by advancing the kingdom of God. He was set to go. He was mature, he had revelation, and he knew where the keys were and what the keys did. He was large and in charge. He learned binding and loosing. He was ready to go...or was he?

Did you know that Jesus taught about three kingdoms in Matthew 16:17-19? Verse 17 makes us aware of God's kingdom when Jesus says that "flesh and blood did not reveal this to you, but My Father who is in heaven." That is God's kingdom. Then in verse 18, we are made aware of the gates of hades or satan's kingdom—Jesus came to destroy the works of the evil one (see 1 John 3:8). Finally, verse 19 reveals the last kingdom: "And I will give you the keys...and whatever you bind on earth shall have been bound in heaven and whatever you loose on earth shall have been loosed in heaven." That kingdom is the kingdom of man working under the direction of God.

If we continue to read Matthew's narrative, however, we see these three kingdoms clash in Matthew 16:21-23. Jesus gave Peter information and revelation, but Peter needed to experience his first lesson in transformation. The word was going to have to become flesh in Peter:

> *From that time Jesus began to show His disciples that He must go to Jerusalem, and suffer many things from the elders and chief priests and scribes, and be killed, and be raised up on the third day. Peter took Him aside and began to rebuke Him, saying, "God forbid it, Lord! This shall never happen to You." But He turned and said to Peter, "Get behind Me, satan! You are a stumbling block to Me; for you are not setting your mind on God's interests, but man's."*
>
> *Then Jesus said to His disciples, "If anyone wishes to come after Me, he must deny himself, and take up his cross and follow Me. For whoever wishes to save his life will lose it; but whoever loses his life for My sake will find it. For what will it profit a man if he gains the whole world and forfeits his soul? Or what will a man give in exchange for his soul?* (Matthew 16:21-26)

Jesus told Peter that He was going to the cross; He told Peter what service in the church and the kingdom was all about—denying yourself for God's sake and the sake of others. This was not what Peter was expecting. Peter tried to do kingdom ministry on Jesus before he had been equipped for ministry in the church. He tried to "bind" Jesus from going to the cross; he tried to "loose" Jesus to another destiny.

He tried to "loose" a cross-less form of Christianity on Jesus. After all, Peter had just taken a class in binding and loosing.

But Jesus knew the voice that was behind Peter's voice. He heard this voice before in the wilderness. What did Jesus do? He bound what had been already bound in Heaven. He said to Peter, "Get behind Me, satan! You are a stumbling block to Me; for you are not setting your mind on God's interests, but man's." That had to be tough on Peter. He still needed some training in ministry before he got into the big stuff in the kingdom.

This is quite an account of the three kingdoms clashing. God's kingdom was in Jesus, satan's kingdom was speaking through a man who needed to do some training and maturing, and man's kingdom was revealed in Peter who still wanted life done his way. Peter was well-intentioned but deceived.

Introducing "His Majesty, the Baby"

How was Jesus going to train Peter's hands for battle? Matthew 16:24 enlightens us. Jesus said, "If anyone desires to come after Me, let him deny himself, and take up his cross, and follow Me." God takes us from the cradle to the cross to the crown. Church is a type of wilderness where we take up the cross. Jesus built His church by taking up the cross; in fact, He set captives free by taking up the cross. Jesus died to Himself in taking up the cross. Similarly, Peter had to learn obedience by taking up his cross so he could follow Jesus into the kingdom.

Church moves us beyond the baby or flesh stage to the maturity stage. It's where we become more Christlike. Church is where we learn to live by every RHEMA that proceeds from the mouth of God. It's where we learn whose voice we are hearing. Think of it. Peter had receptors that allowed satan to talk through him just as, moments earlier, God had talked to and through Peter. When Peter said, "You are the Christ, the Son of the Living God," God was talking *to* humankind and *through* humankind. That is what we call binding and loosing, on earth as it is in Heaven. That's why we are to listen to God, and that's why we need church. There is a bit of Saul (before he became Paul) in us all. Church is where we start the journey from Saul to the apostle Paul. And the first thing we should learn in church is to hear first, speak second. Otherwise, we will be like Peter and speak first and hear second.

Peter went to the school of experience with Jesus and the Father to learn about speaking first and hearing second. Jesus recognized satan speaking through Peter (ouch!). Then the Father showed up at the Mount of Transfiguration in Matthew 17:5 and told the inner group of three (which included Peter), "Hear Him!" They were to hear first and speak second. That was a sign of maturity that comes from being in church. Church is valuable because it moves us beyond the carnal nature of "His Majesty, the Baby," to a fully devoted follower of Jesus Christ, equipped and ready to fulfill God's purposes in our own generation.

Rhema Expands God's Kingdom

In accordance with our analogy of Egypt, wilderness, and Canaan, we are now looking at how RHEMA works in Canaan. We have moved from members to ministers. The guiding verse for RHEMA in the kingdom is Matthew 16:19: "And I will give you the keys of the kingdom of heaven; and whatever you bind on earth shall have been bound in heaven, and whatever you loose on earth shall have been loosed in heaven."

Our definition of kingdom in a geographic sense is any entity or any mountain of culture that is operating contrary to the will of God. In a spiritual sense, a kingdom is any area of culture that is occupied by humanism or any other -ism that is contrary to the knowledge of God. There are areas and spiritual high places that are not under God's jurisdiction.

In a legal sense, "The earth is the Lord's, and the fulness thereof" (Psalm 24:1 KJV). God owns the earth—He has the title deed to that domain. But trespassers are possessing the domain or territory that God owns, much like the Canaanites before the Israelites took possession of Canaan. Binding and loosing is God giving power and authority to His seven-mountain representatives to be process-servers who serve legal notice and dispossess the wisdom-based trespassers. Then marketplace ministers repossess the land and bring it back under God's jurisdiction. Binding is the trespassing notice and loosing is giving it back to its legal owner.

As a marketplace minister, our primary job is to bring light into the darkness that has invaded the marketplace. Look around at your sphere of influence or your mountain in culture—whether it is the mountain of government, business, education, media, arts and entertainment, or family, it's dark there. The only place that is halfway lit is the religion mountain.

Didn't God say, "Let there be light," and light was everywhere? God created light because God is light (see 1 John 1:5). He makes all things into His own image. Light could be because light is! The Light of the World created light so it could be on earth as it is in Heaven. God speaks RHEMA to Christians in the marketplace, then those in the marketplace speak RHEMA in and to their areas of influence. That's being light in the darkness. RHEMA and LOGOS in the kingdom are what take ground and then hold the ground that was taken. Don't think that a group of committed Christians can't do much in their businesses or neighborhoods.

Seven Mountains That Need to Be Transfigured

Six days after Matthew introduces us to the kingdom of Heaven in Matthew 16:19, we see Jesus on top of a mountain in Matthew 17:1-8 with three of His disciples. Here Jesus is taking His A-team to a high mountain where He is transfigured right in front of their eyes. His face shines like the sun, and His garments become as white as light. In other words, Jesus is at the top of the mountain and giving out light. The Light of the World is illuminating the mountaintop. If I were to pick from the seven mountains of society, I would say it is the religion mountain, since Moses and Elijah show up.

Immediately, Peter sees this as a chance to be spiritual. His heart is in the right place. He has a good idea but it's not a God idea. How do I know that? As Peter speaks from his heart (which he'd done with Jesus a few verses earlier), God shows up in a bright cloud and interrupts him. A voice comes out of the cloud saying something different than the first time God said it—and this "something" changes everything: "This is My beloved Son, with whom I am well-pleased; hear Him!" The first time God made this declaration in Matthew 3:17, God said, "This is My beloved Son, in whom I am well-pleased." But notice this time God adds: "Hear Him!" Don't listen to any other voices, but hear Him! Why? Because He hears God.

That's enough for Peter, James, and John. There is no more talk. There are no more good ideas. They hit the deck. If they'd had a church at this point, it could be called Horizontal Christian Fellowship. Jesus then comes along and says, "Don't be afraid." And when they open their eyes, they see only Jesus. I realize this stretches the main meaning of this section of scripture, but we can glean important principles from this account for transforming a runaway culture.

There are seven mountains of culture that need to be transformed back into conformity with the image of Christ. After all, the earth and all its fullness are the Lord's. It all belongs to God. These cultural mountains will underachieve if they listen to any other voice but God's. That is what is happening in today's world. Runaway mountains need to be transfigured and reconfigured back into their original, normal, created design. Here are some keys for marketplace ministers.

First, we need marketplace ministers with Christian thinking who listen to Jesus at the top of each cultural mountain. The mountain didn't transfigure Jesus; rather, Jesus was transfigured first and then the mountain was filled with light. Light is needed at the top of the mountain so the mountain can be transfigured. The anointing always flows downward (see Psalm 133:2). *Transfigured people in high positions transfigure mountains; transformed leaders positioned in high places transform mountains.* People who have the light, shine. Just ask Moses and Elijah. Go light up the top of your mountain!

Second, "hear Him." It's one thing to get to the gates of the seven mountains of society, but it's another thing to have something to say when you get there. There are many Christian business owners and even Christian corporations who are at the top of their mountain, but they don't have too much to say at the top, and so they remain silent. Or they just sound like everyone else. Where's the wisdom? Where's the light? Where's the word of wisdom? Where's the word of knowledge? Where's the solution to the problem like Joseph, Nehemiah, or Daniel had? You have the keys, so go tell it and use it on the mountains.

Share the RHEMA that God has given you with those on your mountain. Adapt a lifestyle of hearing first and speaking second. God is saying to us, "I am using Jesus to talk to you." In the same way, God will be using you to speak to your spheres of influence. Don't be like Peter at this point in his life—having a great heart, but not so great at thinking things through. He didn't learn the lesson from Jesus in Matthew 16:22-23, so God came down to repeat the lesson in Matthew 17:5. I'm not trying to be like Peter, but the truth is that many of us are just like him. The lesson to Peter and to us is, "Hear Him!"

Third, transfigure your mountain as a team. Don't try to do the job alone. Form a microchurch; get a group of people together on your mountain who are motivated, who hear from God, and who have something to say, see, and share. On top of His mountain, Jesus was with a benevolent leader who listened to God most of the time. Jesus was also with a prophet who heard from God. Each listened to God, each had encounters with light, and each spoke what God spoke. Each of them dealt with high-level leaders in society, and each of them transfigured and reconfigured his area of influence. Each had a measure of grace, but together they moved from a measure of grace to grace without measure. Unity brings the anointing and the anointing breaks the yoke.

Fourth, if they can't see us, then they won't be us. We must incarnate. The Word should become flesh on top of the mountains. We need to live God's life, have real solutions to real problems, have favor with God and with others, and go tell it on the mountains. Don't worry about the results, for your job is to deliver the message in word and deed. Illuminate mountains! Illuminate nations! Let your imagination create illuminated nations.

And last, try not to build a monument to yourself like Peter wanted to do. The flesh wants to do that. Don't look at what you can do; look at what God can do. Just look at Jesus, listen to Jesus, and allow God's RHEMA to transfigure you. Then what you say will be what God wanted to say through you. That's how God transfigures mountains.

Transfiguring Your Mountain Through Illumination

The first claim we made in this book is that God speaks. God speaking and the creation of light by the Holy Spirit is called illumination. In First Corinthians 2:10-16, God speaks to the Spirit, and then He speaks through the Spirit to us. When we have ears to hear His voice, we get illumination. We speak that illumination "not in words taught by human wisdom, but in those taught by the Spirit, combining spiritual thoughts and spiritual words" to people in the world. In that way, God says through us, "Let there be light" in the darkness, and there is light. Eyes can't see without light. Real sight comes from real light, and that only comes from hearing an utterance from God. Hearing comes before seeing. Sight needs light. No light, no sight. Illumination comes from hearing God.

Here is the process: when God wants to create something, He simply speaks what He is thinking. The Holy Spirit hears what God speaks, and then the Holy Spirit says it to our spirit and mind. If we have ears to hear, then we will hear what the Spirit is saying. We combine our spiritual thoughts with spiritual words, which don't come from us but come from God. The Word speaks to you a word before you speak a word.

God says to the Spirit, "Let there be light" (or what God wants done and said), then the Holy Spirit says to our spirit, "Let there be light" (or what God wants done or said). If we are listening, we say, "Let there be light" (or what God wants done or said). Where did that word (RHEMA) come from? *We are hearing an utterance that provides illumination, clarity, or direction.* That's what Jesus meant in the Lord's Prayer when He said, "Thy will be done on earth as it is in heaven." RHEMA is a vehicle of God for "Thy kingdom come, Thy will be done!" I call this process *illumination, revelation, transformation, and then perspiration.*

> *How blessed are the people who know the joyful sound! O Lord, they walk in the light of Your countenance* (Psalm 89:15).

Those who hear the joyful sound of the Lord shall walk in the light of His countenance as well as in the light of the Lord. That's illumination, clarity, and direction as we hear first and speak second.

Go Tell It on the Mountains

To those of you working in the marketplace, raising children, retired, or anywhere outside the church walls, it's time to bring the light into the darkness. In order to be effective, however, you need an ear to hear prophetic insights given by the heavenly "insighter" that will occasionally make you seem like an inciter to a stubborn crowd. The time is now to understand, embrace, and utilize the prophetic ministry of Jesus. It's an awareness issue. It's time for marketplace ministers to discover RHEMA, uncover RHEMA, and recover RHEMA so they can change the other six cultural mountains.

Put yourself in a position to succeed by hearing wisdom from God. The best way to do that is to say to the Lord, "Lord, what do You want to say about this business problem, this relationship problem, this financial decision, this promotion opportunity, this possible expansion, this marketing strategy that's not producing?" It's time to say, "Lord, what do You want to do today? What contacts should I make? Whom should I hire? Whom should I fire? What word of wisdom would turn this conflict into a win-win rather than a win-lose?" Worldly wisdom is Clark Kent, but godly illumination is Superman. As Christians who serve God in the marketplace, we have the advantage.

You give God a face and voice within your community. You are filled so you can be spilled. You are a carrier and a courier. You bring the gift of prophetic insight—the voice of God—into a space that needs it. You bring in strategy that is beyond the realm of human reasoning. You bring in a word of wisdom from God. You bring in Christian core values that carry within them the power to create wealth and societal lift. You are an example and a model of wisdom in action, creating influence. You fill the spaces with the glory of the Lord. You bring a servant-leader approach to leadership. You bring unlimited possibilities that would not be options without you. You have a resource that is beyond human education and logic. You have that capacity, and you hopefully have that competency.

When you engage your sphere of influence (your mountain), be like Jesus and look for people who will follow you as you follow Jesus, and then make disciples where you are. The best this world can get is you being you with God all over you. Your roots are in church, but your fruits are in the community. If you're in marketing, then you're not merely marketing; you're manifesting. If you're in management, then you're not merely managing; you're manifesting. Whatever your mountain, you're manifesting. You are making God known outside the church walls. Your career is your ministry and your ministry is your career. You have in your hands what God has in His heart. Let there be light! Let there be a spiritual fountain on top of each mountain!

Consider the seven mountains, or spheres of influence, in society. The problem is not the mountain of government; rather, the problem is that we don't have enough Christians with Christian thinking and values in government. The problem is not the mountain of business; rather, the problem is that we don't have enough Christians with Christian thinking and values in business. The problem is not the mountain of education; the problem is that we don't have enough Christians with Christian thinking and values in education. The problem is not the mountains of media, arts and entertainment, or family per se; rather, the problem is that we don't have enough Christians with Christian thinking and values with the power to influence these mountains.

Kingdom people have always had illumination, but they are not always in a place to use the illumination. Just like Daniel, Joseph, Esther, and Nehemiah were fountains at the top of their mountains, so some of us can and will be too. Culture is transformed from the top down, not the bottom up. We need to be people of influence in places of influence, wherever God has assigned us. Let the Word give you God-inspired, God-breathed, God-empowered RHEMA before you speak a word. The times we are living in require it.

Let There Be Kingdom Light—Outside the Church Walls

At the beginning of this chapter, I quote Joshua Churchyard of Church of the Way in Benoni, South Africa, near Johannesburg. Here is what he says: "As the Son of God, Jesus is an example *for* us. As the Son of Man, Jesus is an example *of* us." That is a profound statement. Jesus the Son of Man was showing us the potential we have, and as Son of Man He was an example of Adam before the fall. Adam walked and talked with God. He experienced God's presence. He experienced Heaven on earth. But as an example *of* us, Jesus limited Himself to doing only what the Father told Him to do. He could have called legions of angels to help Him, but He didn't. Why not? It was because He wanted to show us what it means to be a child of God, a Christian. The word *Christian* means "a little Christ." Little Christs take orders from headquarters. That is the life we were meant to live.

Looking at the ministry of Jesus, we see what He did to show us what we could do if we heard first and spoke second. He wanted us to see what humanity experienced in the garden before the fall. *He was an example of us, if we, like Him, hear first and speak second.* Watch what He did. As Christians, we could do every one of the examples seen below—at least, the potential is certainly there. God is raising up Christians who are ready to do "greater works" atop the seven mountains that need to be transfigured. Jesus serves as an example *for* us and maybe even *of* us in the marketplace or our sphere of influence. As the example of us, He took on the form of the Son of Man. He limited Himself to being dependent on God. How would you like to run your business that way?

He "Forthtold" the Past with the Woman at the Well

> [Jesus said,] *"For you have five husbands, and the one whom you now have is not your husband."...The woman said to Him, "Sir, I perceive that You are a prophet"* (John 4:18-19).

The woman at the well heard the spirit of prophecy, which is the testimony of Jesus! Where did Jesus get that revelation? The Father told Him. Just like God in Genesis, Jesus said, "Woman, let there be light," and there was light. Jesus called her out of darkness and into His marvelous light. He spoke to her what God told Him to speak. She *heard an utterance from God spoken to her concerning her past and present life that provided illumination, clarity, and direction.* His insight illuminated her foresight.

Jesus Discerned Churches

> *To the angel at the church of Sardis write..."I know your deeds, that you have a name that you are alive, but you are dead. Wake up, and strengthen the things that remain..."* (Revelation 3:1-2).

Why did Jesus say this to this church? It was because God told Him to say it. Do you see this? The world would have said to the church of Sardis, "Wow, this church is alive—look at all the ministries, observe all the people, look what the Lord has done!" But the church was in gross darkness. God said, "Jesus, let there be light," and there was light and truth.

He Foretold Coming Events

> *For John baptized with water, but you will be baptized with the Holy Spirit not many days from now* (Acts 1:5).

Jesus foretold and He also "forthtold." How could He know what was going to happen in the future? It was because the Father told Him. Let there be light and there was light. Jesus spoke an utterance from God to Peter so he would be ready for what was going to happen. That communication was for illumination.

He Looks Beyond What Is Evident

> [Jesus said to those standing by,] *"He who is without sin among you, let him be the first to throw a stone at her."... And Jesus said* [to her], *"Go. From now on sin no more"* (John 8:7,11).

A woman was caught in adultery, and the religious right was going to stone the lady. Jesus's response to them opened the eyes of their hearts. Their motives were exposed. Where did Jesus get the wisdom for what He said to the religious leaders? God spoke to Him. Jesus heard first and spoke second. He heard the Father. The wisdom confounded the religious group. They had nowhere to go but out of there. Jesus was, in effect, reliving God's account of creation: let there be light and there was light.

He Revealed Coming Events to Prepare Us

> *For nation will rise against nation, and kingdom against kingdom, and in various places there will be famines and*

> *earthquakes. But all these things are merely the beginning of birth pangs* (Matthew 24:7-8).

Sometimes life is scary. Things go on in the nations—wars and rumors of wars, earthquakes, famines and the like. If we aren't prepared for this, then they could limit our effectiveness at a time when the world might need us the most. God wants us to be prepared. We aren't slaves; we are sons, so we know what the Father is doing. We are family. We are His body. He prepares us beforehand. He speaks to us and He lets us know that despite the horrible circumstances going on around us, He has the big picture under control. He will speak to us so we are prepared to be able to speak to others. Let there be light and there was light, and the light was good.

He Was Sensitive and Discerned God's Timing

> *So Jesus said to them, "My time is not yet here, but your time is always opportune"* (John 7:6).

Jesus knew that in God's divine timetable, His trip to the cross was not yet at hand. How did He know that? Because the Father said it. Notice how Jesus heard first and then spoke second. Remember, as the Son of Man, Jesus lived by every RHEMA that proceeded out of the mouth of God. He learned to discern. You and I can do that too in the marketplace if we learn to hear first, speak second.

He Heard and Then Spoke Provision for God Intersections

> *And He said to them, "Behold, when you have entered the city, a man will meet you carrying a pitcher of water; follow him into the house that he enters. And you shall say to the owner of the house, 'The Teacher says to you, "Where is the guest room in which I may eat the Passover with My disciples?"'"*(Luke 22:10-11)

How did Jesus know this? God spoke it first. Remember, as the Son of Man, Jesus needed to hear from God first and then speak second.

He Foretold Demonic Betrayals, Yet Went by God's Timing

> *And He answered, "He who dipped his hand with Me in the bowl is the one who will betray Me"* (Matthew 26:23).

How did Jesus know that Judas would betray Him? It was because God spoke to Him and there was light.

He Brought a Whole New View of the Ways of God

> *And His disciples asked Him, "Rabbi, who sinned, this man or his parents, that he would be born blind?" Jesus answered, "It was neither that this man sinned, nor his parents; but it was so that the works of God might be displayed in him"* (John 9:2-3).

Jesus knew the exact reason for this man's illness. Common logic at the time didn't have a place for anything other than karma. Jesus, via hearing from the Father, brought a much larger view of God's ways.

He Recognized God-Inspired Revelation

> *Simon Peter answered, "You are the Christ, the Son of the living God." And Jesus said to him, "Blessed are you, Simon Barjona, because flesh and blood did not reveal this to you, but My Father who is in heaven"* (Matthew 16:16-17).

Jesus knew when the voice of God had spoken to someone. And you can too.

He Recognized Evil's Voice in Others

> *Peter took Him aside and began to rebuke Him, saying, "God forbid it, Lord! This shall never happen to you." But He turned and said to Peter, "Get behind Me, satan! You are a stumbling block to me..."* (Matthew 16:22-23).

Jesus knew other voices too. Why? It was because He was used to hearing God's voice.

He Discerned Those Who Were Seeking God

> *Now there was a man of the Pharisees, named Nicodemus, a ruler of the Jews; this man came to Him by night and said to Him, "Rabbi, we know that You have come from God..."* (John 3:1-2).

Because God sees the heart, Jesus could see the heart of Nicodemus.

He Interceded with God's Heart for a Disobedient Nation

> *Jerusalem, Jerusalem, who kills the prophets and stones those who are sent to her! How often I wanted to gather your children together, the way a hen gathers her chicks under her wings, and you were unwilling. Behold, your house is being left to you desolate* (Matthew 23:37-38).

God assigned Jesus the ministry of intercession for us (see Hebrews 7:25). He heard God assign Him this ministry, and He faithfully did it.

He Foretold Peter's Failure and Lifted Peter's Future

> *Simon, Simon, behold, satan has demanded permission to sift you like wheat; but I have prayed for you, that your faith may not fail; and you, when once you have turned again, strengthen your brothers* (Luke 22:31-32).

We can be either accusers or intercessors. The devil is the accuser, but Jesus is the intercessor. He fulfills His ministry because He heard from God.

Listen to Him

Everything Jesus did was prophetic. This was so he could go and tell it and show it on the mountains of this world. How did Jesus do this? Listen to what God says in Matthew 17:5: "This is My beloved Son, with whom I am well-pleased; listen to Him!" Why are we to listen to Jesus? It is because He hears from God. He listens to God. Jesus hears first and speaks second. God is telling the three disciples, "Get the blueprint, Peter, James, and John—and all the other Christians who follow!" Illumination comes first, then communication. Inspiration, revelation, transformation, and then comes perspiration. Let the Word give you a word before you speak a word. Just like God and Jesus, you can say, "Let there be light," wherever you go. While Jesus is in the world, He is the Light of the World, but after Jesus leaves the earth, we will be the light of the world, a city set on a hill. God is light (see 1 John 1:5), Jesus is light (see John 9:5), and Christ-followers are light too (see John 5:14). Jesus said: "He who sent Me is true; and the things which I heard from Him, these I speak to the world" (John 8:26), and "I do nothing on my own initiative, but I speak these things as the Father taught me" (John 8:28).

Upgrading Your Business or Career

God is more concerned about His kingdom coming and His will being done on earth than we are. We have the capacity within us to see this happen via the Holy Spirit. We need to increase our competency. Capacity is what God created you to have on the inside, while competency is what you can do to unleash your capacity. Capacity is Christ in you, but competency is you in Christ. Increase your competency by hearing what God is saying in the kingdom and on the mountains and you will unleash your capacity in influencing your mountain.[3]

Dancing on the Mountaintops to See His Kingdom Come

The following is a chart that Alan Platt of the Doxa Deo Church Network and his team designed to show how cultural transformation starts first with God, then goes through His people to all the cultural influencers in a nation, city, or community. We listen to Him as we ascend the seven mountains of society (Doxa Deo uses eight as seen in this chart) to shift their spiritual realities. We increase so we can inherit.

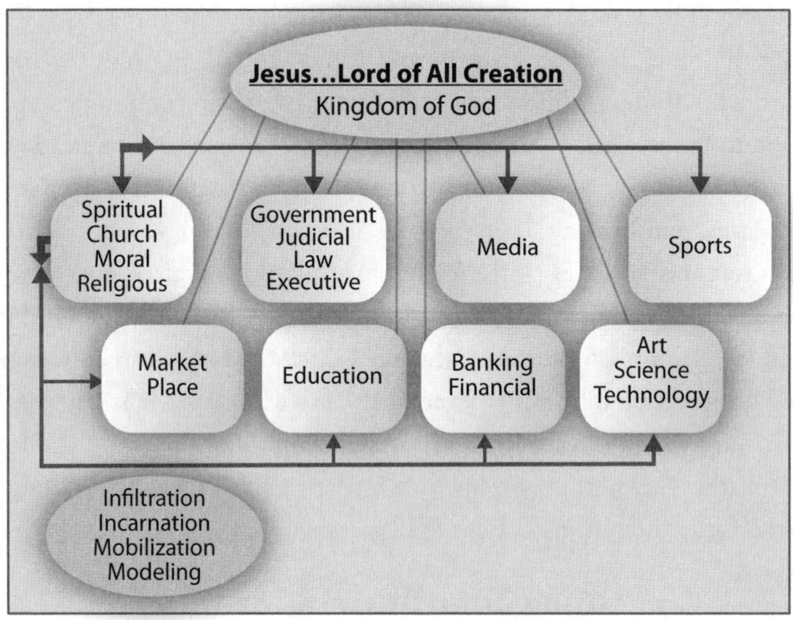

Until we reform, we only revisit. Someday is today and that someone is you. Climb every mountain—all seven of them. Then go tell it on the mountains! When Jesus shows up to transfigure the mountain, start dancing on the mountaintop to see His kingdom come. I hope you dance.

Notes

1. I heard Joseph Garlington say this is one of his sermons at a conference I was attending.
2. Used by permission of Joshua Churchyard.
3. For information on Ed Delph's seminars, including one discussing competency and capacity, visit NationStrategy's website at http://nationstrategy.com/nationstrategy-seminars/.

POWER THOUGHTS ON *Chapter 14*

We can often do more by doing less. God is not particularly interested in quantity production. That is an American standard, not a biblical standard.

—Vance Havner[1]

Don't take the edge off your spirituality on the grindstone of this world. Let it sharpen your ax but not dull it. Everything depends on how you hold the blade! This world will either sharpen your testimony or blunt it. As evil as it is, it can be made to serve a good purpose. After all, you can't sharpen an ax on a cake of butter.

—Vance Havner[2]

A Spirit-filled American and a Spirit-filled Russian will get along. A Spirit-filled white man and a Spirit-filled man of any other color will get along. A Spirit-filled employer and a Spirit-filled employee will get along. Spirit-filled husbands and wives, parents and children, neighbors, will get along. That is the only brotherhood of man that will ever work. Here is the true Fatherhood of God, known only to born-again heart-believers in Jesus Christ.

—Vance Havner[3]

Chapter 14

Illuminating Leaders, Influencers, and Mind Molders

It's one thing to get to the gates of the seven mountains of society. It's quite another thing to have something to say when you get to the gates of the mountains.
—Ed Delph

Here is a wisdom principle for those of you who pastor churches, own businesses, or are involved in any of the seven mountains (or community spheres of influence). It has to do with growth and influence. Solomon, who was the wisest man who ever lived, understood the principle of both/and. He understood the principle of growing up into all aspects *and* combining all the elements of an initiative to bring the initiation to fullness and completion. The points below on Solomon came from my book *Church@Community* that I wrote in 2005. It is as relevant today as then.

Let me ask you a couple of questions: What three elements need to come together in a church for the church to influence or have the potential to change a community for the better? What three elements made the queen of Sheba lightheaded? Let's look at the following verses and draw out another "three-legged stool" of wisdom.

> *So King Solomon became greater than all the kings of the earth in riches and in wisdom* (1 Kings 10:23).
>
> *All the earth was seeking the presence of Solomon, to hear his wisdom which God had put in his heart* (1 Kings 10:24).
>
> *When the queen of Sheba perceived all the wisdom of Solomon, the house that he had built...*(1 Kings 10:4).

The three elements of this stool are having revelation, having a model, and having a platform. First, you need a revelation from God, something to say that is biblically correct, spiritually accurate, or a dream or an idea that comes from God. Without this revelation, you will have nothing to say. Second, you need a model or something to see—a model where God's revelation has become a reality. And third, you need a platform, something to share with others that we shared with you. You are a sample of God's example for others. Let's further explore these concepts.

Something to Say: Solomon Heard from God

Let's explore the first element of *revelation*. First, Solomon had a revelation regarding wisdom. He had illumination on the concept of wisdom. Flesh and blood did not reveal wisdom to him; like Peter in Matthew 16:17, Solomon received his revelation directly from God. The concept of wisdom went from his head to his heart and then to his feet. I call that the "head-heart-feet" principle. The Word became flesh and dwelt among them. It started from Heaven, but it ended up in a real and tangible way on earth. God's revelation to Solomon gave him something to say and something to do. Revelation often works that way.

Solomon's life was purpose-driven around wisdom. He incarnated wisdom. He was not some academic who professed or spoke about wisdom; he was a practitioner of it. The world needed answers and Solomon had the answers to give. He had something special that was uniquely his, and he lived it. The Bible says that all the earth came to hear the wisdom God had put into his heart.

If Solomon had lived in New Testament times, we could say that he was "making known the manifold wisdom of God through the church to the rulers and authorities in heavenly places" (see Ephesians 3:10). Solomon had a revelation on wisdom. However, a revelation on wisdom and a house built on wisdom are two different things entirely.

Something to See: Moving from Revelation to Reality

The second element that will make the "queens" of our communities faint is *model*. Solomon did not merely talk about a model; he had a model that legitimized his revelation on wisdom. The queen of Sheba perceived all the wisdom of Solomon (revelation), and then, according to First Kings 10:7, she saw ("my eyes had seen it") that his revelation worked. This was not theory or hopeful thinking. Solomon possessed both revelation and reality. He made the intangible tangible. The incredible became credible. His evidence demanded a verdict. As Proverbs 9:1 suggests, wisdom has built her house and boy, was it awesome! Revelation without a model will not influence the influencers of the earth. Revelation must always be backed up by model. People of wisdom know this.

Something to Share: Revelation from God Is for Blessing Others

The third element that will make queens faint is what I call *platform*. Platform is the ability to get the word about the revelation and the model out into the community. It is a media issue for the church, business, or revelation. In the case of Solomon, the word-of-mouth method was used and "all the earth was seeking the presence of Solomon." All the earth came for a "home tour" of the house that wisdom built. Solomon had the ability and model to get the word out into all the world. The model was not an end; rather, it was meant to influence the influencers of the world for God. The wisdom of God became real and tangible to the whole world.

This was not about Solomon; rather, this was about a deposit of wisdom into the world for others. The return was the queen of the south hearing about the fame of Solomon concerning the name of the Lord. Solomon, like Jesus, grew in stature and favor with God and others. As a result, he influenced the influencers in a redemptive way. It was a way that the earth could be filled with the glory of God. Platform is essential in creating a "community shift" back to God.

I don't know about you, but I would have liked to have seen Jerusalem in the days of Solomon. I would have loved to have seen and experienced the convergence of revelation, model, and platform all at the same time. Solomon had all the tools in his toolbox. Wisdom understands excellence. Wisdom also understands that no one person or no single church can be excellent in all areas all the time. However, we can pursue excellence and we can be unusually good because excellence draws people to the glory of God.

The church today needs to have these three elements working together to influence the "queens of Sheba" back to God. Possessing one or two of the elements is incomplete. I have been to many churches that have a great "revelation" and yet experience church split after church split. The model is not one that draws healthy people, only dysfunctional people who are looking for a source of significance and security. Other churches are stable and may even be known nationally, but they possess little revelation. Still others have revelation and even a good model, but no one has ever heard of them. They might have favor with God but not favor with people. This is not wise.

A word to those of you in business or other spheres of influence: this principle is true for you also. Your business can grow and thrive if you have a revelation or something that you do that is uniquely yours. Your business needs to be a good model and as well managed as possible. Finally, you need to advertise and get the word out about your business. When you combine revelation, model, and platform, you will usually have success and influence. That's how you cause marketplace ministers from the government mountain to faint like the queen of the south.

My Four Crucial Career Intersections

If you want examples of God speaking to me, I've got lots of them. I could share about how God led my incredible wife, Becky, and me together. I could tell you about particular instances where a Jacob's ladder at the right time assured me, brought clarity, and propelled me further along the path of life. I could tell you about the time right before Christmas at my then-brother-in-law's house when I experienced what I think was an actual appearance of Christ. I could tell you about how God clearly spoke to me, "Jesus is Lord," at my conversion on a snowmobile at three in the morning on a golf course in Pinetop, Arizona. But there are four clarion instances where RHEMA provided illumination and direction in my career path. They may be helpful to marketplace ministers or to those called to ministry outside their churches. Your career is important and holy to God. Your roots are in church but your fruits will be in the community.

Gently Leading, Still Proceeding: The Exodus to Central Bindery

Like how God led Joseph and Mary out of Nazareth to Bethlehem, in 1974 God started repositioning me into my purpose and destiny. Twenty-four years old and equipped with a bachelor's degree in personnel management, I was working as office manager for Grimshaw Mortuaries in Phoenix, Arizona. The company had close to eighty employees, four mortuaries, and one cemetery. I was the secretary of the corporation.

In March of that year, I had received Christ as my Lord and Savior. It was quite a conversion. Right away, I could sense that something was different. I immediately knew I was supposed to leave Grimshaw and start a new business. A print-shop owner from my church mentioned a small book bindery he knew that was for sale. The owners were quite elderly and ready to retire, and the business had dwindled down to a few accounts.

I knew nothing about book binding or printing. My vast experience in the industry was printing funeral folders at the mortuary. I looked at another business, but there was something about the bindery that caught my attention. I was a new Christian, but this was the business for me. I wasn't aware of it, but I had received faith from God for the purchase of that business. It wasn't presumption or a wish dream; rather, it was *a faith-infused utterance from God providing illumination and direction*. From that point on, it was done in Heaven. It just needed to be done on earth. We entered negotiations. And with the helpful eye of my father's wisdom and business sense, we bought the business. That was the start of what is now Central Bindery in Phoenix, Arizona.

I was twenty-four years old and had never been a business owner. I had little to no knowledge of the book-binding industry. The one employee I hired as supervisor was a printing machine operator. The business was dying. The machinery was old. My main competitor was large, territorial, and intimidating. But I had one thing that trumped them all: I had God on my side (more accurately, I was on God's side). I didn't deserve it. I didn't earn it. God gave me the opportunity to be part of what He was doing in my life and many other people's lives also.

The first few years were interesting to say the least. What a learning curve! We built the airplane while it was flying. There were some spins and stalls. God had to carry us at times. I was under construction, and the business was under construction too. There was a whole lot of shaking going on. But after three years, everything started to come together. We became efficient and proficient. We expanded and bought new quality equipment. We formed the greatest team of people I have ever known in the business world.

By the time I was twenty-nine, Central Bindery was the largest book bindery in Arizona, with more than forty employees. The business was running as smoothly as any service business does. I had something to say, something to see, and something to share. I should have been happy, right? I'd arrived—or so I thought. There was something that was changing inside me. Something was stirring. The season was changing. We don't change seasons; we adjust to them. Today, my brother owns Central Bindery and it's grown even larger than when I owned it. Not only did the business change my life, but it also changed my brother's.

What was the key to this? *God spoke and I listened to what He had to say.* It was the same principle as in the creation of the earth. "*Let there be light," and there was light, and God saw that the light was good.* God was gently leading, still proceeding me to His dream, weaving me into His tapestry. And that's a nice place to be.

Gently Leading, Still Proceeding: The Exodus to Being a Single Singles Pastor

While I still owned Central Bindery, the pastor who led me to the Lord, Jerry Landrey, telephoned me one day. That call in 1979 changed my life. Jerry said he was going to Indonesia to speak at some pastors' conferences, and he asked me if I wanted to go with him. All I asked was, "Where is Indonesia?" A few months later, now as a five-year-old Christian, I accompanied Jerry to Jakarta, Malang, and Denpasar, Indonesia. There I met Dr. Harvey Lifsey of Christian Dynamics, which was the ministry conducting the pastors' conferences. Seeing it was my first time overseas, I was stunned by what I experienced. Dr. Lifsey was inspirational and anointed. His speaking introduced me to my first real encounter with RHEMA.

When I listened to him, the Bible came alive. It was truth, but somehow it was more than truth. It was light. It was illumination. It was relatable and it applied to me. Bible verses I knew by memory suddenly jumped off the page. I understood those verses; I didn't just have knowledge about them. For the first time since my salvation experience, I was exposed to both swords. I would never be the same again. Now I had a framework for illumination. I knew by experience the aha moment. Even though I didn't know the word RHEMA, I received a RHEMA on RHEMA.

Flying back from that trip, somewhere between Jakarta and Hong Kong, God spoke to me: "Sell the business. You are now going into the ministry." I was shocked. But His voice was just as clear as when I bought Central Bindery. My first response was, "This can't be You, God. God, do You know how much they pay those pastors?" But God was speaking. It was obvious. This was the next step to something greater. God was weaving the tapestry of my life and many other people's lives. I had faith that it was going to happen. I was like Mary with Gabriel, "Be it done to me according to Your RHEMA."

When I arrived home, I told my father what God had spoken to my heart. My dad is the best businessman I have ever known, having more natural business sense than anyone I had ever met. When I told my father that I wanted to sell the business, he was surprised but nice. He must of thought I was crazy. I imagined him saying to himself, "Sell the business? Is he crazy? He doesn't even know what he has done. Businesses are hard to grow. He has it made." All those thoughts are rational, but when you walk with God, it can get a bit crazy at times.

Central Bindery sold for a large sum of money nine months later, on April 1, 1980. Six years earlier, I had put my last $3,000 into it, and that seed had multiplied exponentially. The business was both successful and significant, having changed the bindery-and-printing culture in Phoenix by being customer-oriented and the first in Arizona to use vastly superior machinery. Efficiency and productivity were increased. Central Bindery also teamed with many then-new print shops that are now some of the largest in the industry. We found new owners to grow with and we all grew together.

There I was, thirty years old, single, unemployed, but with some money. I had a word to go into ministry. I had no seminary degree or formal Bible teaching, but I was attending a singles ministry at Grace Community Church in Tempe, Arizona. Grace was fundamental and their ministers had more degrees than a thermometer.

I started my pursuit for ministry by interviewing at several churches to be a singles pastor. I started with what I had: I'm single, I know something about singles ministry since I attend one, and I have an undergraduate degree. At that time, singles ministry was quite a new phenomenon. Most just dismissed me right away because I had no degree in ministry. All I needed was one church.

The singles ministry I was attending at Grace Community Church had almost four hundred singles in the church's Sunday school program. I played the guitar and was part of the group that led worship, and I eventually began teaching from time to time. The ministry became so large that the church leadership decided they needed an assistant singles pastor. Well, there I was. I was respected by the singles but had no theology degree, but I was cheap because I had some money. I had desire and a heart for singles.

They hired me despite my lack of degree. That was a miracle in itself. Those church guys liked those degrees. In September 1980, I became an assistant pastor at Grace Community Church. God had made a way where there seemed to be no way. Remember what David quoted Gabriel as saying earlier in this book: "No RHEMA spoken by God will not happen"? It never even occurred to me to worry at this point. I had received *a faith-infused utterance from God, giving me clarity and direction in the next step of my life*. I was to be a singles pastor at Grace Community Church for the next seven years (with up to 550 singles) then at Northwest Community Church (with up to 275 singles) in the Metro Phoenix area. Incidentally, the singles ministry at Grace is where I met Becky, my wife and ministry partner since 1983. When you are in God's will by hearing first, speaking second, you find other treasures too. You also change others' lives forever.

But the times were changing as I entered into my eighth year as a singles pastor. Eight is the number of new beginnings. I loved being a singles pastor—I had something to say, something to see, and something to share. But that was yesterday, and yesterday was about to be gone. The "this" was now a "that." Time to adjust to a new season yet once again!

Gently Leading, Still Proceeding: The Exodus to Being a Lead Pastor

From 1982 to 1987, I was singles pastor at Northwest Community Church. It was a wonderful experience where I got to see the singles ministry grow from sixteen singles in the autumn of 1982 to 275 singles by early 1987. The church had grown too. When I started there in 1982, the attendance was about eight hundred people, but by early 1987, there were over three thousand. As a result of the growth, the church facilities needed to expand, so we purchased land at the high prices everyone was paying at that time. Finances were tight. Then the early north winds began to blow preceding Black Monday in October 1987. Offerings decreased along with people's incomes.

In financial crises, generally the first pastors to be let go are the singles pastors. Not only was I a singles pastor, but I had an assistant singles pastor too. I knew one of us would have to go, so I chose to leave but not because of any of the outside influences I mentioned. God was speaking to me once again, and I knew it.

I had been thinking, dreaming, wishing, and wanting to start a church with both Spirit and truth—one that embraced the fullness of Christ, not just one theme or theology emphasis. The fundamentalists were right—well, partially—and the "Spirit-filled" side of the church was right—again, partially. It seemed like each side had what the other needed (much like a marriage). Both the gift-driven and the theology-driven churches were still lacking, wanting and in need of building up into the fullness of Christ.

After allowing God to speak to me in many ways—through others, through circumstances, through the LOGOS of God, and to my innermost being—a group of thirty-six believers started Hosanna Christian Fellowship in the autumn of 1987. That first year, we moved seven times to different rental locations. We called ourselves "The Church on the Move." We grew numerically with no logical explanation. Everything we did broke the church-growth gurus' latest laws. The first 20 percent of every dollar that came in went to missions. We learned about prophecy. We learned about apostolic ministry. We reached the nations. We were deep and wide. We had a strong desire to do what we sensed God wanted to do. It was a fascinating time. It was special and we knew it. But many sensed that ours was a temporary church, "John the Baptist" type of church, a prophetic church that was making the way for something greater. It would be a church for a reason and for a season.

After one year, we knew we needed to build, and I was amazed by the response of the people. Everyone had faith for it. It was expensive, but it never occurred to any of us that this was a big commitment. I gladly signed a personal guarantee. It was a "no brainer" because I had received *a faith-infused utterance from God giving illumination and direction* for the church.

Several years later, our services were near a thousand in attendance. Hosanna, although it wasn't the biggest church in Phoenix, had tremendous influence in the city. I could go on and on about what the church did, but suffice it to say that God initiated and caused the church to grow despite itself. It was birthed prophetically to announce the "Jesus" of apostolic ministry and bring apostolic ministry into the mainstream of Christianity.

God was up to something in my life again. All three stages of my career occurred to get me to the fourth stage of my life. It was time to adjust for yet another season. God wanted to reposition me. My time as a lead pastor was coming to an end. A new season was on its way.

Gently Leading, Still Proceeding: The Exodus to an Apostolic Ministry Called NationStrategy

A time came when I was Hosanna's lead pastor that I knew I needed to minister in and to the nations. God kept prodding me: "Go to the nations. Go to the nations." I felt like I did when I sold Central Bindery. "What is this, God?" I asked. "I'm happy. I'm paid. I have a staff. I love the people. I have something to say, something to see, and something to share. Why should I give all this up?" But I couldn't get any peace. I couldn't go forward and I was slowing the church down. I was a bottleneck.

I brought in two organizational counselors who did a study of the church. They both said to me in a meeting, "Ed, you have two choices: you can minister to eight hundred people or you can change the world." I thought that it wasn't fair—they knew what I would say to that. That did it. "Okay, Lord, I've been down this road before."

Near the end of 2000, several members of the board of directors and I started NationStrategy, which is a nonprofit organization that pastors pastors and leads leaders. To pastors, we are a resource ministry or "guide by their side" in building their churches for their communities. To community and church leaders, we help them envision and empower them for community transformation. We inspire. We care for. We equip. That's called apostolic ministry. That's what apostles do.[4]

In the last sixteen years, we have spoken in well over seven thousand church or community settings. I have been in or ministered in more than a hundred countries. I have written ten books. I have earned my doctorate in faith and culture from Phoenix University of Theology. And I have raised up successors in the Philippines and the United States.

But the most important aspect of my changing career testimony is this: at each intersection or place of advancement, God was there. He wasn't mystical. He wasn't hard to hear. God spoke when I needed a "let there be light" moment, and God provided the faith to do it.

When I needed a RHEMA, it wasn't hard to hear. And each time, as Every Nation leader Steve Murrell says, it wasn't mystical; it was missional. And honestly, most of it wasn't for me; rather, it was for me being where I am supposed to be in God's tapestry so that it uplifts everyone around me. Each successive promotion was both necessary and a learning experience. I learned lessons at Central Bindery that I still apply today. The same is true with singles ministry and being a lead pastor.

If I can work with God in this way, then so can you too. Both swords of the Lord are your weapons—use them. And always build the way God builds. Listen for God's voice so that you will have something to say. Do what you hear God say so you will have something to see. Once what you have heard becomes what they see, something real and tangible, then you will have something to share. When that happens, it opens minds, it opens hearts, and it opens doors of influence into the mountains. It gives you a passport into the mountains. It makes kings and queens faint. You are difference makers with the X factor: you hear God because you know God and know God's voice.

Rhema in Business: David Lake's Journey of Working for God

I (David) never wanted to be in business. I got into the swimming pool industry in 1995 and had a measure of success working for others. I was happy working a good-paying job, collecting my check on payday, and living life. It was nice because I never thought about work unless I was at work. After all, I didn't own the company.

When 2008 rolled around, the economy crashed. My good-paying, secure job was no longer good-paying or secure. Although I was one of the last to be laid off, there was no compensation package. I had no problem believing that God was going to provide for me; He had repeatedly proved over the years that He would take care of me. The only question I had for God was what He wanted me to do next.

I had no money to officially go into business for myself, so I figured I would help people build their swimming pools by consulting for them. They would be the subcontractors and I would point them in the right direction. A couple of people had asked me to do this very thing even though I did not know the people who contacted me. I built their pools and made a little bit of money.

About this time, however, my mother sold some land she had inherited from my grandparents. She suggested I go into business for myself and offered to pay for the license to get started. After I got the license, business continued to be slow. I did some pool-service work and various other jobs God gave me to make a living. A short time later, however, a gentleman approached me regarding the use of my business license. He said he had a financial backer and they wanted to make me the construction manager and pay me a salary if I would help them build the company. I agreed to come on board and we began to build the business.

My task was building the processes of the construction part of the business, working on pricing, and creating a price worksheet that sales could use to sell the pools. We rented offices, hired salespeople, and set up product displays. Salespeople began meeting with potential clients and selling pools. We had a handful of contracts. It seemed like a good start.

It was during this time that God opened a door for me to go on a mission trip. I left on a two-week trip, and when I returned home, the general manager requested a meeting. He informed me that the investor was pulling the plug. They would no longer provide the financing to continue the business. Here is where things got interesting.

I went to the institution that issued my contractor's license, and within two hours I changed the license from the existing business's name back to my company's name. This was a miracle. I immediately became the owner of the company, including all signed contracts and employees. Just like that, God took me from employee to owner through no efforts of my own. Within a couple weeks, the gentleman who talked me into using my license quit, then two of the four remaining salesmen quit. I was left with two salesmen and four contracts that one of the salesmen had negotiated. The only answer I had at that point was God. I did not know how to run a business, nor did I know how to build a business. But this presented no problem to God.

One of the salesmen God left to work with the company was a man I had worked with in the past at another pool company. He was one of the top-producing salesmen in the industry. When he and I worked for the other company, our relationship was adversarial at times. The culture of the company created conditions that tended to pit people against one another, and we both had personalities that tended to speak before we understood what was happening. Neither of us would have been intentional about working together. But again, this presented no problem for God. He gave us a common vision to keep the company going and granted us the grace to execute what He wanted to do. The second salesman left after selling two pools.

So here we were, one guy selling and one guy building. We had no capital to expand. Nobody knew who we were. We were operating job to job and day by day. The first year, we sold just a handful of jobs. God provided enough money to keep us going. The second year, our revenues tripled. The third year, our revenues increased another 40 percent. God continued to open doors for us. Then we opened our first showroom. God provided a comfortable income. I could continue to do ministry and pay for mission trips for the first time in my life.

Up to this point I had not heard much RHEMA. I spent a lot of time with God praying for wisdom to do what I did not know how to do. He led my steps, and I was quite content where He was leading, the pace of His leading, and the fruits of His leading. Then God gave me a RHEMA on a return trip from the Philippines. He gave me a scripture, a LOGOS, that set the stage for the RHEMA:

> *The kingdom of heaven is like a mustard seed, which a man took and sowed in his field, which indeed is the least*

> *of all seeds; but when it is grown it is greater than the herbs and becomes a tree, so that the birds of the air come nest in its branches* (Matthew 13:31-32 NKJV).

God said, "That is what a kingdom business is to be, and that is what I want My kingdom business to be." I knew without a doubt that God wanted to grow the business. I had no idea how to grow a business, but what I did know is that He said, "Grow." And because He said it, it was going to happen.

For a year, I prayed for God to give me wisdom regarding what to do to grow the business. And for an entire year, I got nothing. I returned to the Philippines the following year, and on my return trip home I received a second RHEMA from God: "Now!" God was waiting on His timing regarding our growth. I went home, put additional people on payroll, opened a second showroom, and spent money on advertising. I had no vision to do any of these things, but God had the vision. What God utters, there is no possibility of it not happening.

I still spend a great deal of time with God. We are always talking about what He wants to do with His business. Sometimes He gives me wisdom and sometimes He gives me a RHEMA. LOGOS, His written Word, and RHEMA, His utterances, are both essential for operating a kingdom business that He owns. I don't know where I'd be without it.

Notes

1. Vance Havner, *Pepper 'n' Salt* (Grand Rapids, MI: Fleming H. Revell Company, 1966).
2. Ibid.
3. Ibid.
4. If you would like more information on NationStrategy, visit www.nationstrategy.com.

Section V

CONCLUSION: GOD'S WORDS CREATE GOD'S WORLD

by Ed Delph and David Lake

POWER THOUGHTS FOR *Chapter 15*

"The children of Issachar had understanding of the times and knew what Israel ought to do" (1 Chronicles 12:32). With all the news media today, there is plenty of knowledge of the times, but little understanding. Such understanding will not be gained from news analysts and political experts. It must be based on God's Word and it produces a practical knowledge of what "Israel" people ought to do. We must know the times, we must understand them, and we must know what to do.

—Vance Havner[1]

As Jesus hears God speak, as the Holy Spirit hears Jesus speak, we hear the Holy Spirit speak so that when we speak it is God speaking through us. That way we are creating God's world, not our world. His Words spoken to us then through us create His worlds for us and others!

—Ed Delph

"At the center of all this, Christ rules the church. The church, you see, is not peripheral to the world; the world is peripheral to the church. The church is Christ's body, ***in which He speaks and acts,*** *by which* ***He fills everything with His presence****"* (Ephesians 1:22-23 Message Bible) Do you see this? He speaks. He acts. He fills everything with His Presence. We are a carrier and a courier. It's not I, but Christ.

—Ed Delph

Chapter 15

Mission Possible: Staging for a Rhema Renaissance

Success does not lie in your ability to adjust to change.
Success lies in your ability to anticipate change.
—Alfred Sloan[2]

Let's go back to what may be our future for a moment. Jesus wanted His disciples (and us) to be ready for something that was going to happen on God's calendar. No amount of praying, prophesying, and having conferences was going to change it. This was something God was orchestrating that was beyond human desire or control. God was watching over His Word to perform it. Jesus wanted His disciples to be aware of what was going to happen before it took place so that when it happened they would have peace amid the chaos. They'd see it as a fulfillment of prophecy, not God taking vengeance on them or anyone else. Jesus informed His disciples so they would have the right response to what could be easily misunderstood.

Of course, we are referring to the destruction of Jerusalem in AD 70. The nation of Israel was going to be dispersed all over the world. People were going to have to run and hide in the hills and mountains. Jesus wanted to give them an aha on their future, a future that would come soon enough. He informed them that when they saw Jerusalem surrounded by armies, then the desolation of Jerusalem would be imminent. His followers would not have time to adjust to this change; rather, they were given a RHEMA for this occasion that came right from the LOGOS of God.

This is what was prophesied in Isaiah 63:4, Hosea 9:7, and Daniel 9:24-27. Let's look at the scriptures we are referring to here. It's notable that the same word of prophecy, knowledge, and wisdom is given in Matthew 10:19 and Mark 13:11-13. We will use the version in Luke 21:12-15 to make our point. When three of the four Gospels note this occasion, we need to listen.

> *But before all these things, they will lay their hands on you and will persecute you, delivering you to the synagogues and prisons, bringing you before kings and governors for My name's sake. It will lead to an opportunity for your testimony. So make up your minds not to prepare beforehand to defend yourselves; for I will give you utterance and wisdom which none of your opponents will be able to resist or refute* (Luke 21:12-15).

Concerning the utterance in Luke, Matthew's version notes, "For it is not you who speaks, but it is the Spirit of your Father who speaks in you" (Matthew 10:20), while Mark's version says, "for it is not you who speak, but it is the Holy Spirit" (Mark 13:11).

What If?

Many church leaders and scholars think these verses apply to the future. Bible teacher Bob Yandian refers to this as the Law of Double Reference, meaning that Jesus spoke a prophecy for His disciples' time *and* for a future time also. What if this happened to us in our own time? Would we be ready for it? Would we be at peace during a real storm? We don't mean someone calling you a name because of your belief in Christ, but real persecution, uprooting everything you are familiar with—would you have peace in that midst of that?

What if we were imprisoned for our Christianity? What if we were put on trial for our faith? What if we didn't have a lawyer to defend us? What if our family or friends betrayed us, reporting our faith in Jesus to the police, and we were imprisoned for it? Would we be ready for a future in which we were real victims, not just self-proclaimed victims who needed a safe zone at some university? Jerusalem in AD 70 had no safe zone in the physical realm, but there was a safe zone in the kingdom of God. Just ask those three university students—Shadrach, Meshach, and Abednego. They understood the safest place in Babylon was in the fire with Jesus.

We have a feeling that the response of the average churchgoer in the Western culture would be dismal if rough times came. Most church people would be freaked out at these circumstances. There would be weeping and gnashing of teeth inside the church. Many would respond with faithlessness. Why? It is because faith comes from hearing all the Word of God, not just the parts of the Word of God that make people feel good about themselves. Maybe it's time to equip and prepare people in our churches to heard first and speak second in order to empower the church for times such as these. We need to give the LOGOS an opportunity to speak a RHEMA to the people. That is wisdom, and that is biblical. Jesus said to do this for such a time as then and now. Let's make sure we equip those in the church to understand beforehand that something like what happened in AD 70 could happen again in our own day, just in case it happens. It's like the old saying about the rapture, "Pray for pre-tribulation, but prepare for post-tribulation."

In that courtroom, one will have to give more than the LOGOS or a Bible verse out of context. It will require the right Bible verse or principle, at the right time, for the right people, which is the right testimony lighting up the courtroom. The God-inspired utterance infused with faith we give in that courtroom will have to be clear, relevant wisdom from above. It will have to be specific and timely. It will have to be accurate for the occasion. It will need to be God presently speaking through us. It will have to be a word which none of the opponents will be able to resist or refuse. In that time, the LOGOS will give the accused a RHEMA to say to those in the courtroom.

Culture, nations, and societies all over the world are generally getting darker and darker. The possibility of facing a trial like this is becoming more of a reality. Yes, there will be ebbs and flows of outpourings and the like, but at the end of the ages, some tough stuff happens. It happened then and it may happen again in our own day and age. Be prepared beforehand about the necessity and reality of the two swords from the Lord that are given to every believer for times such as these.

We wish we will all be ready. That's one of the reasons we wrote this book! We need to be ready whether the end times are imminent or coming later.

Times of Ambiguity: Hitting a Moving Target

Years ago, John Maxwell spoke the following in his "Injoy Life" series on how your success today can become your failure tomorrow: "How we love success. Once we get a little piece of it, we want to hold on to it forever...and that's the problem. Life changes, and no set plan will last long. What got you there won't keep you there." He went on to say, "In dynamic times, times of ambiguity and change, success can't be engineered by 'how-tos.' Success is cultivated by moving to 'who-tos.' 'Who-tos' are those who know how to thrive in ambiguity, capitalize on turbulence, and master crisis."

Regarding times of chaos and change, American billionaire industrialist J. Paul Getty has been quoted as saying, "Experience is your worst enemy. Experience only helps in situations that have a degree of predictability; it is deadly in situations that require a fresh approach." And mid-twentieth-century auto-industry executive Alfred Sloan shared his thoughts on anticipating change: "Success does not lie in your ability to adjust to change. Success lies in your ability to anticipate change."[3]

There is no doubt that we are living in times of ambiguity and change. The prophet Daniel said this phenomenon would exist in the end times:

> *Now at that time Michael, the great prince who stands guard over the sons of your people, will arise. And there will be a time of distress such as never occurred since there was a nation until that time; and at that time your people, everyone who is found written in the book, will be rescued. Many of those who sleep in the dust of the ground will awake, these to everlasting life, but the others to disgrace and everlasting contempt. Those who have insight will shine brightly like the brightness of the expanse of heaven, and those who lead the many to righteousness, like the stars forever and ever. But as for you, Daniel, conceal these words and seal up the book until the end of time; many will go back and forth, and knowledge will increase* (Daniel 12:1-4).

> *Many will be purged, purified and refined, but the wicked will act wickedly; and none of the wicked will understand, but those* [the instructors] *who have insight will understand....But as for you* [Daniel], *go your way to the end; then you will enter into rest and rise again for your allotted portion at the end of the age"* (Daniel 12:10,13).

First, if you have received Christ, then you are rescued and going to Heaven forever. Michael is there to make sure that what Christ did for us on the cross will get done. Remember, no RHEMA spoken by God will not happen. Your contribution on earth is secure and your future is sure because of what Jesus had done through His death and resurrection.

Second, there are people known as "people of insight." Because the best sight is insight, those individuals will shine brightly with the light of God. They know how to say, "Let there be light!" There will be another group of people who have the grace and calling for leading many to righteousness, both in salvation and discipleship. God speaks through them because they listen. They thrive amid chaos and ambiguity; they will have insight that is beyond human ability. They will stand out by being outstanding. In fact, they will be like the sons of Issachar, "men who understood the times, with knowledge of what Israel should do..." (1 Chronicles 12:32). Many know the times but have no idea what to do in those times. But these men trust God for both and have faith for both. How did they do that? Faith comes by hearing God. Wherever you see faith, someone heard something from God.

Third, this is a commentary on the times in which all of this will be happening. Many will go back and forth, and knowledge will increase. Sounds like times such as these, doesn't it? This could mean that there will be many who travel on planes and the like, but it could also mean going back and forth in their beliefs and values, ways of living, driven by winds, waves, and fads everywhere. But one thing is for sure—the times are ambiguous. There are no homes, family, and values. The only thing that is real is whatever is trending. Everything will be shadow, not substance. Chaotic times create chaotic people unless they have insight that comes from hearing God.

In the end times, people need "the light" giving them insight on what is right. We need people bringing light into darkness. In the end times, people will want someone and something they can trust and rely on. That is being the "who-to" John Maxwell mentioned. People will want revelation that creates transformation. They will want the sun, not the moon. The moon only reflects light, but it is the sun that produces light. How do you become a "who-to"? One thing is for sure: you must learn how to hear first, speak second. Daniel was a "who-to." Kings sought him out; they came to him. Daniel's gift made room for him and put him in the presence of kings. Daniel knew how to hit a moving target. He tuned into the *frequent-see* of God. Frequent seeing comes from frequent hearing what God is saying.

Last, God says, "Daniel, just go your way to the end." We don't know many people to whom God says, "Go your way because I'm not worried about you anymore; I've got your back." Why could Daniel go his way to the end? It was because God knew Daniel's way was His way. These people who listen to God in the end times have God's way in mind, using both swords of the Lord for God's purposes. Then they can receive their allotted portion at the end of the age, and then cast their portion back at Christ's feet! Those people have insight. We hope we all will rise to this level of work and ministry. The world is waiting for the "instructors" with insight to give to others so they will have insight.

Whether end times are here, people today want insight, illumination, and revelation. People in the church want clarity, but clarity is a rarity. Pastors and kingdom leaders, let's equip people for life, not just church life, with LOGOS and RHEMA. Feed them the whole counsel of God's Word, not just the momentary fad. There ought to be one or two aha moments for everyone, both young and old Christians, in every service or meeting where people are gathered together in His name. Inspire and equip people to be people of light and insight. His people, like John the Baptist, are not "the light" but they bear witness to the light (see John 1:8). The light is what empowers us to be the lights of the world.

Staging for God's Rhema Renaissance

Both of us are ardent fishermen. We love to fish in the springtime at several of the lakes near Phoenix, Arizona, when the largemouth bass are getting ready to spawn. When the water warms to a certain temperature, something triggers the bass to reproduce. They rise from the depths of the lakes and swim to the shores in search of a partner. They begin preparing nests by clearing out rocks or debris. This process is called staging, which is the first sign something has changed.

The fish have always been in the lake, but now they can be seen near the shore. What was hidden in darkness is now revealed by the light. Then the spawning begins. There is action. New life is created. This happens because it is the right season, the right time, and the right temperature for something special to begin *en masse,* with both frequency and potency. Staging changes everything. It confirms that spring has sprung; it is the sign of a shift to something new and special.

There were times in Israel's past when visions, revelations, miracles, Holy Spirit downloads and the like were infrequent. For example, Israel was enslaved in Egypt for over four hundred years. The glory of God was absent in Israel for four hundred years before Jesus was born. These were winter times—but winter times always turn into spring. God begins again in the fullness of time to create something special.

Such was the case in Israel in First Samuel 3:1. Things looked hopeless, barren, and dark. Then, suddenly, God began staging by creating a RHEMA *Renaissance:* "Now the boy Samuel was ministering to the Lord before Eli. And word from the Lord was rare in those days, visions were infrequent" (1 Samuel 3:1). "Visions were infrequent" in this Hebrew text means "no vision spread abroad." The Bible goes on to explain that three times God spoke to Samuel, calling him by name. Samuel thought it was Eli calling, so each time Samuel heard his name he went to Eli asking if he'd called him. Even though Samuel was a prophet's servant living in the prophet's house, he did not know God.

> *Then the Lord came and stood and called as at other times, "Samuel! Samuel!" And Samuel said, "Speak, for Your servant is listening." The Lord said to Samuel, "Behold, I am about to do a thing in Israel at which both ears of everyone who hears it will tingle"* (1 Samuel 3:10-11).

Did you notice the hear first, speak second principle in action here? Three times the Lord spoke to Samuel before God revealed Himself to Samuel. Samuel, even though he didn't know God, said "Speak, for Your servant is listening." Then God revealed what He was going to do in Israel. From that dark hour, God raised up Samuel, David, Solomon, and some of the greatest days Israel had ever known.

We sense God staging something wonderful, especially since the beginning of 2016. God shows up in dark times. In the United States, terrible division and chaos surrounded the 2016 presidential election. Families were divided. Mainstream media reports were maddening. The political climate was crazy. Then out of the woodwork came someone and something different. That happened with Cyrus, Samuel, the apostle Paul, Moses, and many others who didn't start out as spiritual giants. Don't get messed up on who God chooses. This isn't about politics; it's the principle that matters. The bubble of the flesh-based Eli-way of doing things has burst—God is staging something special.

It is in the darkest hour where God's greatest power lies. God creates light so we can have insight. Samuel started his ministry in the "when man is revealed, God is concealed" era. But he finished in the "when God is revealed, man is concealed" era. What happened in between? God was speaking, the Holy Spirit was hovering and listening for a new beginning for Israel and for Samuel, which was already written in the LOGOS. Now there would be a season of great things happening, but later it would become another season of not-so-great things. Springtime and harvest are both in God's kingdom.

We are sensing that God is in the beginning stages of a RHEMA *Renaissance*. We believe RHEMA for many Christians will increase in both frequency and potency during these times. Christians have always received RHEMA, but now there will be a significant difference: people will have ears to hear what the Spirit is saying so they can speak it or do what they have heard. They will know they have heard RHEMA because there will be faith attached to what they hear. There will be no doubt about it. They will do what the Father says just like Jesus did. Faith will come from hearing the spoken, present, specific word of the Lord for advancing God's kingdom.

People will frequently see what the Lord has done because they will frequently hear what the Spirit says to the church. They will have faith. Wherever faith exists, someone heard a word from God. More listening and hearing produces more seeing. *Prophetic people tend to hear from God and then receive from God the faith to speak on what they have heard.* This is why Paul assures us in Romans, "Since we have gifts that differ according to the grace given to us, each of us is to exercise them accordingly: if prophecy, according to the proportion of his faith" (Romans 12:6).

Where did their faith come from? It came from God. Leaders will not only have the faith to climb each of the seven mountains of culture but will also have something from God to say when they get to the gates at the top of the mountain. What they carry in their hearts will come out of their mouths—a word of faith right on time for the occasion.

Reformation within the Church Created Renaissance in the Community

Talk about transfigured people transfiguring mountains! Martin Luther was such a person. The Reformation began in Wittenberg, Germany, when Martin Luther nailed his Ninety-Five Theses to the door of the Castle Church on October 31, 1517. Why did he do that? He heard from God. The great Reformation that opened the door to the Renaissance started when Martin Luther received a RHEMA on LOGOS from God. He received the revelation in the wilderness of the Dark Ages. That RHEMA, which returned the Bible or LOGOS back to all the people, transformed the culture, the church, and society.

Martin Luther ascended the church mountain. He stood at the gate of that mountain, supplied with God-infused faith. He spoke ninety-five revolutionary principles to the church mountain. He was a transfigured man who had heard from God to transfigure the church. When the church mountain was transformed, the other six mountains were also transformed as a result.

Many would have told him he was on mission impossible. Taking on the Catholic Church in that day was quite a feat. But with an utterance from God, all things are possible. After Martin Luther received a RHEMA on restoring LOGOS back to the church, it became mission possible. He embraced the possibility, not the impossibility, of inevitable, undeniable change. It wasn't change for change's sake, however; it was change in the direction God wanted for His purposes and the world's benefit. When God is behind the change, then everyone wins.

The Reformation preceded the Renaissance by only a short time. The Reformation was about the church, but the Renaissance was about the intellect, or the six other mountains besides the church mountain. When God used Martin Luther to transform the church, it changed the other mountains also. The people who went to church but worked outside the church were transformed. They, in turn, transformed the mountain where they worked or lived. As LOGOS spread, RHEMA spread, transforming the world. The Dark Ages ended when the Bible was reintroduced to the common person. The result was upgrades in art, machinery, human relations, awareness, and so on. It was a Renaissance created by a RHEMA. And it all started with listening.

What is the meaning of Renaissance? It means "rejuvenation, a renewal, resurgence, a revival, an awakening, regeneration, an invigoration, or a new dawning." That's what we expect. Amid gross darkness in our culture today, people who truly hear from God will appear. There will be a Renaissance in many sectors of society that is created by RHEMA and LOGOS working together. How long it will last is up to God. But we know this: God is getting ready to speak.

Change will happen one way or another. That is undeniable. The question is, which way will things change? That is where we come in. Christians, arise! You are agents of change for doing things God's way, not in humanism's way. Embrace it. Climb your mountain. Speak to your mountain. But make sure that you are speaking what God is speaking. Be armed with the two swords of the Lord. Be bold but be wise. Don't just present Christ; represent Him to the world.

Embracing the Lifestyle of Hear First, Speak Second

How do you make hear first, speak second a lifestyle? How do you make listening for what God is saying automatic? How do you let the Word speak a word before you speak a word consistently and clearly? First, embracing a lifestyle of hear first and speak second starts by revelation. We need to have an aha moment; we need to see this as primary, not secondary.

Consider the Hebrew mind-set on the concept of hearing. In the ancient Hebrew mind-set, hearing and doing were understood to be the same. *Hearing* implied *doing what was heard*. In other words, you haven't heard if you haven't done what you heard.[4] In the Greek mind-set, however, hearing and doing are two separate and distinct ideas. One can hear and not do because they are different modes. This idea is demonstrated by the Holy Spirit in Genesis 1:1-3. God spoke, the Holy Spirit heard and then did what the Father spoke. The Holy Spirit didn't respond to God with, "Wow, God, that is really good! I am inspired. I am informed. I am impressed. What good revelation! I have been fed. What a good word. I'll be back next week for more." No, the Holy Spirit did what He heard God say because He heard/did it. This is probably where the Hebrew concept for hearing came from. New worlds and new creations are formed in this way.

And so it is with us. We do what the Holy Spirit says. *Faith is a fact that is expressed in an act*. Faith comes from hearing. The response comes from faith, and we know that faith comes from hearing. So when God speaks and it is really God who is speaking, we hear and do what God spoke. Throughout this book, we have used the hear first, speak second idea to get this point across. If you hear, then it's implied you will speak and act on what you have heard. Once this lifestyle moves from your head to your heart, then and only then can it move to your feet.

After you receive a revelation of this concept, how can you move it from your heart to your feet? Hear first, speak second becomes a habit. What is on the outside of us needs to get inside. Make a great habit, and your great habit will make you. Let's illustrate.

Many years ago, I (Ed) learned how to fly a private airplane. I loved flying, and it worked well for the book-binding business I owned. I learned to fly in a small two-seat airplane, a Cessna 150. At first, learning to fly was intimidating, especially takeoffs and landings, and those big power lines at the end of the runway. However, after several months, flying became easier because piloting an airplane became a habit. It became automatic. What was unnatural became natural. That's the power of habit.

Then I became a one-third owner in a much more complex airplane. It was a six-passenger Piper Comanche 260. It had retractable landing gear, a variable-speed propeller, wing flaps, exhaust-gas temperature controls, fuel-injection mixture controls, and big horsepower for its 200-mph speed. This airplane had the same high-performance wing design as the P-51 Mustang from World War II. It was a handful on the descent for landing. I remember taking off with my right foot to the floor trying to keep the airplane straight because the torque from the propeller wanted to turn the plane sideways. On top of that, I had to listen to the tower tell me when to taxi, where to taxi, when to take off, what runway to use, and what the altimeter pressure was. After the takeoff, they even told me which direction to take.

The first time I flew this airplane was with my instructor. I already knew how to fly from the Cessna days, but this was a whole new experience. I had to learn how to fly this plane while flying it. That's why I had an instructor. It was intimidating. There were so many new controls and things going on that had consequences if I didn't fly the plane right. I thought I would never get comfortable taking off in that plane. Flaps up, throttle back, back off on propeller speed, gear up, lean out the mixture, keep airspeed up, take right foot off pedal, keep nose up—but not too far, listen to tower, try not to ignore instructor and tower freaking out. And time is too short to tell you about landing that slippery plane!

But after flying the Comanche for a few weeks, everything became easier. I didn't have to think about all those adjustments anymore. Taking off and landing became second nature. After a month, I could carry on a conversation with a passenger in the front seat while I was taking off and landing because what was necessary to fly the plane became a habit.

The same is true when learning to listen to God. Get in the habit of thinking about God first. Initially it may seem hard. You will have to remember, concentrate, and apply. But after a while, you will be a beneficiary of the habit of hearing first and speaking second. "God, what do You want to do today? What wisdom do You want me to speak to this hurting person right now? What solution do You have for this problem in my company? Where do You want me to invest money? What do You want for my marriage? Whom do you want me to marry? Should I change jobs? How can I mend that relationship with my former friend? What is Your highest and utmost for me?" It becomes a habit. It's the Christian's normal way of life. It's flying the high-performance airplane of life!

Conclusion

There you go! Hear first, speak second has to become a revelation to you. Then after that revelation comes the power of habit as you choose consistently to hear first and speak second. Why not be like King David and fulfill the purposes of God in your generation? Use your life wisely and then "fall asleep," much like David did during his generation (Acts 13:36).

As we said in the Introduction, our twofold desire in writing this book was that you would live your life in all areas by the hear first, speak second paradigm; and second, that you would receive a RHEMA on RHEMA. It's your birthright. Desire RHEMA and acquire RHEMA, because we all require RHEMA. As a result, God has a voice—your voice—on Earth as it is in Heaven.

Here is a world-changing, society-transforming, giant-slaying, runaway culture-shifting statement for you: *If you truly hear from God, then God speaks through you a relevant, personal truth that is biblically correct and spiritually accurate for his or her situation*. That's high octane. Use it, but use it wisely. The way is yours—take it!

Notes

1. Vance Havner, *Pepper 'n' Salt* (Grand Rapids, MI: Fleming H. Revell Company, 1966).
2. Alfred Sloan, https://soundfaith.com/sermons/23192-the-5-big-challenges-in-life, accessed March 27, 2017.
3. Ibid.
4. I learned this from my Hebrew-thinking friend from South Africa, Joshua Churchyard.

About David Lake

David Lake is an ordained pastor and business owner, as well as marketplace minister. He is passionate about running his life, business, and ministry by hearing the voice of God. God has placed in his heart a burden to equip other business owners, pastors, churches, and Christians how to live their lives by seeking first the kingdom of God.

David has been in ministry since the early '90s, working with both youth and adults. He served as a youth pastor at Hosanna Christian Fellowship, led home fellowship groups, and has ministered in the mission field in several countries. He has traveled abroad with Men and Women of Action, doing building projects. David was also a pastor at Church at Community with Ed Delph. He currently pastors a seasonal church in Tonopah, Arizona, and continues traveling abroad ministering with Ed for NationStrategy. He has been married to Rhonda since 1984. They have four grown children and six grandchildren.

About Dr. Ed Delph

Dr. Ed Delph has been a pastor at three different churches since 1980 in the Phoenix, Arizona, area. He is a noted author of ten books, weekly columnist in several newspapers worldwide, teacher, business owner, and speaker having traveled to more than a hundred countries. He is currently president of a worldwide ministry, NationStrategy, a nonprofit organization involved in community and societal transformation. Ed earned his business degree from Arizona State University and his Doctorate of Ministry in Faith in Culture from Phoenix University of Theology in 2004.